UN-
COMMONS

UN-COMMONS

COLLECTING TREASURES

1950's EDITION
With 1948 & 49

By Ken Hanaway

authorHOUSE®

AuthorHouse™
1663 Liberty Drive
Bloomington, IN 47403
www.authorhouse.com
Phone: 1-800-839-8640

First published by AuthorHouse 1/5/2010

ISBN: 978-1-4490-6358-0 (sc)
ISBN: 978-1-4490-6359-7 (e)

Printed in the United States of America
Bloomington, Indiana

This book is printed on acid-free paper.

Table of Contents

STUFF

These common players did some "uncommon" things during their careers. Some of the things they have done can never be repeated, and some you wouldn't want repeated. The list goes from tragic deaths to triumphant achievements. Somewhere in this STUFF, you will find a reason to collect some of these commons.

t=topps   b=bowman   er=error   dp=double print

ABRAMS, CAL : []152 b'51 []86 b'52 []98 t'53 []91 b'54 []55 b'55

Was thrown out at the plate in the bottom of the 9th to help Brooklyn lose the Pennant to the 1950 Whiz Kids of Philadelphia.

ALOMA, LUIS : []231 b'51 []308 t'52 []134 b'54 []57 t'54

Had the highest career Winning percentage .871 with a minimum 20 decisions.

BARRETT, RED : []213 b'49

With Boston Braves threw only 58 pitches in a 9 inning game to beat Cincinnati 2-0 on 8/10/44

BAUMHOLTZ, FRANK : []195 b'52 []225 t'52 []221 b'54 []60 t'54 []227 b'55 []172 t'55 []274 t'56

Was the only batter that Stan Musial pitched to in the majors. Frank was also a Pro Basketball player

BEARD, TED : []308 b'51 []150 t'52

Cleared the right field stands at Forbes Field with a Homerun, only others to do it were *Babe Ruth* and *Mickey Mantle*.

BEARDEN, GENE : []173 b'52 []229 t'52

Won the 1st play-off game in American League history in '48 for Cleveland. Was runner up to Alvin Dark for Rookie of the Year '48.

BELL, GUS : []118dp t'53

Hits for cycle with Pirates on 6/4/51. Was replaced in the starting All Star line-up in '56 because of ballot stuffing.

BENTON, AL : []374 t'52

Only pitcher to face both *Babe Ruth* and *Mickey Mantle*. With Detroit Al set a Major League record with 2 sacrifices in the same inning. In 1968 at 57 years old he was killed in a motel fire/explosion.

BERNIER, CARLOS : []243dp t'53 []171 b'54

In '89 at age 62 Carlos hanged himself.

BIRRER, BABE : []84 t'56

On 7/19/55 he hit a pair of 3-run Homers (only RBI's in 3 year career).

BLADES, RAY : []243 t'54

Managed the Brooklyn Dodgers in '48 for one game, and Won.

BONHAM, ERNIE : []77 b'49

On 9/15/49 he died suddenly of an appendectomy during season.

BOROWY, HANK : []134 b'49 []177 b'50 []250 b'51

With the Cubs he beats the Pirates to clinch Pennant 9/29/45

BOUCHEE, ED : []314 t'57 []39 t'59

In '57 Ed is 2nd in Rookie of the Year votes behind Jack Sanford.

BROWN, TOMMY : []236 b'52 []42 b'53

With the Dodgers, he becomes the youngest player in the Major Leagues to Homer (16 yrs 8 mos) on 8/20/45

BRUTON, BILL : []165 t'59 — With the Braves he hits 2 bases loaded Triples vs. Cards 8/2/59.

BYRD, HARRY : []38 b'53 []131dp t'53 []49 b'54 []159 b'55 []154 t'58 — Harry was the AL Rookie of the Year in '52 with the Athletics.

CAIN, BOB : []236 b'50 []197 b'51 []19 b'52 []56 b'53 []266 t'53 []195 b'54 []61 t'54 — Bob walked midget Eddie Gaedel on 4 pitches on 8/19/51

CHAPMAN, BEN : []391er t'52 — Poor guy, his only card is a picture of Sam Chapman. In '42 as a Minor League manager he was suspended for a year for punching an umpire.

CHAPMAN, SAM : []104 b'50 []9 b'51 — On 5/5/39, with the Athletics, he hit for the cycle.

COURTNEY, CLINT : []70 b'53 []127dp t'53 []69 b'54 []34 b'55 []159 t'56 []51 t'57 []92 t'58 []483 t'59 — Was the first catcher to wear glasses behind the plate. In '52 he was second in AL Rookie of the Year voting, behind Harry Byrd.

CRANDALL, DEL : []567as t'59 — In '49 Del was second in NL Rookie of the Year voting behind Don Newcombe.

CROWE, GEORGE : []254 t'56 []73 t'57 []12 t'58 []337 t'59 — George was also a Pro Basketball player.

CUNNINGHAM, JOE : []168 t'58 []285 t'59 — With the Cards on 7/1/54 Joe set a record with 3 Homers in his first two games in the Majors.

DELSING, JIM : []279 b'51 []157 b'52 []44w b,53 []239 t'53 []55 b'54 []111 t'54 []274 b'55 []338 t'56 []386 t'59 — On 8/19/51 Jim pinch ran after midget Eddie Gaedel was walked.

DEMETER, DON : []244 t'58 []324 t'59 — With the Phillies, Don didn't make an error in 266 consecutive games.

DERRINGTON, JIM : []129 t'58 — On 9/30/56 he became the youngest (modern day) pitcher to START a Major league game 16 yrs 10 mos (White Sox)

DREWS, KARL : []188 b'50 []113 b'53 []59dp t'53 []191 b'54 — In '63, at age 43, Karl was killed by a drunk driver.

DORISH, HARRY : []266 b'51 []303 t'52 []145dp t'53 []86 b'54 []110 t'54 []248 b'55 []167 t'56 — With the Browns, he is the last AL pitcher to steel home 6/2/50. It is his only stolen base in a 10 year career.

DROPO, WALT : []235 t'52 []257 t'57 []158 t'59 — Was AL Rookie of the Year in '50 with Detroit. In '52 Walt had a record setting 12 consecutive hits.

EASTER, LUKE : []2dp t'53 — On 6/23/50 Luke hit's the longest Homer at Cleveland Stadium off Joe Haynes. In '79 Luke was shot to death by two robbers during a payroll robbery, he was 63.

ESSEGIAN, CHUCK : []278 t'59

In '59 he became the 2nd (*Jackie Jensen*, the 1st) to play in the Rose Bowl and the World Series.

EVERS, HOOT : []42 b'49
[]41 b'50 []23 b'51 []111 b'52
[]222 t'52 []25 b'53 []18 b'54

On 9/7/50 he hit for the cycle. On 6/13/50 with Detroit he hit's a 9th inning homer to set a Major League record for Home Runs (11) in a game by two teams (Yankees).

FACE, ROY : []246 t'53

Had the most consecutive Wins (22) by a relief pitcher ('58-'59)

FARRELL, DICK : []78 t'58

In '77 Dick was killed in an auto accident in England he was 43.

FERRISS, BOO : []211 b'49

On 6/16/45 he loses to the Yankees after starting his career with 8 Wins (4 shut-outs). Was Chicago Chapter ROY in '45.

FINIGAN, JIM : []14 t'55
[]22 t'56 []248 t'57 []136 t'58
[]47 t'59

Was 2nd in Rookie of the Year voting in '54 behind Bob Grim

FITZGERALD, ED : []109 b'49
[]178 b'50 []180 b'52 []236 t'52
[]168 b'54 []208 b'55 []198 t'56
[]367 t'57 []236 t'58 []33 t'59

With 2 outs in the 9th inning Ed pinch-hit a double to ruin a Perfect game being pitched by *Billy Pierce* in '58

FORNIELES, MIKE : []154 t'54
[]266 b'55 []116 t'57 []361 t'58
[]473 t'59

On 9/2/52 with the Senators Mike pitches a 1 hitter in his Major League debut against the Athletics.

FOWLER, DICK : []171 b'49
[]214 b'50 []190 b'52 []210 t'52

On 9/9/46 with the A's Dick throws a no-hitter against the Browns.

FOX, HOWIE : []80 b'50
[]180 b'51 []125 b'52 []209 t'52
[]158 b'53 []22 t'53 []246 t'54

In '55 Howie was stabbed to death in a bar fight, he was 34.

FRANCONA, TITO : []184r t'57
[]268 t'59

In '56 Tito was 2nd in Rookie of the Year voting behind *Luis Aparicio*

GALAN, AUGIE : []39 b'48
[]233 t'54

Augie played an entire 154-game season without hitting into a double play.

GORBOUS, GLEN : []174 t'56

Threw a baseball a record 445 feet 10 inches on 8/1/57.

GORDON, SID : []101 b'49
[]109 b'50 []19 b'51 []60 b'52
[]5 b'53 []117dp t'53 []11 b'54

On 7/4/50 he tied a Major League record with 4th Grand Slam of the season.

GREENGRASS, JIM : []209 t'53
[]28 b'54 []22 t'54 []49 b'55
[]275 t'56

Opening day 4/13/54 Jim hits 4 Doubles for Cincinnati.

GRIM, BOB : []36 t'57

In '54 Bob is voted AL Rookie of the Year.

GROMEK, STEVE : []198 b'49
[]131 b'50 []115 b'51 []203 b'52
[]63w b'53 []199 b'54 []203 b'55
[]310 t'56 []258 t'57

On 5/4/46 with the Indians Steve stops *Cecil Travis'* hitting streak after six consecutive hits.

HADDIX, HARVEY : []256dp t'57

On 5/26/59 he pitches 12 perfect innings and loses to the Braves 1-0 in the 13th. Was 2nd in Rookie of the Year voting *Junior Gilliam* won in '53.

HAMRIC, BERT : []336 t'58

Never played in the field, 9 pinch-hit at bats, one hit (double).

HANEY, FRED : []75 t'54
[]551as t'59

Was the 1st Manager to lead the Braves to 2 Pennants ('57-'58)

HARDY, CARROLL : []168 t'59

Pinch hit for both *Ted Williams* and *Roger Maris*.

HAYNES, JOE : []191 b'49
[]240 b'51 []103 b'52 []145 t'52
[]223 t'54

On 6/23/50, Joe gave up the longest Home Run hit at Cleveland Stadium to Luke Easter.

HEARN, JIM : []190 b'49
[]208 b'50 []49 b'52 []76 b'53
[]38dp t'53 []220 b'55 []202 t'56
[]348 t'57 []298 t'58 []63 t'59

Two months after retiring, Jim records a Loss. (suspended game)

HIGGINS, MIKE : []150 t'55

Pinky hits for the cycle when with the A's on 8/6/33.

HOPP, JOHNNY : []207 b'49
[]122 b'50

With the Pirates on 5/14/50 Johnny went 6 for 6 against the Cubs with 2 Home Runs and 4 Singles.

HUDSON, SID : []17 b'50
[]169 b'51 []123 b'52 []60 t'52
[]29 b'53 []251 t'53 []194 b'54
[]93 t'54 []318 b'55

On 4/27/47 Sid ruined the Yankees *Babe Ruth* Day by beating them 1-0 for Washington.

JACKSON, LARRY : []97 t'58
[]399 t'59

With the Cardinals in '57, Larry has beaten every NL team.

JANSEN, LARRY : []40w b'53

Larry was 2nd in NL Rookie of the Year voting in '47 behind *Jackie Robinson*.

JOHNSON, BILLY : []122 b'52
[]83 t'52 []21 t'53

Was the Chicago Chapter Rookie of the Year in '43 as a Yankee.

JONES, NIPPY : []238 b'50
[]213 t'52

While pinch-hitting for Spahn in '57 Nippy turned a called ball into a hit-by-pitch by showing the umpire the ball had SHOE POLISH on it.

KEEGAN, BOB : []196 t'53
[]100 t'54 []10 t'55 []54 t'56
[]99 t'57 []200 t'58

On 8/20/57, with the White Sox, Bob throws a no-hitter against Wash.

KELLNER, ALEX : []222 b'49
[]14 b'50 []57 b'51 []226 b'52
[]201 t'52 []107 b'53 []51 b'54
[]53 b'55 []176 t'56 []280 t'57
[]3 t'58 []101 t'59

Was 2nd in the AL '49 Rookie of the Year voting behind Roy Sievers.

KINDALL, JERRY : []221r t'58

Had the lowest batting average (.213) in the 1900's with 2000+ at-bats.

KLAUS, BILLY : []150 b'55 []217 t'56 []292 t'57 []89 t'58 []299 t'59

Was 2nd in the AL '55 Rookie of the Year voting behind *Herb Score*.

LANIER, MAX : []207 b'50 []230 b'51 []110 b'52 []101 t'52

In '46 Max defected to the Mexican League, and was later granted amnesty to return.

LAWRENCE, BROOKS : []75r b'55 []305 t'56 []66 t'57 []374 t'58 []67 t'59

On 7/21/56, Brooks has a 13 game Win streak snapped by a *Roberto Clemente* 3 run Homer.

LEE, DON : []379 t'57 []132rp t'59

Don and his father Thornton have both given up Home Runs to *Ted Williams*, 21 years apart.

LEJA, FRANK : []99 t'55

On 9/19/54 Frank got his only hit in the Majors, it was also the last Hit at the A's Shibe Park before they moved to Kansas City.

LEMON, JIM : []103r t'54 []262 b'55

Set an all-time record in '56 by striking out 138 times. In '59 Jim hit 2 Home Runs in the same inning.

LINDELL, JOHNNY : []209 b'50 []203dp t'53 []159 b'54 []51 t'54

In '47 he drives in a World Series high 7 runs, while going 9 for 18.

MALZONE, FRANK : []558as t'59

Was 2nd in '57 AL Rookie of the Year voting behind *Tony Kubek*

MANTILLA, FELIX : []17 t'58 []157 t'59

Scored the winning run in Haddix's 12 inning Perfect game loss.

MAPES, CLIFF : []13 b'52 []103 t'52

Wore 3 retired uniforms, Ruth #3, Mantle #7, Greenberg #4. Cliff had to change to #13 when they retired Ruth's number on 6/13/48. (number 13 will probably be retired when *Alex Rodriguez* retires)

MASTERSON, WALT : []157 b'49 []153 b'50 []307 b'51 []205 b'52 []186 t'52 []9w b'53

On 6/29/41 Walt gives up a hit to *Joe DiMaggio* to set a record of a 42 game hitting streak.

McCAHAN, BILL : []31 b'48 []80 b'49

Also played Pro Basketball

McCULLOUGH, CLYDE : []163 b'49 []124 b'50 []94 b'51 []99 b'52 []218 t'52

On 7/26/52 Clyde hit 3 Home Runs in a row for the Cubs in a losing effort against the Phillies.

McDANIEL, VON : []65r t'58

On 6/15/58 Von has the best debut of a teenage pitcher with a 2 Hit Shut-out against Brooklyn.

MEYER, JACK : []269 t'56 []162 t'57 []186 t'58 []269 t'59

Was 2nd in '55 NL Rookie of the Year voting behind *Bill Virdon*. In '67 Jack was killed in an auto accident at age 34.

MITCHELL, DALE : []239 b'52 []26dp t'53

In '49 Dale had more Triples (23) than strike-outs (11). On 10/8/56 he struck out to give *Don Larson* a Perfect World Series Game. That strike-out was his last at-bat of an 11 year career.

MIZELL, WILMER : []128dp t'53

Set a NL record by walking 9 batters and pitching a shut-out 9/1/58.

NELSON, ROCKY : []199 t'54 []446 t'59

Hits an inside-the-glove 2 run Homer on 4/30/49 as the umpire ruled Andy Pafko trapped the ball.

NICHOLS, CHET : []120 b'52 []72 b'55 []278 t'56

Was 2nd in '51 NL Rookie of the Year voting behind *Willie Mays*.

NOREN, IRV : []63 b'52 []45w b'53 []35dp t'53 []298 t'57

Also played Pro Basketball.

NUXHALL, JOE : []105dp t'53

On 6/10/44 becomes the youngest pitcher in the Majors 15yrs 10mos.

O'NEIL, STEVE : []201 b'51 []127 t'54

Hit a Home Run in the game that saw the only death in a Major League game. *Carl Mays* beaned *Ray Chapman*, 8/16/20.

PARNELL, MEL : []241 b'52 []19dp t'53 []313 t'57

On 7/14/56 Mel pitched a no-hitter against the White Sox, at Fenway.

PHILLIPS, JACK : []240 t'52 []228 b'55 []307 t'57

Jack was accidentally electrocuted in '58 he was 39.

PIERETTI, MARINO : []217 b'49 []181 b'50

On 6/21/50 he gave up *Joe DiMaggio's* 2'000th hit (single).

PILLETTE, DUANE : []316 b'51 []82 t'52 []59w b'53 []269 t'53 []133 b'54 []107 t'54 []244 b'55 []168 t'55

Beat the Yankees to end their winning streak at 18 and stopped the Browns team record losing streak at 14. Duane and his father are the only father/son to be league-leaders in Losses.

RAMOS, PEDRO : []49 t'56 []326 t'57 []331 t'58 []78 t'59

On 5/30/56 he gave up a Home Run to Mantle that was within 18 inches of leaving Yankee Stadium. Set an AL record giving up 43 HR in '57.

REYNOLDS, ALLIE : []141dp t'53

Among his many accomplishments are 2 no-hitters in '51, 7/12 - 9/28.

RICE, DEL : []125 b'50 []107 b'52 []100 t'52 []53 b'53 []68 t'53 []30 b'54 []106 b'55 []193 t'57 []51 t'58

Also played Pro Basketball

RIDDLE, JOHN : []274 t'53 []147 t'54 []98 t'55

Was the oldest (42) catcher to battery with brother (Elmer) in '48.

RIDZIK, STEVE : []223 b'54 []111 b'55 []123 t'57

Gave up 38th HR *to Frank Robinson* to tie rookie HR record 9/11/56.

ROBERTS, CURT : []242 t'54 []107 t'55 []306 t'56

In '69 Curt was hit by a car and killed while changing a flat, he was 40.

ROBERTSON, SHERRY : []161 b'50 []95 b'51 []245 t'52

While warming up he threw a ball over 1st base and it struck and killed a fan. In '70 Sherry was killed in a car accident, he was 51.

ROBINSON, AARON : []133 b'49 []95 b'50 []142 b'51

Hit a Home Run to stop the Indians 47 scoreless innings pitching streak on 8/21/48.

ROLFE, RED : []296 t'52

On 8/9/39, Red starts a record 18 game scoring streak.

ROSAR, BUDDY : []10 b'48
[]138 b'49 []136 b'50 []236 b'51

On 7/19/40 Buddy hits for the cycle. In '46 he becomes the only catcher to field 1.000 in a season of more than 100 games (117).

ROSEN, AL : []135dp t'53

In '53 "Flip" is voted the American League MVP.

RUDOLPH, DON : []347 t'58
[]179 t'59

In '68 Don was crushed by a dump truck he was 37.

RYBA, MIKE : []237 t'54

Was the only player to both pitch and catch in both leagues. In '71 Mike died when he fell off a ladder while trimming branches (68)

SAUER, HANK : []111dp t'53

In '52 Hank is voted the National League MVP.

SCHEIB, CARL : []25 b'49
[]213 b'50 []83 b'51 []46 b'52
[]116 t'52 []150 b'53 []57 t'53
[]67 b'54 []118 t'54

On 9/6/43, with the A's, Carl becomes the youngest (16 yrs 8 mos) in the American League.

SCHULTZ, BOB : []144dp t'53
[]59 b'54

In '79 Bob was shot and killed in a bar, he was 62.

SEMINICK, ANDY : []51 b'51
[]297 t'52 []7w b'53 []153dp t'53
172 b'54 []93 b'54 []296 t'56

In '49 with the Phillies, Andy had two Homers in the same inning.

SEWELL, RIP : []234 b,49

Threw the EEPHUS to *Ted Williams* in the '46 All-Star game, and Teddy hit it for a Home Run. Rip set a NL record with 11 assists on 6/6/41, pitching with the Pirates.

SHEA, FRANK : []230 b'52
[]248 t'52 []141 b'53 []164dp t'53
[]104 b'54 []207 b'55

In the '47 All-Star game "Spec" became the 1st Rookie to record a Win. Spec also won 2 games in the '47 World Series.

SIEVERS, ROY : []67dp t'53
[]566as t'59

In '49 Roy was voted AL Rookie of the Year.

SISLER, DICK : []127 b'52
[]10w b'53

On 10/1/50 Dick hit's a 3 run Homer off of *Don Newcombe* to clinch the Pennant for the Phillies.

SMALLEY, ROY : []115 b'50
[]44 b'51 []173 t'52 []56w b'53
[]109 b'54 []231 t'54 []252 b'55
[]397 t'57

On 6/28/50 with the Cubs, Roy hits for the cycle.

SMITH, BOB W : []445 t'58

In 2003 Bob died from injuries from a tractor accident, he was 68.

SMITH, MAYO : []130 t'55
[]60 t'56

Mayo managed the World Series winning Tigers in '68.

SOUTHWORTH, BILLY : []207 b'51

Billy was inducted into the Hall of Fame in 2008. He is credited for Scouting *Jackie Robinson*.

STALLCUP, VIRGIL : []81 b'49
[]116 b'50 []108 b'51 []6 b'52
[]69 t'52 []180 t'53

In '49 he had the fewest walks in a season with 500+ at-bats (9). In '89 Virgil shot himself, he was 67.

STOBBS, CHUCK : []62 t'52 []89dp t'53 []185 t'54 []41 t'55 []68 t'56 []101 t'57 []239 t'58 []26 t'59

On 4/17/53, Chuck pitched Mantle's 565 ft Home Run that went out of Griffith Stadium.

STONE, DEAN : []114 t'54 []60 t'55 []87 t'56 []381 t'57 []286 t'59

On 7/13/53, Dean recorded an All-Star game Win with out throwing a pitch, *Red Schoendienst* was picked off stealing home.

SURKONT, MAX : []12 b'52 []302 t'52 []156 b'53 []75 b'54 []83 b'55 []209 t'56 []310 t'57

On 5/25/53, Max strikes out a record 8 batters in a row.

THOMPSON, HANK : []249 b'52 []64 t'54 []109 t'57

On 8/16/50 Hank hits 2 inside-the-park Home Runs.

THURMAN, BOB : []279 t'57 []34 t'58 []541 t'59

Hits 3 homers to help set a NL record of 10 HR's in a 9 inning game. Redlegs and the Braves

TRIANDOS, GUS : []80 t'56 []568as t'59

On 9/20/58 Gus hit a HR to help *Hoyt Wilhelm* get a no-hitter. In a 13 year career, he records a 1.000 stolen base percentage (1 for 1)

TROUT, DIZZY: []134 b'50

On 4/30/52 Dizzy gives up a HR to *Ted Williams* in the last game Ted plays before going to the Korean War.

TRUCKS, VIRGIL : []198 b'54

Virgil pitches 2 no-hitters in '52, 5/15 vs. WAS and 8/25 vs. NY.

TURLEY, BOB : []570as t'59

In '58 Bob wins the Cy Young award and the World Series MVP.

UMPHLETT, TOM : []88 b'54 []45 b'55

Was 2nd in '53 AL Rookie of the Year voting behind *Harvey Kuenn*.

VALO, ELMER : []66 b'49 []49 b'50 []206 b'52 []34 t'52 []122 t,53 []145 t'54 []145 t'55 []54 t'57 []323 t'58

On 8/2/50 Elmer hits for the Cycle. (A's)

VOLLMER, CLYDE : []53 b'50 []91 b'51 []57 b'52 []255 t'52 []152 b'53 []32 t'53 []136 b'54 []13 b'55

On 6/8/50 Clyde sets a Major League record with 8 plate appearances in 8 innings.

WAITKUS, EDDIE : []28 b'51 []158 t'52

Was the Chicago Chapter Rookie of the Year in '46. On 6/15/49 Eddie was shot in the chest by Ruth Steihagen , but returned to baseball in '50.

WALKER, HARRY : []130 b'49

Along with Fred, they are the only brothers with Batting titles. Fred in '44 and Harry in '47 (363)

WALL, MURRAY : []217 t'53 []410 t'58

In '71 Murray shot himself, he was 45

WALLS, LEE : []82 b'55 []52 t'57 []66 t'58 []105 t'59

On 7/2/57 Lee hits for the Cycle (Cubs)

WERTZ, VIC : []244 t'52

On 9/14/47 Vic hits for the Cycle (Tigers)

WESTLAKE, WALLY : []45 b'49
[]69 b'50 []38 t'52 []192 t'53
[]92 t'54 []102 t'55 []81 t'56

Wally hit for the Cycle twice, on 7/30/48 and then again on 6/14/49 while with the Pirates.

WRIGHT, TAFT : []96 b'49

Taft drove in at least 1 Run in a record 13 consecutive games ('41)

YOST, EDDIE : []173 t'58

On 8/12/54 Eddie draws his 100th Walk for the 5th year in a row.

BORN (on this day) TO PLAY

Everyone has birthdays and since there is a maximum of 366 of them we must share our special day with others. I personally have collected all the players that share July 1st with me. Since I gathered that information, my next project was to collect the cards of the players that were born in the same state (Indiana).

JANUARY

01 1919	[] ROBERTSON, SHERRY	
01 1921	[] LINT, ROYCE	
01 1924	[] BISHOP, CHARLIE	
01 1924	[] TORGESON, EARL	
01 1927	[] SCHEIB, CARL	
01 1931	[] CASTLEMAN, FOSTER	
02 1907	[] KRESS, RALPH	
03 1915	[] HUDSON, SID	
03 1922	[] STALLCUP, VIRGIL	
04 1914	[] FRANKS, HERMAN	
04 1925	[] GORMAN, TOM	
04 1929	[] VALENTINE, CORKY	
04 1930	[] McMAHON, DON	
04 1933	[] MONZANT, RAY	
05 1918	[] KRAMER, JACK	
05 1924	[] MARSH, FRED	
05 1928	[] OLDIS, BOB	
05 1935	[] BATTEY, EARL	
06 1915	[] FERRICK, TOM	
06 1917	[] MASI, PHIL	
06 1931	[] TOMANEK, DICK	
06 1933	[] WALLS, LEE	
06 1934	[] GREEN, LENNY	
07 1910	[] McCARTHY, JOHN	
07 1920	[] HOWELL, DIXIE M	
07 1921	[] BEARD, TED	
07 1924	[] PENDLETON, JIM	
07 1931	[] SEMPROCH, ROMAN	
07 1931	[] STEWART, BUNKY	
08 1915	[] COOPER, WALKER	
08 1921	[] RICKERT, MARV	
08 1923	[] BUSBY, JIM	
08 1933	[] TASBY, WILLIE	
08 1934	[] FREESE, GENE	
08 1935	[] BERTOIA, RENO	
08 1937	[] DILLARD, DON	
10 1922	[] CHAMBERS, CLIFF	
10 1926	[] STRICKLAND, GEORGE	
10 1928	[] DITTMER, JACK	
10 1936	[] BOWSFIELD, TED	
10 1937	[] O'TOOLE, JIM	
11 1922	[] BERRY, NEIL	
13 1930	[] MARGONERI, JOE	
14 1892	[] MEYER, BILLY	

14 1923	[] JOHNSON, KEN	
14 1930	[] DALEY, PETE	
15 1903	[] OLIVER, TOM	
15 1920	[] GROMEK, STEVE	
16 1917	[] RAMAZZOTTI, BOB.	
16 1924	[] WOOTEN, EARL	
16 1934	[] OWENS, JIM	
17 1915	[] SMITH, MAYO	
17 1920	[] THOMPSON, JOHN	
17 1922	[] MERSON, JOHN	
17 1933	[] PORTER, J W	
17 1935	[] BROWN, DICK	
18 1931	[] PEPPER, HUGH	
18 1932	[] FORNIELES, MIKE	
18 1933	[] RAYDON, CURT	
19 1932	[] SADOWSKI, ED	
20 1917	[] DOBSON, JOE	
20 1929	[] WADE, GALE	
20 1933	[] STEPHENS, GENE	
21 1914	[] DONNELLY, BLIX	
21 1923	[] MELE, SAM	
21 1927	[] O'CONNELL, DANNY	
22 1925	[] YOUNG, BOBBY	
22 1925	[] BUCHA, JOHNNY	
23 1918	[] GUMPERT, RANDY	
23 1923	[] DEAL, ELLIS	
23 1924	[] AMALFITANO, JOE	
23 1928	[] CARRASQUEL, CHICO	
23 1930	[] SULLIVAN, FRANK	
24 1932	[] ORAVETZ, ERNIE	
24 1934	[] BRIGGS, JOHN	
24 1936	[] STIGMAN, DICK	
25 1933	[] ROACH, MEL	
25 1934	[] KAZANSKI, TED	
25 1936	[] PRITCHARD, BUDDY	
27 1926	[] BORKOWSKI, BOB	
27 1929	[] KLINE, BOB	
28 1916	[] MUNCRIEF, BOB	
28 1922	[] ARFT, HANK	
28 1928	[] RUNNELS, PETE	
28 1929	[] BERNIER, CARLOS	
29 1918	[] RIGNEY, BILL	
29 1919	[] EDWARDS, HANK	
29 1927	[] NIEMAN, BOB	

29 1929	[] ROBERTSON, AL	30 1925	[] LAWRENCE, BROOKS
30 1917	[] HARRIS, MICKEY	31 1929	[] MAAS, DUKE
30 1923	[] DROPO, WALT	31 1931	[] ALSTON, TOM
30 1925	[] GLYNN, BILL	31 1932	[] AGUIRRE, HANK

FEBRUARY

01 1918	[] WYSE, HANK	14 1931	[] CAFFIE, JOE
01 1921	[] MADISON, DAVE	16 1926	[] JUDSON, HOWIE
01 1931	[] SMITH, BOB G	16 1936	[] LANDRUM, DON
01 1934	[] CONLEY, BOB	17 1921	[] LADE, DOYLE
02 1922	[] JONES, SHELDON	17 1926	[] CRIMIAN, JACK
03 1922	[] DYCK, JIM	17 1934	[] KIRKLAND, WILLIE
03 1925	[] BYRD, HARRY	17 1935	[] DOUGLAS, WHAMMY
03 1935	[] KAISER, DON	18 1923	[] TIPTON, JOE
05 1923	[] DIERING, CHUCK	18 1927	[] WEHMEIER, HERM
05 1928	[] HOAK, DON	18 1927	[] ARROYO, LUIS
05 1929	[] WORTHINGTON, AL	18 1929	[] NEEMAN, CAL
06 1926	[] CALDERONE, SAM	18 1930	[] HOUSE, FRANK
07 1926	[] LANE, JERALD HAL	19 1935	[] NIXON, RUSS
07 1927	[] LONNETT, JOE	20 1920	[] GUSTINE, FRANK
07 1928	[] SMITH, AL	20 1922	[] WILSON, JIM
07 1936	[] LEJA, FRANK	20 1924	[] YVARS, SAL
07 1938	[] PIZARRO, JUAN	20 1928	[] FACE, ROY
08 1921	[] MARSHALL, WILLARD	22 1920	[] DREWS, KARL
08 1921	[] EVERS, HOOT	22 1928	[] WILSON, BOB
08 1922	[] BASGALL, MONTE	22 1930	[] LUTTRELL, LYLE
09 1916	[] HUGHSON, TEX	22 1931	[] NICHOLS, CHET
09 1925	[] WERTZ, VIC	23 1914	[] TRESH, MIKE
09 1928	[] PALICA, ERV	23 1924	[] HAUGSTAD, PHIL
10 1915	[] REYNOLDS, ALLIE	23 1932	[] BOLGER, JIM
10 1926	[] JACKSON, RANDY	24 1919	[] WILBER, DEL
10 1933	[] DAVIE, JERRY	24 1930	[] PHILLIPS, BUBBA
10 1933	[] HEMAN, RUSS	25 1921	[] PAFKO, ANDY
11 1924	[] RICE, HAL	25 1924	[] LOHRKE, JACK
11 1929	[] BEARD, RALPH	26 1915	[] ROE, PREACHER
11 1933	[] O'DELL, BILLY	26 1930	[] NEGRAY, RON
12 1917	[] DiMAGGIO, DOM	26 1930	[] JANOWICZ, VIC
12 1919	[] DUBIEL, WALT	26 1934	[] LEE, DON
12 1921	[] BOLLWEG, DON	27 1920	[] RYAN, CONNIE
12 1922	[] MAIN, FORREST	27 1933	[] TAYLOR, SAMMY
12 1922	[] CLARK, MIKE	28 1928	[] KOKOS, DICK
12 1939	[] WALKER, JERRY	28 1930	[] NICHOLS, DOLAN
13 1921	[] CASTIGLIONE, PETE	28 1930	[] MALZONE, FRANK
13 1927	[] BRIDEWESER, JIM	28 1930	[] SAMFORD, RON
14 1915	[] BARRETT, RED	29 1924	[] ROSEN, AL

MARCH

01 1921	[] FOX, HOWIE			15 1922	[] NOBLE, RAY
01 1924	[] THOMPSON, CHUCK			15 1928	[] KING, NELSON
01 1925	[] USHER, BOB			16 1927	[] COURTNEY, CLINT
01 1927	[] VAN CUYK, CHRIS			16 1930	[] LANDRITH, HOBIE
01 1928	[] HAMRIC, BERT			16 1932	[] BLASINGAME, DON
01 1932	[] ZANNI, DOM			17 1919	[] SAUER, HANK
02 1921	[] STARR, DICK			18 1911	[] BENTON, AL
02 1924	[] ABRAMS, CAL			18 1916	[] LAKE, EDDIE
02 1926	[] TAYLOR, BILL			18 1919	[] WHITE, HAL
02 1932	[] FERNANDEZ, CHICO			18 1925	[] HATFIELD, FRED
02 1936	[] BRADY, JIM			18 1926	[] LITTLEFIELD, DICK
03 1919	[] SOUCHOCK, STEVE			18 1932	[] TATE, LEE
04 1917	[] McCULLOUGH, CLYDE			19 1904	[] FITZPATRICK, JOHN
04 1918	[] QUEEN, MEL			19 1931	[] SMITH, PAUL LESLIE
04 1926	[] MICHAELS, CASS			20 1915	[] SPENCE, STAN
05 1921	[] VALO, ELMER			20 1925	[] WIDMAR, AL
05 1930	[] CRANDALL, DEL			20 1927	[] WILLIS, JIM
06 1915	[] SWIFT, BOB			20 1928	[] CRAWFORD, RUFUS
06 1924	[] PODBIELAN, BUD			20 1933	[] ALTMAN, GEORGE
06 1933	[] ABERNATHY, TED.			20 1937	[] KUHN, KEN
07 1921	[] FUSSELMAN, LES			21 1923	[] HUGHES, JIM
07 1930	[] ACKER, TOM			21 1927	[] FRIEND, OWEN
07 1931	[] RAND, DICK			22 1923	[] CROWE, GEORGE
07 1933	[] BOUCHEE, ED			22 1933	[] SCHROLL, AL
08 1912	[] MUELLER, RAY			22 1936	[] OLIVER, GENE
08 1917	[] SALKELD, BILL			23 1927	[] LOGAN, JOHNNY
08 1924	[] ATWELL, TOBY			23 1928	[] LEMON, JIM
08 1930	[] GRIM, BOB			23 1932	[] MEYER, JACK
08 1937	[] SMALL, JIM			24 1922	[] ROGOVIN, SAUL
09 1893	[] SOUTHWORTH, BILLY			24 1925	[] KRYHOSKI, DICK
09 1930	[] RAINES, LARRY			25 1909	[] LEONARD, DUTCH
09 1932	[] KLINE, RON			25 1930	[] MINARCIN, RUDY
09 1932	[] MARTIN, JAKE			25 1932	[] CRADDOCK, WALT
09 1934	[] LANDIS, JIM			25 1932	[] HELD, WOODY
10 1925	[] LIMMER, LOU			27 1932	[] COVINGTON, WES
10 1921	[] BLATNICK, JOHNNY			28 1919	[] RASCHI, VIC
13 1918	[] PELLAGRINI, EDDIE			28 1920	[] MARTIN, BABE
13 1922	[] MAPES, CLIFF			28 1929	[] MacDONALD, BILL
13 1923	[] ROSSI, JOE			30 1921	[] FOWLER, DICK
13 1928	[] GREENWOOD, BOB			31 1918	[] GRISSOM, MARV
13 1931	[] BESSENT, DON			31 1920	[] KOSLO, DAVE
14 1921	[] KENNEDY, BILL			31 1931	[] SNYDER, GENE

APRIL

01 1921	[] MURFF, JOHN			02 1930	[] JONES, GORDON
01 1926	[] THIES, JAKE			03 1926	[] GRAMMAS, ALEX
01 1935	[] QUALTERS, TOM			03 1929	[] DITMAR, ART
02 1919	[] JOHNSON, EARL			03 1939	[] TAYLOR, BOB
02 1924	[] AVILA, BOBBY			04 1916	[] RAMSDELL, WILLARD
02 1930	[] CECCARELLI, ART			04 1928	[] SMITH, FRANK

04 1929	[] GILBERT, TOOKIE		20 1917	[] PECK, HAL
04 1937	[] GEIGER, GARY		21 1919	[] ROJEK, STAN
05 1921	[] HOGUE, BOB		21 1935	[] BURK, MACK
07 1933	[] DEL GRECO, BOBBY		22 1933	[] SCHMIDT, BOB
08 1915	[] HIGBE, KIRBY		23 1917	[] LUPIEN, TONY
08 1933	[] MERRITT, LLOYD		23 1926	[] HARMON, CHUCK
08 1934	[] FARRELL, DICK		23 1935	[] BLACKBURN, RON
11 1916	[] CHAPMAN, SAM		24 1919	[] HOWELL, DIXIE H
11 1918	[] McCOSKY, BARNEY		24 1936	[] HOBBIE, GLEN
11 1921	[] HEARN, JIM		25 1898	[] HANEY, FRED
12 1924	[] WIGHT, BILL		26 1919	[] TRUCKS, VIRGIL
12 1926	[] MORYN, WALT		26 1920	[] NORTHY, RON
14 1935	[] KEOUGH, MARTY		26 1922	[] DENTE, SAM
14 1935	[] SECREST, CHARLIE		26 1927	[] HAMNER, GRANNY
15 1910	[] MAYO, ED		26 1929	[] ELSTON, DON
15 1931	[] BAILEY, ED		27 1924	[] THOMAS, KEITH
16 1916	[] SUDER, PETE		28 1927	[] MAXWELL, CHARLIE
17 1923	[] HEMUS, SOLLY		28 1930	[] STURDIVANT, TOM
18 1922	[] BURTSCHY, ED		28 1934	[] BRANDT, JACKIE
18 1929	[] KRALY, STEVE		28 1935	[] RAMOS, PEDRO
18 1939	[] McDANIEL, VON		29 1929	[] RIDZIK, STEVE

MAY

01 1917	[] MARRERO, CONRADO		13 1928	[] SMITH, BOB W
01 1919	[] ZARRILLA, AL		13 1932	[] SHEPARD, JACK
01 1930	[] PALYS, STAN		14 1921	[] THURMAN, BOB
02 1932	[] BRESSOUD, EDDIE		14 1925	[] MOSS, LES
03 1892	[] BAKER, DEL		15 1926	[] BACZEWSKI, FRED
03 1916	[] SILVESTRI, KEN		16 1919	[] OVERMIRE, FRANK
03 1926	[] JOK, STAN		16 1920	[] PHILLEY, DAVE
05 1925	[] RUTHERFORD, JOHN		16 1926	[] WALKER, RUBE
05 1934	[] BUDDIN, DON		17 1932	[] HOEFT, BILLY
06 1917	[] McCORMICK, MIKE		17 1933	[] VIRGIL, OZZIE
06 1921	[] CHESNES, BOB		18 1922	[] COAN, GIL
06 1921	[] WAKEFIELD, DICK		18 1923	[] LUND, DON
06 1926	[] COLE, DICK		18 1933	[] HARDY, CARROLL
06 1932	[] RABE, CHARLEY		19 1915	[] EARLY, JAKE
07 1919	[] PAPAI, AL		19 1927	[] McDONALD, JIM
09 1927	[] KATT, RAY		19 1927	[] ANTONELLO, BILL
09 1932	[] BARTIROME, TONY		20 1930	[] MORGAN, TOM
09 1935	[] SHIPLEY, JOE		21 1924	[] FITZGERALD, ED
10 1920	[] GRASSO, MICKEY		21 1927	[] TAPPE, ELVIN
10 1931	[] BOWMAN, BOB		21 1930	[] REGALADO, RUDY
11 1907	[] SEWELL, RIP		21 1934	[] THACKER, MOE
11 1920	[] HERMANSKI, GENE		21 1936	[] LATMAN, BARRY
11 1922	[] KENNEDY, MONTE		22 1934	[] VALDIVIELSO, JOSE
11 1923	[] ORTIZ, LOUIS		23 1925	[] KING, CLYDE
11 1924	[] CAMPOS, FRANK		24 1926	[] MIRANDA, WILLIE
12 1916	[] BOROWY, HANK		25 1912	[] GALAN, AUGIE
12 1922	[] HETKI, JOHN		25 1925	[] LIDDLE, DON
12 1930	[] UMPHLETT, TOM		25 1932	[] MARSHALL, JIM
13 1917	[] STRINGER, LOU		26 1935	[] HAAS, EDDIE
13 1924	[] FANNIN, CLIFF		27 1909	[] HIGGINS, MIKE

27 1924	[] HURD, TOM	29 1928	[] SCHMIDT, WILLARD
27 1935	[] KINDALL, JERRY	30 1922	[] HOOPER, BOB
28 1923	[] KUZAVA, BOB	30 1924	[] LOWN, TURK
28 1934	[] SMITH, BOBBY GENE		

JUNE

01 1926	[] MOORE, RAY	17 1925	[] POPE, DAVE
01 1931	[] SMITH, HAL R	17 1928	[] NIXON, WILLARD
02 1929	[] VALDES, RENE	17 1932	[] DANIELS, BENNIE
02 1929	[] LILLIS, BOB	18 1933	[] PHILLIPS, TAYLOR
02 1931	[] JACKSON, LARRY	19 1923	[] ALOMA, LUIS
02 1932	[] SKIZAS, LOU	19 1924	[] BLACKBURN, JIM
02 1933	[] LUMPE, JERRY	19 1929	[] FERRARESE, DON
04 1922	[] COLEMAN, RAY	20 1926	[] KOSHOREK, CLEM
04 1928	[] HUNTER, BILLY	20 1928	[] MAHONEY, BOB
04 1930	[] CASAGRANDE, TOM	20 1928	[] SCHULT, ART
05 1916	[] JOOST, EDDIE	20 1929	[] BURNETTE, WALLY
05 1924	[] BRISSIE, LOU	21 1927	[] COLLUM, JACK
06 1927	[] TALBOT, BOB	22 1920	[] MASTERSON, WALT
06 1931	[] ARIAS, RUDOLPH	22 1931	[] THRONEBERRY, FAYE
06 1931	[] WILLEY, CARL	23 1915	[] ROBINSON, AARON
07 1921	[] McCAHAN, BILL	24 1907	[] HEMSLEY, ROLLIE
08 1930	[] PAINE, PHIL	24 1923	[] HODERLEIN, MEL
08 1935	[] BRUNET, GEORGE	24 1925	[] BANTA, JACK
09 1903	[] RYBA, MIKE	25 1930	[] LUNA, MEMO
09 1911	[] McCORMICK, FRANK	25 1930	[] ROBINSON, HUMBERTO
09 1925	[] PEARCE, JIM	25 1935	[] DEMETER, DON
09 1926	[] SMALLEY, ROY	26 1918	[] SINGLETON, BERT
10 1928	[] LEHMAN, KEN	26 1921	[] POLLET, HOWIE
10 1929	[] FOILES, HANK	26 1933	[] GREEN, GENE
12 1928	[] CUSICK, JOHN	27 1923	[] KRETLOW, LOU
12 1928	[] PARKS, JACK	27 1923	[] ZERNIAL, GUS
13 1920	[] RODRIGUEZ, HECTOR	27 1925	[] TERWILLIGER, WAYNE
13 1922	[] PARNELL, MEL	27 1929	[] MARLOWE, DICK
14 1928	[] PLEWS, HERB	27 1930	[] TROWBRIDGE, BOB
14 1933	[] CONSTABLE, JIMMY	27 1931	[] COLES, CHUCK
15 1916	[] STEWART, ED	27 1932	[] KASKO, EDDIE
15 1925	[] BAKER, GENE	28 1935	[] BLAYLOCK, BOB
15 1927	[] FLOWERS, BENNET	29 1915	[] TROUT, DIZZY
16 1922	[] SURKONT, MAX	29 1925	[] JONES, NIPPY
16 1923	[] CLARK, ALLIE	29 1925	[] CONNELLY, BILL
16 1924	[] JOHNSON, ERNIE	29 1926	[] MORGAN, BOBBY
16 1926	[] MILLER, BOB	29 1933	[] SHAW, BOB
16 1934	[] HERRERA, FRANK	30 1931	[] GROSS, DON

JULY

01 1920	[] LEHNER, PAUL	01 1936	[] DROTT, DICK
01 1924	[] WOOD, KEN	02 1929	[] STOBBS, CHUCK
01 1928	[] FREEMAN, HERSHALL	02 1930	[] BURNSIDE, PETE
01 1935	[] BAUMAN, FRANK	03 1914	[] ROSAR, BUDDY

03 1922	[] FOWLER, ART	18 1916	[] HOPP, JOHNNY
03 1930	[] PILARCIK, AL	18 1920	[] KAZAK, EDDIE
04 1928	[] BIRRER, BABE	18 1925	[] McCALL, WINDY
04 1929	[] TREMEL, BILL	18 1928	[] HARRELL, BILLY
04 1929	[] TUTTLE, BILL	19 1927	[] GARDNER, BILLY
04 1931	[] MALKMUS, BOB	19 1930	[] SOLIS, MARCELINO
05 1922	[] KOZAR, AL	21 1927	[] SMITH, DICK
05 1923	[] FRICANO, MARION	21 1929	[] SNYDER, JERRY
05 1926	[] HAWES, ROY LEE	22 1922	[] RIVERA, JIM
05 1928	[] BAXES, JIM	22 1934	[] STEVENS, R C
05 1931	[] PORTOCARRERO, ARNIE	23 1917	[] SCARBOROUGH, RAY
06 1891	[] O'NEILL, STEVE	23 1926	[] GROTH, JOHNNY
06 1924	[] KELLERT, FRANK	24 1922	[] PILLETTE, DUANE
06 1930	[] OLSON, KARL	24 1927	[] WARD, PRESTON
07 1926	[] CLARK, MEL	26 1914	[] KINDER, ELLIS
07 1926	[] SPENCER, GEORGE	26 1917	[] BLOODWORTH, JIMMY
07 1928	[] WHITE, SAMMY	26 1920	[] SISTI, SIBBY
07 1929	[] ROMONOSKY, JOHN	26 1921	[] SAFFELL, TOM
08 1929	[] POWERS, JOHN	26 1925	[] MAYO, JACKIE
08 1930	[] GORBOUS, GLEN	26 1926	[] MILLER, BILL
08 1939	[] KEEGAN, BOB	26 1932	[] BRODOWSKI, DICK
09 1931	[] FODGE, GENE	26 1933	[] SIEBERN, NORM
09 1932	[] CLEVENGER, TEX	26 1935	[] JACKSON, LOU
09 1932	[] VEAL, COOT	27 1898	[] TAYLOR, ZACK
11 1931	[] GRAY, DICK	27 1923	[] BOONE, RAY
12 1919	[] WYROSTEK, JOHNNY	27 1933	[] KUCKS, JOHNNY
12 1927	[] HARSHMAN, JACK	28 1901	[] FITZSIMMONS, FRED
12 1931	[] PENSON, PAUL	28 1930	[] LEPCIO, TED
13 1920	[] HILLER, FRANK	28 1931	[] KERIAZAKOS, GUS
13 1921	[] DORISH, HARRY	29 1920	[] DUSAK, ERV
13 1927	[] GOMEZ, RUBEN	29 1934	[] MANTILLA, FELIX
13 1929	[] SPENCER, DARYL	30 1922	[] COLEMAN, JOE
13 1938	[] PAVLETICH, DON	30 1923	[] MINNER, PAUL
14 1929	[] PURKEY, BOB	30 1928	[] HALL, BILL
15 1923	[] EDWARDS, BRUCE	30 1928	[] NUXHALL, JOE
15 1925	[] WELLMAN, BOB	30 1930	[] TRIANDOS, GUS
15 1931	[] WILL, BOB	31 1916	[] HITCHCOCK, BILLY
15 1935	[] MILLER, BOB G	31 1927	[] ABER, AL
16 1910	[] NORMAN, BILL	31 1927	[] SHANTZ, WILMER
16 1920	[] JANSEN, LARRY	31 1931	[] COLEMAN, RIP
17 1930	[] LYNCH, JERRY	31 1931	[] DURHAM, JOE
17 1930	[] McMILLAN, ROY		

AUGUST

02 1906	[] POSEDEL, BILL	05 1925	[] JACOBS, ANTHONY
02 1924	[] MERRIMAN, LLOYD	05 1927	[] KRSNICH, ROCKY
03 1917	[] CANDINI, MILO	06 1896	[] BLADES, RAY
03 1928	[] HYDE, DICK	06 1926	[] LABINE, CLEM
04 1915	[] EASTER, LUKE	06 1928	[] MOFORD, HERB
04 1918	[] KOLLOWAY, DON	07 1927	[] BRIDGES, ROCKY
04 1929	[] PIGNATANO, JOE	07 1927	[] HOUTTEMAN, ART
05 1921	[] ST CLAIRE, EBBA	07 1931	[] CRONE, RAY
05 1924	[] YUHAS, ED	07 1936	[] NELSON, BOB

08 1917	[] RAFFENSBERGER, KEN	18 1920	[] KENNEDY, BOB
08 1918	[] STUART, MARLIN	18 1927	[] BOWMAN, ROGER
08 1928	[] TEMPLE, JOHNNY	18 1934	[] CONSOLO, BILLY
09 1919	[] SANFORD, FRED	19 1928	[] FINIGAN, JIM
09 1923	[] VICO, GEORGE	20 1919	[] HARRIST, EARL
09 1930	[] BOLLING, MILT	20 1924	[] ZUVERINK, GEORGE
09 1930	[] MEJIAS, ROMAN	20 1925	[] MIGGINS, LARRY
09 1931	[] ESSEGIAN, CHUCK	21 1916	[] DICKSON, MURRY
10 1911	[] WRIGHT, TAFT	21 1920	[] PLATT, MIZELL
10 1922	[] HARTUNG, CLINT	21 1920	[] STALEY, GERRY
10 1923	[] PORTERFIELD, BOB	22 1909	[] KEELY, BOB
10 1927	[] CHAKALES, BOB	22 1930	[] SPEAKE, BOB
11 1907	[] NEWSOM, BOBO	22 1931	[] BARCLAY, CURT
11 1915	[] SCHEFFING, BOB	23 1918	[] HOLCOMBE, KEN.
11 1932	[] KORCHECK, STEVE	23 1921	[] MITCHELL, DALE
12 1917	[] GORDON, SID	23 1924	[] LOLLAR, SHERM
12 1928	[] BUHL, BOB	23 1924	[] ROMANO, JOHN
12 1928	[] WHITE, CHUCK	23 1930	[] BELLA, ZEKE
12 1936	[] BURTON, ELLIS	24 1928	[] GRIGGS, HAL
13 1930	[] MIZELL, WILMER	24 1932	[] WOODESHICK, HAL
13 1930	[] WIESLER, BOB	25 1926	[] MILLIKEN, BOB
13 1935	[] GRANT, JIM	25 1928	[] JOHNSON, DARRELL
14 1929	[] PISONI, JIM	26 1924	[] KELLNER, ALEX
14 1930	[] COOGAN, DALE	26 1925	[] DeMARS, BILLY
15 1930	[] MARTYN, BOB	26 1929	[] POHOLSKY, TOM
15 1934	[] MOREHEAD, SETH	26 1935	[] SILVERA, AL
15 1936	[] BUZHARDT, JOHN	27 1915	[] VERBAN, EMIL
16 1913	[] BONHAM, ERNIE	27 1918	[] LOWREY, PEANUTS
16 1922	[] WOODLING, GENE	27 1931	[] CUNNINGHAM, JOE
16 1925	[] JONES, WILLIE	27 1932	[] KING, JIM
16 1929	[] ROBERTS, CURT	27 1935	[] BROGLIO, ERNIE
16 1931	[] RUDOLPH, DON	28 1925	[] PRAMESA, JOHNNY
17 1920	[] BICKFORD, VERN	28 1928	[] TRICE, BOB
17 1933	[] DAVENPORT, JIM	28 1937	[] HARTMAN, BOB
18 1915	[] LANIER, MAX	29 1919	[] COX, BILLY
29 1928	[] McDERMONT, MICKEY	30 1918	[] JOHNSON, BILLY
29 1930	[] COLE, DAVE	30 1927	[] GOLDSBERRY, GORDON
29 1939	[] ZUPO, FRANK	31 1916	[] LITWHILER, DANNY
30 1916	[] LINDELL, JOHNNY	31 1925	[] HOSKINS, DAVE

SEPTEMBER

01 1922	[] ASTROTH, JOE	06 1921	[] PHILLIPS, JACK
01 1927	[] BOYER, CLOYD	06 1922	[] PERKOWSKI, HARRY
01 1930	[] STONE, DEAN	06 1924	[] FRIDLEY, JIM
03 1920	[] CONSUEGRA, SANDY	06 1924	[] JEFFCOAT, HAL
03 1922	[] MARTIN, MORRIE	06 1924	[] SCHMEES, GEORGE
03 1931	[] BREWER, TOM	07 1917	[] PARTEE, ROY
03 1936	[] BOROS, STEVE	08 1926	[] SLEATER, LOU
04 1919	[] WAITKUS, EDDIE	08 1932	[] WISE, CASEY
04 1928	[] SANTIAGO, JOSE	09 1931	[] AVERILL, EARL
05 1920	[] BEARDEN, GENE	10 1931	[] ANDERSON, HARRY
05 1930	[] BELARDI, WAYNE	11 1926	[] MIKSIS, EDDIE

16

12 1916	[] HAMNER, RALPH	19 1930	[] TURLEY, BOB
12 1920	[] SEMINICK, ANDY	20 1898	[] DRESSEN, CHUCK
12 1924	[] CHURCH, BUBBA	20 1922	[] LOMBARDI, VIC
12 1925	[] LOPATA, STAN	21 1917	[] HAYNES, JOE
12 1926	[] FREESE, GEORGE.	21 1930	[] MUFFETT, BILLY
13 1931	[] SUSCE, GEORGE	21 1934	[] ZIMMERMAN, JERRY
14 1927	[] HILLMAN, DAVE	22 1923	[] WRIGHT, TOMMY
15 1907	[] OSTERMUELLER, FRITZ	22 1929	[] BRIGHT, HARRY
15 1924	[] DAVIS, JIM	22 1931	[] ASPROMONTE, KEN
15 1928	[] LENNON, BOB	23 1920	[] PIERETTI, MARINO
15 1929	[] WHEAT, LEROY	23 1924	[] RESTELLI, DINO
16 1908	[] MILLS, BUSTER	24 1921	[] VOLLMER, CLYDE
16 1923	[] DEMPSEY, CON	26 1921	[] MADDERN, CLARENCE
16 1928	[] VALENTINETTI, VITO	26 1924	[] ERAUTT, ED
16 1930	[] MROZINSKI, RON	27 1928	[] KIPPER, THORNTON
17 1917	[] GETTELL, AL	27 1930	[] HALL, DICK
17 1918	[] DILLINGER, BOB	27 1933	[] CASALE, JERRY
17 1923	[] PEDEN, LES	28 1916	[] EVANS, AL
17 1936	[] CARROLL, TOMMY	28 1917	[] TUCKER, THURMAN
18 1925	[] HADDIX, HARVEY	28 1917	[] MOULDER, GLEN
19 1924	[] BENSON, VERN	28 1928	[] GERNERT, DICK
19 1926	[] WALL, MURRAY	29 1924	[] McGHEE, ED
19 1927	[] SARNI, BILL	29 1935	[] ANDERSON, BOB
19 1929	[] SHEARER, RAY	30 1929	[] BLAYLOCK, MARV

OCTOBER

01 1918	[] RUSSELL, JIM	10 1929	[] TIEFENAUER, BOB
01 1926	[] BOYD, BOB	11 1912	[] GUERRA, MIKE
01 1928	[] NARAGON, HAL	11 1918	[] CHIPMAN, BOB
01 1931	[] KIPP, FRED	11 1926	[] GINSBERG, JOE
02 1920	[] SHEA, FRANK	11 1929	[] KELL, EVERETT
02 1924	[] SERENA, BILL	11 1930	[] FISCHER, BILL
02 1930	[] SCULL, ANGEL	11 1931	[] BLAYLOCK, GARY
03 1905	[] RIDDLE, JOHN	12 1917	[] MURRAY, RAY
03 1928	[] MELTON, DAVE	12 1925	[] OSBORNE, LARRY
03 1932	[] CLARK, PHIL	13 1924	[] SILVERA, CHARLIE
04 1918	[] MUNGER, GEORGE	13 1926	[] YOST, EDDIE
04 1922	[] LENHARDT, DON	14 1914	[] JOLLY, DAVE
04 1927	[] KELLY, ROBERT	14 1915	[] HEINTZELMAN, KEN
04 1927	[] REPULSKI, RIP	14 1924	[] RENNA, BILL
05 1925	[] HOFMAN, BOBBY	14 1934	[] CHENEY, TOM
06 1922	[] FRAZIER, JOE	15 1927	[] HENRY, BILL
07 1918	[] BAUMHOLTZ, FRANK	15 1931	[] HARRIS, GAIL
07 1921	[] SIMA, AL	15 1936	[] SWANSON, ART
07 1922	[] HATTON, GRADY	16 1921	[] BATTS, MATT
07 1923	[] DALEY, BUD	16 1924	[] CAIN, BOB
07 1928	[] PRESKO, JOE	16 1931	[] SISLER, DAVE
08 1902	[] SCHREIBER, PAUL	17 1908	[] ROLFE, RED
08 1910	[] MOSES, WALLY	17 1915	[] SANDLOCK, MIKE
08 1921	[] METKOVICH, GEORGE	17 1927	[] KLIPPSTEIN, JOHNNY
08 1929	[] MABE, BOB	17 1933	[] POWELL, LEROY
09 1912	[] HAEFNER, MICKEY	18 1927	[] ROTBLATT, MARV
10 1916	[] BAKER, FLOYD	18 1935	[] NUNN, HOWIE

19 1913	[] BRAZLE, AL	24 1927	[] HOGUE, CAL
19 1930	[] KOPPE, JOE	25 1913	[] MARCHILDON, PHIL
19 1933	[] ALVAREZ, OSSIE	25 1923	[] MEYER, RUSS
20 1928	[] MICELOTTA, BOB	25 1925	[] HARTSFIELD, ROY
21 1913	[] CHRISTMAN, MARK	26 1920	[] BYERLY, BUD
21 1930	[] THOMAS, VALMY	26 1923	[] GLAVIANO, TOMMY
21 1933	[] GORYL, JOHN	26 1926	[] BOKELMAN, DICK
22 1918	[] WALKER, HARRY	27 1919	[] RICHMOND, DON
22 1933	[] JACKSON, RON	27 1922	[] RICE, DEL
23 1920	[] STEPHENS, VERN	29 1931	[] ALLIE, GAIR
23 1930	[] DRAKE, SOLLY	31 1924	[] FONDY, DEE
24 1927	[] GREENGRASS, JIM		

NOVEMBER

01 1917	[] MULLIN, PAT	15 1928	[] ROY, NORMAN
01 1931	[] KEMMERER, RUSS	15 1930	[] BEVAN, HAL
01 1932	[] PYBURN, JIM	15 1937	[] WEBSTER, RAY
02 1914	[] McBRIDE, TOM	16 1930	[] FOYTACK, PAUL
02 1920	[] SISLER, DICK	16 1931	[] BOLLING, FRANK
02 1927	[] WILLIAMS, DAVE	16 1932	[] CHITI, HARRY
02 1928	[] ROSS, BOB	17 1919	[] LaMANNO, RAY
03 1919	[] GOLIAT, MIKE	17 1927	[] WEIK, DICK
04 1925	[] JACOBS, FORREST	17 1929	[] ZAUCHIN, NORM
04 1927	[] SAWATSKI, CARL	17 1933	[] PENA, ORLANDO
04 1933	[] FRANCONA, TITO	17 1936	[] BELL, GARY
05 1909	[] GUMBERT, HARRY	18 1924	[] NELSON, ROCKY
05 1924	[] DIXON, SONNY	18 1926	[] SIEVERS, ROY
06 1922	[] KERR, BUDDY	18 1932	[] McDEVITT, DANNY
06 1925	[] ADDIS, BOB	20 1917	[] DOBERNIC, JESS
06 1928	[] WILSON, BILL	20 1929	[] BERBERET, LOU
07 1916	[] HATTON, JOE	21 1908	[] RICHARDS, PAUL
07 1933	[] HALE, BOB	21 1924	[] HACKER, WARREN
08 1920	[] WESTLAKE, WALLY	24 1930	[] FRIEND, BOB
09 1919	[] PRIDDY, JERRY	25 1923	[] WILSON, AL
09 1920	[] WHITMAN, DICK	25 1928	[] NARLESKI, RAY
10 1896	[] DYKES, JIMMY	25 1933	[] WAUGH, JIM
10 1912	[] TEBBETTS, BIRDIE	26 1922	[] MUIR, JOE
10 1922	[] LIPON, JOHNNY	26 1922	[] WADE, BEN
10 1930	[] KING, CHARLES	27 1920	[] SCHMITZ, JOHNNY
11 1929	[] DELOCK, IKE	27 1923	[] SCHULTZ, BOB
11 1931	[] DOTTERER, DUTCH	27 1927	[] QUINN, FRANK
12 1924	[] HANSEN, ANDY	27 1933	[] MORAN, BILLY
12 1926	[] JOHNSON, DON	28 1922	[] WESTRUM, WES
12 1927	[] HANEBRINK, HARRY	28 1927	[] PAULA, CARLOS
13 1915	[] WILKS, TED	29 1924	[] NOREN, IRV
13 1925	[] DELSING, JIM	29 1939	[] DERRINGTON, JIM
13 1928	[] BILKO, STEVE	30 1901	[] SUKEFORTH, CLYDE
15 1916	[] OSTROWSKI, JOE	30 1929	[] KIELY, LEO
15 1928	[] BELL, GUS	30 1931	[] MAYER, ED

DECEMBER

01 1921	[] SAVAGE, BOB	11 1914	[] NICHOLSON, BILL
01 1925	[] McLISH, CAL	11 1919	[] COMBS, MERRILL
02 1934	[] RODGERS, ANDRE	11 1924	[] BROWN, HECTOR
03 1925	[] SIMPSON, HARRY	11 1927	[] GRAY, JOHNNY
03 1926	[] CORWIN, AL	11 1930	[] O'BRIEN, JOHNNY
04 1933	[] RICKETTS, DICK	11 1930	[] O'BRIEN, EDDIE
05 1921	[] FERRISS, BOO	12 1917	[] KLUTTZ, CLYDE
05 1928	[] URBAN, JACK	12 1921	[] HOWERTON, BILL
06 1920	[] NIARHOS, GUS	12 1930	[] SANCHEZ, RAUL
06 1925	[] PLESS, RANCE	13 1916	[] MAJESKI, HANK
06 1927	[] BROWN, TOMMY	13 1929	[] LOES, BILLY
06 1934	[] DOBBEK, DAN	14 1921	[] ADAMS, BOBBY
07 1930	[] FREEMAN, MARK	14 1923	[] LaPALME, PAUL
07 1930	[] SMITH, HAL W	14 1925	[] JONES, SAM
07 1935	[] CARDWELL, DON	14 1929	[] WHISENANT, PETE
071927	[] DONOVAN, DICK	14 1932	[] McDANIEL, JIM
08 1918	[] ZOLDAK, SAM	14 1933	[] SCHOONMAKER, JERRY
08 1925	[] THOMPSON, HANK	15 1919	[] TRINKLE, KEN
09 1921	[] KRESS, CHUCK	15 1920	[] ROBINSON, EDDIE
09 1928	[] DeMAESTRI, JOE	15 1929	[] HERBERT, RAY
09 1928	[] KLAUS, BILLY	15 1931	[] ESPOSITO, SAMMY
09 1930	[] HAZLE, BOB	16 1931	[] CHRISLEY, NEIL
10 1931	[] ROSELLI, BOB	17 1926	[] JABLONSKI, RAY
17 1934	[] HADLEY, KENT	24 1916	[] GRAHAM, JACK
18 1929	[] CIMOLI, GINO	24 1938	[] HENRICH, BOB
18 1930	[] BAXES, MIKE	25 1908	[] CHAPMAN, BEN
19 1917	[] POAT, RAY	25 1925	[] GARVER, NED
19 1935	[] TAYLOR, TONY	25 1928	[] BLYZKA, MICHAEL
20 1931	[] BECQUER, JULIO	25 1934	[] BEAMON, CHARLIE
21 1925	[] PETERSON, KENT	26 1927	[] SCHELL, DANNY
21 1925	[] RUSH, BOB	27 1922	[] JOHNSON, CONNIE
21 1927	[] DANIELS, JACK	28 1921	[] BURBRINK, NELSON
21 1930	[] KRAVITZ, DANNY	29 1926	[] UPTON, TOM
21 1930	[] WERLE, BILL	30 1923	[] ELLIOTT, HARRY
21 1936	[] LUMENTI, RALPH	30 1929	[] TAYLOR, JOE
22 1923	[] HALL, BOB	30 1930	[] GRAFF, MILT
22 1929	[] BRUTON, BILL	31 1919	[] BYRNE, TOMMY
23 1925	[] BLAKE, ED	31 1924	[] GRAY, TED
23 1929	[] CICOTTE, AL		

STATE OF MINE

None of us really had anything to do with it, but there is a soft spot for the State, or Country in, which we were born. It just so happened to be where mother was at the time. Here is a checklist of where these UN-COMMONS' mothers just happened to be.

ALABAMA

[] BOLLING, FRANK
[] BRUTON, BILL
[] CAFFIE, JOE
[] CHURCH, BUBBA
[] DANIELS, BENNIE
[] DAVENPORT, JIM
[] FREEMAN, HERSHALL
[] GRAMMAS, ALEX
[] HATFIELD, FRED

[] HITCHCOCK, BILLY
[] HOUSE, FRANK
[] KIRKLAND, WILLIE
[] LEHNER, PAUL
[] LINT, ROYCE
[] MORAN, BILLY
[] NIARHOS, GUS
[] OLIVER, TOM
[] PARKS, JACK

[] POPE, DAVE
[] POWERS, JOHN
[] PYBURN, JIM
[] SEWELL, RIP
[] TAYLOR, BILL
[] TRUCKS, VIRGIL
[] WORTHINGTON, AL

ARIZONA

[] HEMUS, SOLLY
[] KELLNER, ALEX

[] LEE, DON

[] MADDERN, CLARENCE

ARKANSAS

[] BEARDEN, GENE
[] BLAYLOCK, MARV
[] DRAKE, SOLLY
[] JACKSON, RANDY
[] KELL, EVERETT

[] KINDER, ELLIS
[] KING, JIM
[] LOLLAR, SHERM
[] McGHEE, ED
[] SMITH, HAL R

[] STEPHENS, GENE
[] STUART, MARLIN
[] TATE, LEE
[] WYSE, HANK

BAHAMAS

[] RODGERS, ANDRE

CALIFORNIA

[] ADAMS, BOBBY
[] AGUIRRE, HANK
[] AMALFITANO, JOE
[] BARRETT, RED
[] BATTEY, EARL
[] BAXES, JIM
[] BAXES, MIKE
[] BEAMON, CHARLIE
[] BELARDI, WAYNE
[] BERBERET, LOU

[] BOCKMAN, EDDIE
[] BONHAM, ERNIE
[] BOONE, RAY
[] BOWMAN, BOB
[] BRESSOUD, EDDIE
[] BRIGGS, JOHN
[] BROGLIO, ERNIE
[] BURTON, ELLIS
[] CANDINI, MILO
[] CHAPMAN, SAM

[] CHESNES, BOB
[] CIMOLI, GINO
[] CLEVENGER, TEX
[] COLE, DICK
[] COLEMAN, RAY
[] COMBS, MERRILL
[] COOGAN, DALE
[] CRANDALL, DEL
[] DALEY, BUD
[] DALEY, PETE

[] DAVIS, JIM
[] DeMAESTRI, JOE
[] DEMPSEY, CON
[] DERRINGTON, JIM
[] DILLINGER, BOB
[] DiMAGGIO, DOM
[] ELLIOTT, HARRY
[] FERRARESE, DON
[] FITZGERALD, ED
[] GALAN, AUGIE
[] GLAVIANO, TOMMY
[] GOLDSBERRY, GORDON
[] GREEN, GENE
[] GRISSOM, MARV
[] HARSHMAN, JACK
[] HELD, WOODY
[] HEMAN, RUSS
[] HOWERTON, BILL
[] JONES, NIPPY
[] JOOST, EDDIE
[] KEOUGH, MARTY
[] KRESS, RALPH
[] LAKE, EDDIE
[] LaMANNO, RAY
[] LANDIS, JIM

[] LANDRUM, DON
[] LATMAN, BARRY
[] LILLIS, BOB
[] LOHRKE, JACK
[] LOMBARDI, VIC
[] LOWREY, PEANUTS
[] MacDONALD, BILL
[] MAIN, FORREST
[] MAYER, ED
[] McCALL, WINDY
[] McCORMICK, MIKE
[] McDANIEL, JIM
[] MERRIMAN, LLOYD
[] METKOVICH, GEORGE
[] MORGAN, TOM
[] OLSON, KARL
[] ORTIZ, LOUIS
[] PALICA, ERV
[] PARTEE, ROY
[] POSEDEL, BILL
[] PRIDDY, JERRY
[] PRITCHARD, BUDDY
[] RAND, DICK
[] REGALADO, RUDY
[] RENNA, BILL

[] RIGNEY, BILL
[] ROSELLI, BOB
[] ROSS, BOB
[] ROSSI, JOE
[] SARNI, BILL
[] SERENA, BILL
[] SHEPARD, JACK
[] SILVERA, AL
[] SILVERA, CHARLIE
[] STEWART, ED
[] SULLIVAN, FRANK
[] TALBOT, BOB
[] TAYLOR, JOE
[] TRIANDOS, GUS
[] USHER, BOB
[] VICO, GEORGE
[] WALLS, LEE
[] WEBSTER, RAY
[] WERLE, BILL
[] WESTLAKE, WALLY
[] WIGHT, BILL
[] WILSON, AL
[] WILSON, JIM
[] ZARRILLA, AL
[] ZUPO, FRANK

CANADA

[] BOWSFIELD, TED
[] FOWLER, DICK

[] GORBOUS, GLEN
[] MARCHILDON, PHIL

[] ROBERTSON, SHERRY
[] RUTHERFORD, JOHN

COLORADO

[] LINDELL, JOHNNY

CONNECTICUT

[] BELLA, ZEKE
[] CASAGRANDE, TOM
[] CASTIGLIONE, PETE

[] CECCARELLI, ART
[] DROPO, WALT
[] DUBIEL, WALT

[] GARDNER, BILLY
[] SANDLOCK, MIKE
[] SHEA, FRANK

CUBA

[] ALOMA, LUIS
[] ALVAREZ, OSSIE
[] ARIAS, RUDOLPH
[] BECQUER, JULIO
[] CAMPOS, FRANK
[] CONSUEGRA, SANDY

[] FERNANDEZ, CHICO
[] FORNIELES, MIKE
[] GUERRA, MIKE
[] HERRERA, FRANK
[] MARRERO, CONRADO
[] MEJIAS, ROMAN

[] MIRANDA, WILLIE
[] NOBLE, RAY
[] PAULA, CARLOS
[] PENA, ORLANDO
[] RAMOS, PEDRO
[] RODRIGUEZ, HECTOR

[] SANCHEZ, RAUL
[] SCULL, ANGEL
[] TAYLOR, TONY
[] VALDES, RENE
[] VALDIVIELSO, JOSE

CZECHOSLOVAKIA

[] VALO, ELMER

DELEWARE

[] JACOBS, FORREST

DOMINICAN REPUBLIC

[] VIRGIL, OZZIE

FLORIDA

[] BESSENT, DON
[] BLOODWORTH, JIMMY
[] GRANT, JIM
[] GRAY, JOHNNY
[] HALE, BOB
[] HANSEN, ANDY
[] HOGUE, BOB
[] KLINE, BOB
[] PLATT, MIZELL
[] SCHREIBER, PAUL
[] TAYLOR, ZACK

GEORGIA

[] BISHOP, CHARLIE
[] CHENEY, TOM
[] CLARK, PHIL
[] GRIGGS, HAL
[] HALL, BILL
[] HARTSFIELD, ROY
[] HAYNES, JOE
[] HEARN, JIM
[] JOHNSON, CONNIE
[] KENNEDY, BILL
[] MOSES, WALLY
[] NIXON, WILLARD
[] OSBORNE, LARRY
[] PHILLIPS, TAYLOR
[] SIMPSON, HARRY
[] STEVENS, R C
[] TIPTON, JOE
[] TRICE, BOB
[] VEAL, COOT

IDAHO

[] HADLEY, KENT
[] JACKSON, LARRY
[] MARTYN, BOB
[] SALKELD, BILL

ILLINOIS

[] ASTROTH, JOE
[] BARCLAY, CURT
[] BLADES, RAY
[] BLAKE, ED
[] BOKELMAN, DICK
[] BOLLWEG, DON
[] BURNSIDE, PETE
[] CHITI, HARRY
[] DOBERNIC, JESS
[] DRESSEN, CHUCK
[] DUSAK, ERV
[] EDWARDS, BRUCE
[] ESPOSITO, SAMMY
[] FINIGAN, JIM
[] FRIEND, OWEN

[] GEIGER, GARY
[] GROTH, JOHNNY
[] GUSTINE, FRANK
[] HACKER, WARREN
[] HAEFNER, MICKEY
[] HAWES, ROY LEE
[] HOBBIE, GLEN
[] HUGHES, JIM
[] HYDE, DICK
[] JABLONSKI, RAY
[] JACOBS, ANTHONY
[] JUDSON, HOWIE
[] KENNEDY, BOB
[] KLAUS, BILLY
[] KOKOS, DICK
[] KOLLOWAY, DON
[] LANDRITH, HOBIE

[] LENHARDT, DON
[] LEONARD, DUTCH
[] LIDDLE, DON
[] LUTTRELL, LYLE
[] MARSHALL, JIM
[] MASI, PHIL
[] MAYO, JACKIE
[] McCARTHY, JOHN
[] MEYER, RUSS
[] MILLER, BOB G
[] NEEMAN, CAL
[] O'TOOLE, JIM
[] OLIVER, GENE
[] OSTERMUELLER, FRITZ
[] PAPAI, AL
[] POAT, RAY

[] RAYDON, CURT
[] ROBERTSON, AL
[] ROMONOSKY, JOHN
[] ROTBLATT, MARV
[] SILVESTRI, KEN
[] SKIZAS, LOU
[] SMITH, HAL W
[] STONE, DEAN
[] TAPPE, ELVIN
[] TAYLOR, BOB
[] TURLEY, BOB
[] TUTTLE, BILL
[] VERBAN, EMIL
[] WAKEFIELD, DICK
[] WHEAT, LEROY
[] WILL, BOB
[] WYROSTEK, JOHNNY

INDIANA

[] ANDERSON, BOB
[] CROWE, GEORGE
[] FITZSIMMONS, FRED
[] FODGE, GENE

[] FRIEND, BOB
[] HARMON, CHUCK
[] KRALY, STEVE
[] MUFFETT, BILLY

[] PILARCIK, AL
[] TRINKLE, KEN
[] TROUT, DIZZY
[] WISE, CASEY

IOWA

[] BAKER, GENE
[] COLLUM, JACK

[] DITTMER, JACK
[] HATTON, JOE

[] OLDIS, BOB
[] WEIK, DICK

ITALY

[] BERTOIA, RENO

[] PIERETTI, MARINO

KANSAS

[] BANTA, JACK
[] BASGALL, MONTE
[] CAIN, BOB
[] HENRICH, BOB
[] HETKI, JOHN
[] JOHNSON, KEN

[] KIPP, FRED
[] MARSH, FRED
[] MUELLER, RAY
[] PENSON, PAUL
[] RAMSDELL, WILLARD
[] SCHMIDT, WILLARD

[] SPENCER, DARYL
[] STURDIVANT, TOM
[] SWIFT, BOB
[] THOMAS, KEITH
[] THURMAN, BOB

KENTUCKY

[] BELL, GUS
[] BICKFORD, VERN
[] BLACKBURN, JIM

[] CONLEY, BOB
[] FANNIN, CLIFF
[] HAAS, EDDIE

[] HOWELL, DIXIE H
[] HOWELL, DIXIE M
[] KUHN, KEN

[] MOFORD, HERB [] SPENCE, STAN [] THACKER, MOE
[] SCHULTZ, BOB

LOUISIANA

[] BEVAN, HAL [] JACKSON, LOU [] SCHROLL, AL
[] COURTNEY, CLINT [] KRAMER, JACK [] STRICKLAND, GEORGE
[] GILBERT, TOOKIE [] PARNELL, MEL [] SWANSON, ART
[] HAMNER, RALPH [] POLLET, HOWIE [] TASBY, WILLIE
[] HARRIST, EARL [] RYAN, CONNIE [] WILLIS, JIM

MAINE

[] SUKEFORTH, CLYDE [] WILLEY, CARL

MARYLAND

[] ANDERSON, HARRY [] MERSON, JOHN [] NICHOLSON, BILL
[] BEARD, TED [] MOORE, RAY [] RUDOLPH, DON
[] BYRNE, TOMMY [] MUIR, JOE [] YOUNG, BOBBY

MASSACHUSETTS

[] COLEMAN, JOE [] LaPALME, PAUL [] QUINN, FRANK
[] DITMAR, ART [] LEJA, FRANK [] RASCHI, VIC
[] DONOVAN, DICK [] LUMENTI, RALPH [] ROY, NORMAN
[] ESSEGIAN, CHUCK [] LUPIEN, TONY [] THOMPSON, JOHN
[] FARRELL, DICK [] MAYO, ED [] WAITKUS, EDDIE
[] HERMANSKI, GENE [] PELLAGRINI, EDDIE

MEXICO

[] AVILA, BOBBY [] LUNA, MEMO [] SOLIS, MARCELINO
[] GREENWOOD, BOB

MICHIGAN

[] BERRY, NEIL [] GROSS, DON [] MAAS, DUKE
[] BLYZKA, MICHAEL [] HERBERT, RAY [] MAXWELL, CHARLIE
[] BOROS, STEVE [] HOUTTEMAN, ART [] MICHAELS, CASS
[] BRUNET, GEORGE [] JACKSON, RON [] MILLER, BOB
[] BUHL, BOB [] KAZANSKI, TED [] OVERMIRE, FRANK
[] CICOTTE, AL [] KOPPE, JOE [] PILLETTE, DUANE
[] DAVIE, JERRY [] KOSHOREK, CLEM [] POHOLSKY, TOM
[] DELOCK, IKE [] KUZAVA, BOB [] POWELL, LEROY
[] DOBBEK, DAN [] LITTLEFIELD, DICK [] RUSH, BOB
[] GRAY, TED [] LOPATA, STAN [] SCHELL, DANNY
[] GREEN, LENNY [] LUND, DON [] STRINGER, LOU
[] GROMEK, STEVE [] LYNCH, JERRY [] TERWILLIGER, WAYNE

[] WILBER, DEL   [] ZAUCHIN, NORM   [] ZUVERINK, GEORGE

MINNESOTA

[] BACZEWSKI, FRED   [] KINDALL, JERRY   [] REPULSKI, RIP
[] DONNELLY, BLIX   [] MAHONEY, BOB   [] STIGMAN, DICK
[] GRAHAM, JACK   [] MORYN, WALT   [] WESTRUM, WES

MISSISSIPPI

[] BLASINGAME, DON   [] HOSKINS, DAVE   [] PEPPER, HUGH
[] BOLLING, MILT   [] MADISON, DAVE   [] PHILLIPS, BUBBA
[] BOYD, BOB   [] MIZELL, WILMER   [] WALKER, HARRY
[] FERRISS, BOO   [] NICHOLS, DOLAN

MISSOURI

[] ARFT, HANK   [] HOFMAN, BOBBY   [] SISLER, DICK
[] BAUMAN, FRANK   [] KEELY, BOB   [] SLEATER, LOU
[] BLAYLOCK, GARY   [] LUMPE, JERRY   [] SMALLEY, ROY
[] BOYER, CLOYD   [] MARTIN, MORRIE   [] SMITH, BOB W
[] BRIGHT, HARRY   [] MERRITT, LLOYD   [] SMITH, MAYO
[] BYERLY, BUD   [] NORMAN, BILL   [] SMITH, AL
[] CHRISTMAN, MARK   [] PENDLETON, JIM   [] SPEAKE, BOB
[] COOPER, WALKER   [] PISONI, JIM   [] THIES, JAKE
[] CRAWFORD, RUFUS   [] PRESKO, JOE   [] TIEFENAUER, BOB
[] DICKSON, MURRY   [] RESTELLI, DINO   [] UPTON, TOM
[] DIERING, CHUCK   [] SCHEFFING, BOB   [] WADE, GALE
[] EASTER, LUKE   [] SCHMIDT, BOB   [] WARD, PRESTON
[] EVERS, HOOT   [] SCHOONMAKER, JERRY   [] WIESLER, BOB
[] HALL, DICK   [] SIEBERN, NORM   [] WILSON, BILL
[] HANEBRINK, HARRY   [] SIEVERS, ROY
[] HEINTZELMAN, KEN   [] SISLER, DAVE

MONTANA

[] BOUCHEE, ED   [] PLEWS, HERB

NEBRASKA

[] BRANDT, JACKIE   [] JONES, SHELDON   [] URBAN, JACK
[] DYCK, JIM   [] LADE, DOYLE   [] ZIMMERMAN, JERRY
[] HOPP, JOHNNY   [] MAPES, CLIFF
[] JOHNSON, DARRELL   [] SOUTHWORTH, BILLY

NEW HAMPSHIRE

[] ROLFE, RED

[] SAVAGE, BOB

[] SMITH, BOB G

NEW JERSEY

[] ACKER, TOM
[] BOROWY, HANK
[] BRADY, JIM
[] BRODOWSKI, DICK
[] CALDERONE, SAM
[] CLARK, ALLIE
[] CLARK, MIKE
[] CUNNINGHAM, JOE
[] CUSICK, JOHN
[] DENTE, SAM

[] GLYNN, BILL
[] GRASSO, MICKEY
[] HILLER, FRANK
[] HOOPER, BOB
[] JOHNSON, BILLY
[] KASKO, EDDIE
[] KERIAZAKOS, GUS
[] KIELY, LEO
[] KRYHOSKI, DICK
[] KUCKS, JOHNNY

[] MALKMUS, BOB
[] MIKSIS, EDDIE
[] NARLESKI, RAY
[] O'BRIEN, EDDIE
[] O'BRIEN, JOHNNY
[] O'CONNELL, DANNY
[] ROMANO, JOHN
[] SIMA, AL
[] VALENTINETTI, VITO

NEW MEXICO

[] HANEY, FRED

[] STEPHENS, VERN

NEW YORK

[] ANTONELLO, BILL
[] ASPROMONTE, KEN
[] BIRRER, BABE
[] BOWMAN, ROGER
[] BROWN, TOMMY
[] CARROLL, TOMMY
[] CASALE, JERRY
[] CHIPMAN, BOB
[] COLEMAN, RIP
[] CORWIN, AL
[] DeMARS, BILLY
[] DOTTERER, DUTCH
[] DREWS, KARL
[] FACE, ROY
[] FERRICK, TOM
[] FRICANO, MARION
[] GINSBERG, JOE
[] GORDON, SID
[] GORMAN, TOM
[] GREENGRASS, JIM
[] GRIM, BOB

[] HARRIS, MICKEY
[] JOK, STAN
[] KEEGAN, BOB
[] KERR, BUDDY
[] LANE, JERALD HAL
[] LENNON, BOB
[] LEPCIO, TED
[] LIMMER, LOU
[] LOES, BILLY
[] LOGAN, JOHNNY
[] LOWN, TURK
[] MAJESKI, HANK
[] MALZONE, FRANK
[] McCORMICK, FRANK
[] McDERMONT, MICKEY
[] McDEVITT, DANNY
[] McMAHON, DON
[] MELE, SAM
[] MICELOTTA, BOB
[] MIGGINS, LARRY
[] NOREN, IRV

[] PHILLIPS, JACK
[] PIGNATANO, JOE
[] PORTOCARRERO, ARNIE
[] RIDZIK, STEVE
[] RIVERA, JIM
[] ROGOVIN, SAUL
[] ROJEK, STAN
[] ROSAR, BUDDY
[] SCHULT, ART
[] SHAW, BOB
[] SISTI, SIBBY
[] SMITH, FRANK
[] ST CLAIRE, EBBA
[] TROWBRIDGE, BOB
[] WHITE, HAL
[] WILKS, TED
[] YOST, EDDIE
[] YVARS, SAL
[] ZANNI, DOM
[] ZOLDAK, SAM

NORTH CAROLINA

[] ABERNATHY, TED.
[] ALLIE, GAIR
[] ALSTON, TOM
[] ALTMAN, GEORGE
[] BENSON, VERN
[] BLACKBURN, RON
[] BREWER, TOM
[] BROWN, HECTOR
[] CARDWELL, DON
[] CHAKALES, BOB
[] COAN, GIL
[] COVINGTON, WES
[] DIXON, SONNY

[] DOUGLAS, WHAMMY
[] EARLY, JAKE
[] EVANS, AL
[] FLOWERS, BENNET
[] FRAZIER, JOE
[] HOLCOMBE, KEN
[] JOLLY, DAVE
[] KING, CLYDE
[] KLUTTZ, CLYDE
[] LANIER, MAX
[] MARLOWE, DICK
[] MURRAY, RAY
[] NUNN, HOWIE

[] PEARCE, JIM
[] SCARBOROUGH, RAY
[] STALLCUP, VIRGIL
[] STEWART, BUNKY
[] TEMPLE, JOHNNY
[] UMPHLETT, TOM
[] WADE, BEN
[] WALKER, RUBE
[] WHISENANT, PETE
[] WHITE, CHUCK
[] WOOD, KEN
[] WRIGHT, TAFT
[] WRIGHT, TOMMY

NORTH DAKOTA

[] COLE, DAVE

OHIO

[] ABER, AL
[] ADDIS, BOB
[] AVERILL, EARL
[] BAUMHOLTZ, FRANK
[] BEARD, RALPH
[] BLATNICK, JOHNNY
[] BOLGER, JIM
[] BORKOWSKI, BOB
[] BRIDEWESER, JIM
[] BURBRINK, NELSON
[] BURTSCHY, ED
[] CONSOLO, BILLY
[] CRADDOCK, WALT
[] DROTT, DICK
[] EDWARDS, HANK
[] ELSTON, DON

[] GARVER, NED
[] HADDIX, HARVEY
[] HEMSLEY, ROLLIE
[] HODERLEIN, MEL
[] HOGUE, CAL
[] JANOWICZ, VIC
[] JONES, SAM
[] KAZAK, EDDIE
[] KELLY, ROBERT
[] LAWRENCE, BROOKS
[] LIPON, JOHNNY
[] NARAGON, HAL
[] NEGRAY, RON
[] NELSON, ROCKY
[] NIEMAN, BOB
[] NIXON, RUSS

[] NUXHALL, JOE
[] PRAMESA, JOHNNY
[] RICE, DEL
[] SCHMEES, GEORGE
[] SEMPROCH, ROMAN
[] SPENCER, GEORGE
[] TOMANEK, DICK
[] VALENTINE, CORKY
[] VOLLMER, CLYDE
[] WAUGH, JIM
[] WEHMEIER, HERM
[] WELLMAN, BOB
[] WIDMAR, AL
[] WOODLING, GENE
[] YUHAS, ED

OKLAHOMA

[] BENTON, AL
[] BLAYLOCK, BOB
[] BRAZLE, AL
[] DEAL, ELLIS
[] DEMETER, DON
[] DOBSON, JOE
[] FITZPATRICK, JOHN
[] FUSSELMAN, LES

[] KAISER, DON
[] KELLERT, FRANK
[] KRETLOW, LOU
[] McDANIEL, VON
[] McLISH, CAL
[] MITCHELL, DALE
[] MORGAN, BOBBY
[] MOSS, LES

[] MOULDER, GLEN
[] MUNCRIEF, BOB
[] PORTER, J W
[] REYNOLDS, ALLIE
[] SNYDER, JERRY
[] THOMPSON, HANK
[] WALKER, JERRY

OREGON

[] BAKER, DEL
[] CHAMBERS, CLIFF
[] ERAUTT, ED
[] FOX, HOWIE

[] JANSEN, LARRY
[] JOHNSON, DON
[] JONES, GORDON
[] McDONALD, JIM

[] SMALL, JIM
[] SMITH, BOBBY GENE
[] WHITMAN, DICK

PANAMA

[] ROBINSON, HUMBERTO

PENNSYLVANIA

[] ABRAMS, CAL
[] BARTIROME, TONY
[] BILKO, STEVE
[] BUCHA, JOHNNY
[] COLES, CHUCK
[] COX, BILLY
[] CRIMIAN, JACK
[] DANIELS, JACK
[] DEL GRECO, BOBBY
[] DORISH, HARRY
[] DYKES, JIMMY
[] FOYTACK, PAUL
[] FRANCONA, TITO
[] GERNERT, DICK
[] GOLIAT, MIKE
[] GRAFF, MILT
[] GRAY, DICK
[] GUMBERT, HARRY
[] GUMPERT, RANDY
[] HALL, BOB
[] HARRELL, BILLY
[] HOAK, DON
[] HUNTER, BILLY
[] KEMMERER, RUSS
[] KING, NELSON
[] KLINE, RON

[] KORCHECK, STEVE
[] KOZAR, AL
[] KRAVITZ, DANNY
[] KRESS, CHUCK
[] LITWHILER, DANNY
[] LONNETT, JOE
[] MARGONERI, JOE
[] MARTIN, JAKE
[] MASTERSON, WALT
[] McCAHAN, BILL
[] McCOSKY, BARNEY
[] MEYER, JACK
[] MILLER, BILL
[] MINARCIN, RUDY
[] MINNER, PAUL
[] MROZINSKI, RON
[] MULLIN, PAT
[] NORTHY, RON
[] O'NEILL, STEVE
[] ORAVETZ, ERNIE
[] OSTROWSKI, JOE
[] OWENS, JIM
[] PALYS, STAN
[] PURKEY, BOB
[] QUALTERS, TOM
[] QUEEN, MEL

[] RAFFENSBERGER, KEN
[] RAMAZZOTTI, BOB
[] RICHMOND, DON
[] RICKETTS, DICK
[] RUSSELL, JIM
[] RYBA, MIKE
[] SADOWSKI, ED
[] SAUER, HANK
[] SAWATSKI, CARL
[] SCHEIB, CARL
[] SECREST, CHARLIE
[] SHANTZ, WILMER
[] SHEARER, RAY
[] SMITH, DICK
[] SMITH, PAUL LESLIE
[] SNYDER, GENE
[] SOUCHOCK, STEVE
[] STARR, DICK
[] SUDER, PETE
[] SUSCE, GEORGE
[] THOMPSON, CHUCK
[] TREMEL, BILL
[] TRESH, MIKE
[] WERTZ, VIC
[] WOODESHICK, HAL

PUERTO RICO

[] ARROYO, LUIS
[] BERNIER, CARLOS

[] GOMEZ, RUBEN
[] MANTILLA, FELIX

[] PIZARRO, JUAN
[] SANTIAGO, JOSE

RHODE ISLAND

[] GORYL, JOHN
[] LABINE, CLEM

[] PAINE, PHIL
[] NICHOLS, CHET

[] SURKONT, MAX

SOUTH CAROLINA

[] BRISSIE, LOU
[] BUDDIN, DON
[] BUZHARDT, JOHN
[] BYRD, HARRY
[] CHRISLEY, NEIL
[] DILLARD, DON

[] FOWLER, ART
[] HAZLE, BOB
[] HIGBE, KIRBY
[] JEFFCOAT, HAL
[] JONES, WILLIE
[] NEWSOM, BOBO

[] O'DELL, BILLY
[] RIDDLE, JOHN
[] ROBINSON, AARON
[] ROSEN, AL
[] TAYLOR, SAMMY
[] WOOTEN, EARL

SOUTH DAKOTA

[] HARDY, CARROLL

TENNESSEE

[] BAILEY, ED
[] CASTLEMAN, FOSTER
[] CHAPMAN, BEN
[] CONSTABLE, JIMMY
[] CRONE, RAY

[] FREEMAN, MARK
[] HUDSON, SID
[] KING, CHARLES
[] McCULLOUGH, CLYDE
[] MEYER, BILLY

[] PLESS, RANCE
[] SAFFELL, TOM
[] SHIPLEY, JOE
[] THRONEBERRY, FAYE

TEXAS

[] BATTS, MATT
[] BELL, GARY
[] BRIDGES, ROCKY
[] BURK, MACK
[] BUSBY, JIM
[] FONDY, DEE
[] HARTUNG, CLINT
[] HATTON, GRADY
[] HENRY, BILL
[] HIGGINS, MIKE
[] HUGHSON, TEX

[] KATT, RAY
[] McBRIDE, TOM
[] McMILLAN, ROY
[] MELTON, DAVE
[] MILLS, BUSTER
[] MOREHEAD, SETH
[] MUNGER, GEORGE
[] MURFF, JOHN
[] NELSON, BOB
[] PEDEN, LES
[] PHILLEY, DAVE

[] RABE, CHARLEY
[] RICHARDS, PAUL
[] ROBERTS, CURT
[] ROBINSON, EDDIE
[] RUNNELS, PETE
[] SAMFORD, RON
[] TUCKER, THURMAN
[] WALL, MURRAY
[] WILLIAMS, DAVE
[] ZERNIAL, GUS

UTAH

[] FRANKS, HERMAN
[] PETERSON, KENT

[] SANFORD, FRED

[] SINGLETON, BERT

VENEZUELA

[] CARRASQUEL, CHICO

[] MONZANT, RAY

29

VIRGIN ISLANDS

[] THOMAS, VALMY

VIRGINIA

[] ATWELL, TOBY
[] BAKER, FLOYD
[] BURNETTE, WALLY
[] CONNELLY, BILL
[] DURHAM, JOE
[] FOILES, HANK

[] GETTELL, AL
[] HAMNER, GRANNY
[] HARRIS, GAIL
[] HILLMAN, DAVE
[] HURD, TOM
[] KENNEDY, MONTE

[] LEMON, JIM
[] MABE, BOB
[] MARSHALL, WILLARD
[] PERKOWSKI, HARRY
[] PORTERFIELD, BOB
[] ROACH, MEL

VERMONT

[] JOHNSON, ERNIE

[] TEBBETTS, BIRDIE

WASHINGTON

[] JOHNSON, EARL
[] LEHMAN, KEN
[] MARTIN, BABE

[] PODBIELAN, BUD
[] RICKERT, MARV
[] STALEY, GERRY

[] TORGESON, EARL
[] WHITE, SAMMY

WASHINGTON D C

[] KLIPPSTEIN, JOHNNY

WEST VIRGINIA

[] BROWN, DICK
[] CLARK, MEL
[] FREESE, GENE
[] FREESE, GEORGE

[] FRIDLEY, JIM
[] HAMRIC, BERT
[] MILLIKEN, BOB
[] RAINES, LARRY

[] RICE, HAL
[] SEMINICK, ANDY
[] STOBBS, CHUCK

WISCONSIN

[] DELSING, JIM
[] FISCHER, BILL
[] HARTMAN, BOB
[] HAUGSTAD, PHIL
[] HOEFT, BILLY

[] KIPPER, THORNTON
[] KOSLO, DAVE
[] KRSNICH, ROCKY
[] PAFKO, ANDY
[] PAVLETICH, DON

[] PECK, HAL
[] SCHMITZ, JOHNNY
[] VAN CUYK, CHRIS
[] WILSON, BOB

ONLY COMMON CARD

When collecting cards of players with only one card, you need a few qualifiers. I have listed: (a) it is their only "common card" even though they might not be listed as common in another year: (b) these are commons from 1948 to 1959, they might have cards earlier than 1948: (c) they might be listed as "DP" (double print) which made them monetarily common: (d) some players have more than one card, but they are in the same year, or different make. Not all of these cards are as easy to find as you might think.

(ob) ONLY BOWMAN / (ot) ONLY TOPPS / (oy) ONLY YEAR / (np) NEVER PLAYED

1948 BOWMAN

[] 042 POAT, RAY

1949 BOWMAN

[] 074 McBRIDE, TOM
[] 077 BONHAM, ERNIE
[] 089 PLATT, MIZELL
[] 091 WAKEFIELD, DICK
[] 096 WRIGHT, TAFT
[] 099 GUSTINE, FRANK
[] 102 SPENCE, STAN
[] 106 EARLY, JAKE
[] 113 LaMANNO, RAY
[] 121 CHRISTMAN, MARK
[] 123 BLATNICK, JOHNNY
[] 130 WALKER, HARRY
[] 141 LUPIEN, TONY
[] 146 McCORMICK, MIKE
[] 149 PARTEE, ROY
[] 152 MADDERN, CLARENCE
[] 159 MOULDER, GLEN
[] 166 TRESH, MIKE
[] 167 MARTIN, BABE

[] 182 PECK, HAL
[] 187 MARCHILDON, PHIL
[] 189 WOOTEN, EARL
[] 193 TRINKLE, KEN
[] 195 BOCKMAN, EDDIE
[] 199 HUGHSON, TEX
[] 200 DOBERNIC, JESS
[] 204 SAVAGE, BOB
[] 211 FERRISS, BOO
[] 212 HAMNER, RALPH
[] 213 BARRETT, RED
[] 215 HIGBE, KIRBY
[] 220 McCARTHY, JOHN
[] 221 MUNCRIEF, BOB
[] 227 OSTERMUELLER, FRITZ
[] 228 MAYO, JACKIE
[] 234 SEWELL, RIP
[] 236 SANFORD, FRED
[] 239 McCORMICK, FRANK

1950 BOWMAN

[] 123 RESTELLI, DINO
[] 145 GRAHAM, JACK
[] 224 COOGAN, DALE (ob)

[] 224 BANTA, JACK
[] 235 GILBERT, TOOKIE (ob)
[] 245 PAPAI, AL

1951 BOWMAN

[] 130 SAFFELL, TOM
[] 182 FERRICK, TOM
[] 185 BLOODWORTH, JIMMY
[] 192 WYSE, HANK
[] 201 O'NEILL, STEVE (ob)
[] 204 LOMBARDI, VIC
[] 207 SOUTHWORTH, BILLY
[] 215 PETERSON, KENT
[] 221 WHITMAN, DICK
[] 222 TUCKER, THURMAN
[] 239 MacDONALD, BILL (ob)
[] 255 CANDINI, MILO
[] 264 RICHMOND, DON
[] 269 NOBLE, RAY

[] 276 QUINN, FRANK
[] 278 ROY, NORMAN
[] 280 OVERMIRE, FRANK (ob)
[] 286 USHER, BOB (ob)
[] 293 JOHNSON, KEN
[] 303 ROTBLATT, MARV
[] 304 GETTELL, AL
[] 308 BEARD, TED (ob)
[] 310 DUSAK, ERV (ob)
[] 313 MUELLER, RAY
[] 315 TAYLOR, ZACK
[] 320 WHITE, HAL
[] 383 DUBIEL, WALT (ob)

1952 BOWMAN

[] 114 HILLER, FRANK (oy)
[] 192 CUSICK, JOHN
[] 210 WILSON, AL (oy)
[] 227 SUKEFORTH, CLYDE (ob)

[] 234 FITZSIMMONS, FRED
[] 242 KELL, EVERETT
[] 245 SCHMEES, GEORGE

1952 TOPPS

[] 009 HOGUE, BOB
[] 018 COMBS, MERRILL
[] 019 BUCHA, JOHNNY (ot)
[] 041 WELLMAN, BOB
[] 044 DEMPSEY, CON
[] 050 RICKERT, MARV
[] 051 RUSSELL, JIM (ot)
[] 053 VAN CUYK, CHRIS
[] 058 MAHONEY, BOB
[] 061 GILBERT, TOOKIE (ot)
[] 071 UPTON, TOM
[] 074 HANSEN, ANDY
[] 087 COOGAN, DALE (ot)
[] 095 HOLCOMBE, KEN (ot)
[] 101 LANIER, MAX (ot)
[] 103 MAPES, CLIFF (ot)
[] 105 PRAMESA, JOHNNY (ot)
[] 114 RAMSDELL, WILLARD (ot)
[] 124 KENNEDY, MONTE (ot)
[] 128 BOLLWEG, DON (ot)
[] 130 JONES, SHELDON (ot)
[] 132 KLUTTZ, CLYDE
[] 134 TIPTON, JOE (ot)

[] 138 MacDONALD, BILL (ot)
[] 139 WOOD, KEN (ot)
[] 141 HARTUNG, CLINT (ot)
[] 144 BLAKE, ED
[] 150 BEARD, TED (ot)
[] 152 EVANS, AL (ot)
[] 154 MUIR, JOE
[] 155 OVERMIRE, FRANK (ot)
[] 156 HILLER, FRANK (oy)
[] 160 FRIEND, OWEN (ot)
[] 163 ROJEK, STAN (ot)
[] 164 DUBIEL, WALT (ot)
[] 167 HOWERTON, BILL (ot)
[] 178 MICHAELS, CASS (ot)
[] 183 DUSAK, ERV (ot)
[] 194 HATTON, JOE (ot)
[] 198 HAUGSTAD, PHIL
[] 206 OSTROWSKI, JOE
[] 207 HARRIS, MICKEY (ot)
[] 210 FOWLER, DICK (ot)
[] 211 COLEMAN, RAY (ot)
[] 213 JONES, NIPPY (ot)
[] 218 McCULLOUGH, CLYDE (ot)

[] 222 EVERS, HOOT (ot)
[] 228 BRAZLE, AL (ot)
[] 229 BEARDEN, GENE (ot)
[] 231 ZOLDAK, SAM (ot)
[] 234 SOUCHOCK, STEVE (ot)
[] 245 ROBERTSON, SHERRY (ot)
[] 247 GUMPERT, RANDY (ot)
[] 256 SUDER, PETE (ot)
[] 260 CASTIGLIONE, PETE (ot)
[] 278 CLARK, ALLIE (ot)
[] 279 STEWART, ED (ot)
[] 284 ARFT, HANK (ot)

[] 292 BAKER, FLOYD (ot)
[] 296 ROLFE, RED
[] 304 DENTE, SAM (ot)
[] 327 WILSON, AL (oy)
[] 336 KOSLO, DAVE (ot)
[] 348 KELLY, ROBERT
[] 374 BENTON, AL
[] 375 MERSON, JOHN
[] 383 WILBER, DEL (ot)
[] 387 MEYER, BILLY (ot)
[] 391 CHAPMAN, BEN

1953 BOWMAN

[] 008w THOMAS, KEITH (oy)
[] 021w PODBIELAN, BUD (ob)
[] 083 DANIELS, JACK

[] 094 ADDIS, BOB (ob)
[] 098 RODRIGUEZ, HECTOR
[] 142 MIGGINS, LARRY

1953 TOPPS

[] 015 NEWSOM, BOBO
[] 126 CONNELLY, BILL
[] 129 THOMAS, KEITH (oy)
[] 136 HEINTZELMAN, KEN (ot)
[] 178 WAUGH, JIM
[] 193 CLARK, MIKE

[] 204 BOKELMAN, DICK
[] 229 KRSNICH, ROCKY
[] 243 BERNIER, CARLOS (ot)
[] 245 NORMAN, BILL
[] 256 PEDEN, LES

1954 BOWMAN

[] 102 HODERLEIN, MEL
[] 118 BOYD, BOB (ob)

[] 171 BERNIER, CARLOS (ob)
[] 222 LUNA, MEMO

1954 TOPPS

[] 067 WILLIS, JIM
[] 097 LANE, JERALD HAL
[] 127 O'NEILL, STEVE (ot)
[] 143 HEMSLEY, ROLLIE
[] 152 BLYZKA, MICHAEL
[] 176 KEELY, BOB
[] 196 JOK, STAN (ot)
[] 204 SCULL, ANGEL (np)
[] 207 OLIVER, TOM
[] 212 MICELOTTA, BOB
[] 213 FITZPATRICK, JOHN

[] 219 KRESS, CHUCK
[] 224 WEIK, DICK
[] 227 MILLS, BUSTER
[] 229 TALBOT, BOB (ot)
[] 233 GALAN, AUGIE (ot)
[] 236 PENSON, PAUL
[] 237 RYBA, MIKE
[] 243 BLADES, RAY
[] 244 WHEAT, LEROY
[] 247 MAYO, ED
[] 272 ANTONELLO, BILL

1955 BOWMAN

[] 014 KERIAZAKOS, GUS
[] 036 BELARDI, WAYNE
[] 042 GREENWOOD, BOB
[] 062 LINT, ROYCE
[] 077 McDONALD, JIM
[] 079 MIRANDA, WILLIE (ob)
[] 084 FREESE, GEORGE
[] 091 MARLOWE, DICK
[] 113 HALL, BOB
[] 115 BOWMAN, ROGER
[] 120 BURTSCHY, ED
[] 121 CRAWFORD, RUFUS

[] 129 NARAGON, HAL (ob)
[] 142 REGALADO, RUDY
[] 148 CHAKALES, BOB (ob)
[] 175 SHANTZ, WILMER
[] 206 BEARD, RALPH
[] 211 DIXON, SONNY
[] 254 FLOWERS, BENNET
[] 257 ALSTON, TOM
[] 268 HAWES, ROY LEE
[] 287 MROZINSKI, RON
[] 292 BLAYLOCK, MARV (ob)

1955 TOPPS

[] 012 THIES, JAKE
[] 023 PARKS, JACK (np)
[] 044 VALENTINE, CORKY
[] 073 SHEPARD, JACK
[] 079 SCHELL, DANNY
[] 101 GRAY, JOHNNY
[] 103 WHITE, CHUCK
[] 114 ORTIZ, LOUIS (NP)

[] 136 STEWART, BUNKY
[] 137 ELLIOTT, HARRY
[] 139 KRALY, STEVE
[] 167 CASAGRANDE, TOM (np)
[] 170 PEARCE, JIM
[] 173 KLINE, BOB
[] 183 JACOBS, ANTHONY
[] 196 WADE, GALE

1956 TOPPS

[] 027 BURBRINK, NELSON
[] 059 SANTIAGO, JOSE
[] 084 BIRRER, BABE
[] 126 BRADY, JIM
[] 129 MARTIN, JAKE
[] 137 SILVERA, AL
[] 144 POWELL, LEROY

[] 169 NELSON, BOB
[] 174 GORBOUS, GLEN
[] 204 SWANSON, ART
[] 265 CONSUEGRA, SANDY (ot)
[] 291 KELLERT, FRANK
[] 339 PLESS, RANCE

1957 TOPPS

[] 022 SNYDER, JERRY (ot)
[] 191 MARGONERI, JOE
[] 224 BLAYLOCK, MARV (ot)
[] 266 KUHN, KEN
[] 268 COLLUM, JACK (ot)

[] 276 PYBURN, JIM, JIM
[] 321 MURFF, JOHN
[] 337 VALDES, RENE
[] 382 BRIDEWESER, JIM (ot)
[] 386 LUTTRELL, LYLE

1958 TOPPS

[] 065 McDANIEL, VON
[] 083 HAZLE, BOB
[] 096 DURHAM, JOE
[] 126 PALYS, STAN
[] 129 DERRINGTON, JIM
[] 131 HENRICH, BOB
[] 151 PRITCHARD, BUDDY
[] 182 CAFFIE, JOE
[] 218 RAND, DICK
[] 229 ZUPO, FRANK

[] 231 MERRITT, LLOYD
[] 243 RAINES, LARRY
[] 283 SHEARER, RAY
[] 376 RABE, CHARLEY
[] 391 MELTON, DAVE
[] 442 PAINE, PHIL
[] 445 SMITH, BOB W
[] 449 FODGE, GENE
[] 451 TAYLOR, JOE
[] 461 MAYER, ED

1959 TOPPS

[] 049 HALL, BILL
[] 091 MOFORD, HERB
[] 120 COLES, CHUCK
[] 121 CONLEY, BOB
[] 134 McDANIEL, JIM (np)
[] 140 SECREST, CHARLIE (np)
[] 192 BEAMON, CHARLIE
[] 211 BLAYLOCK, BOB
[] 214 SOLIS, MARCELINO
[] 254 BELLA, ZEKE

[] 281 CRADDOCK, WALT
[] 283 HEMAN, RUSS
[] 362 NICHOLS, DOLAN
[] 504 ALVAREZ, OSSIE
[] 522 SNYDER, GENE
[] 532 FREEMAN, MARK
[] 537 ARIAS, RUDOLPH
[] 538 KING, CHARLES (ot)
[] 539 BLAYLOCK, GARY
[] 544 TATE, LEE

DEBUT AND DEPARTURE

Every season Major League Baseball welcomes a new batch of want-a-be stars, and says good-bye to others. The lists below are the debut season of common cards, and the cards of player's last season. In most cases these are listed as "rookie" cards in various guides, but I will list them as "debut cards" depicting the season they played in their first game. The departure or retired cards represent the last season in which they played in a game. The card companies, in some cases, have produced cards for some of these players beyond retirement.

t=topps - b=bowman

1948 Debut

No common debut cards found

1949 Debut

HOFMAN, BOBBY : []223 b'49 NY N   KRYHOSKI, DICK : []218 b'49 NY A

1950 Debut

COOGAN, DALE : []244 b'50 PIT   MORGAN, BOBBY : []222 b'50 BKN
GILBERT, TOOKIE : []235 b'50 NY N

1951 Debut

NOBLE, RAY : []269 b'51 NY N

1952 Debut

DELOCK, IKE : []250 b'52 BOS A   LEPCIO, TED : []335 t'52 BOS A
FRIDLEY, JIM : []399 t'52 CLE   ROSSI, JOE : []379 t'52 CIN
GERNERT, DICK : []343 t'52 BOS A   SCHMEES, GEORGE : []245 b'52 STL A
KELL, EVERETT : []242 b'52 PHI A   SNYDER, JERRY : []246 b'52 WAS
KOSHOREK, CLEM : []380 t'52 PIT   THRONEBERRY, FAYE : []376 t'52 BOS A

1953 Debut

ANTONELLO, BILL : []272 t'53 BKN   KEEGAN, BOB : []196 t'53 CHI A
FACE, ROY : []246 t'53 PIT   MILLIKEN, BOB : []221 t'53 BKN
FOILES, HANK : []252 t'53 CIN   O'BRIEN, EDDIE : []249 t'53 PIT
HUNTER, BILLY : []166 t'53 STL A   O'BRIEN, JOHNNY : []223 t'53 PIT
JABLONSKI, RAY : []189 t'53 STL N   OLDIS, BOB : []262 t'53 WAS
JANOWICZ, VIC : []222 t'53 PIT   PEDEN, LES : []256 t'53 WAS

PENDLETON, JIM : []185 t'53 MIL
REPULSKI, RIP : []172 t'53 STL N

SCHULT, ART : []167 t'53 NY A

1954 Debut

ALLIE, GAIR : []179 t'54 PIT
CRONE, RAY : []206 t'54 MIL
GRAMMAS, ALEX : []151 t'54 STL N
HARMON, CHUCK : []182 t'54 CIN
JACOBS, FORREST : []129 t'54 PHI A
JOK, STAN : []196 t'54 PHI N
LUNA, MEMO : []222 b'54 STL
LYNCH, JERRY : []234 t'54 PIT

MICELOTTA, BOB : []212 t'54 PHI N
PENSON, PAUL : []236 t'54 PHI N
PORTOCARRERO, ARNIE : []214 t'54 PHI A
ROBERTS, CURT : []242 t'54 PIT
ROBERTSON, AL : []211 b'54 []149 t'54 PH A
TAYLOR, BILL : []74 t'54 NY N
THOMPSON, CHUCK : []209 b'54 BKN
WHEAT, LEROY : []244 t'54 PHI A

1955 Debut

DALEY, PETE : []206 t'55 BOS
FERRARESE, DON : []185 t'55 BAL
KLINE, BOB : []173 t'55 WAS
MINARCIN, RUDY : []174 t'55 CIN
OWENS, JIM : []202 t'55 PHI

PHILLIPS, BUBBA : []228 b'55 DET
ROBINSON, HUMBERTO : []182 t'55 MIL
SMITH, HAL W : []8 t'55 BAL
WADE, GALE : []196 t'55 CHI N

1956 Debut

BRADY, JIM : []126 t'56 DET

PLESS, RANCE : []339 t'56 KC

1957 Debut

ANDERSON, HARRY : []404 t'57 PHI
BARCLAY, CURT : []361 t'57 NY N
CARDWELL, DON : []374 t'57 PHI
CHRISLEY, NEIL : []320 t'57 WAS
GRAFF, MILT : []369 t'57 KC
KASKO, EDDIE : []363 t'57 STL
LEE, DON : []379 t'57 DET

MILLER, BOB : []46 t'57 PHI
NEEMAN, CAL : []353 t'57 CHI N
PIZARRO, JUAN : []383 t'57 MIL
RODGERS, ANDRE : []377 t'57 NY N
SMITH, BOBBY GENE : []384 t'57 STL
VALDES, RENE : []337 t'57 BKN
WISE, CASEY : []396 t'57 CHI N

1958 Debut

BLACKBURN, RON : []459 t'58 PIT
CLARK, PHIL : []423 t'58 STL
DAVENPORT, JIM : []413 t'58 SF
ESSEGIAN, CHUCK : []460 t'58 PHI
FODGE, GENE : []449 t'58 CHI N
GRANT, JIM : []394 t'58 CLE
GRAY, DICK : []146 t'58 LA

KIRKLAND, WILLIE : []128 t'58 SF
MORAN, BILLY : []388 t'58 CLE A
SCHMIDT, BOB : []268 t'58 SF
SEMPROCH, ROMAN : []474 t'58 PHI
SMITH, BOB W : []445 t'58 BOS
STEVENS, R C : []470 t'58 PIT
TAYLOR, SAMMY : []281 t'58 CHI N

1959 Debut

ALTMAN, GEORGE : []512 t'59 CHI N
ARIAS, RUDOLPH : []537 t'59 CHI A
BAXES, JIM : []547 t'59 LA
BLAYLOCK, GARY : []539 t'59 STL
BROGLIO, ERNIE : []296 t'59 STL
DAVIE, JERRY : []256 t'59 DET
DILLARD, DON : []123 t'59 CLE
DOBBEK, DAN : []124 t'59 WAS

FREEMAN, MARK : []532 t'59 KC
HARTMAN, BOB : []128 t'58 MIL
NUNN, HOWIE : []549 t'59 STL
OLIVER, GENE : []135 t'59 STL
RICKETTS, DICK : []137 t'59 STL
SNYDER, GENE : []522 t'59 LA
WEBSTER, RAY : []531 t'59 CLE

Baseball says good-bye

1948 Retired

No common retired cards found

1949 Retired

BARRETT, RED : []213 b'49 BOS N
BOCKMAN, EDDIE : []195 b'49 PIT
BONHAM, ERNIE : []77 b'49 PIT
CHRISTMAN, MARK : []121 b'49 WAS
DOBERNIC, JESS : []200 b'49 CIN
EARLY, JAKE : []106 b'49 WAS/CHI N
HAMNER, RALPH : []212 b'49 CHI N
HUGHSON, TEX : []199 b'49 BOS A
McCAHAN, BILL : []80 b'49 PHI A

PECK, HAL : []182 b'49 CLE
PLATT, MIZELL : []89 b'49 STL A
SAVAGE, BOB : []204 b'49 STL A
SEWELL, RIP : []234 b'49 PIT
SPENCE, STAN : []102 b'49 STL A/BOS A
TRESH, MIKE : []166 b'49 CLE
TRINKLE, KEN : []193 b'49 PHI N
VICO, GEORGE : []122 b'49 DET ([]49 t'53)
WRIGHT, TAFT : []96 b'49 PHI

1950 Retired

BANTA, JACK : []224 b'50 BKN
CHESNES, BOB : []70 b'50 PIT
COOGAN, DALE : []244 b'50 PIT ([]87 t'52)
GUMBERT, HARRY : []171 b'50 PIT
HAEFNER, MICKEY : []183 b'50 BOS N/CHA
KOZAR, AL : []15 b'50 CHI A/WAS

LADE, DOYLE : []196 b'50 CHI N ([]139 b'51)
LAKE, EDDIE : []240 b'50 DET ([]140 b'51)
PIERETTI, MARINO : []181 b'50 CLE
SALKELD, BILL : []237 b'50 CHI A
STRINGER, LOU : []187 b'50 BOS A

1951 Retired

BLACKBURN, JIM : []287 b'51 CIN
BLOODWORTH, JIMMY : []185 b'51 PHI N
BOROWY, HANK : []250 b'51 DET
CANDINI, MILO : []255 b'51 PHI N
CHAPMAN, SAM : []9 b'51 CLE/PHI A
DeMARS, BILLY : []43 b'51 STL A
DILLINGER, BOB : []63 b'51 CHI A/PIT
DONNELLY, BLIX : []208 b'51 BOS N
EVANS, AL : []38 b'51 BOS A ([]152 t'52)
GUERRA, MIKE : []202 b'51 BOS A/WAS
JOHNSON, EARL : []321 b'51 DET

KERR, BUDDY : []171 b'51 BOS N
KRAMER, JACK : []200 b'51 NY A/NY N
LITWHILER, DANNY : []179 b'51 CIN
MUELLER, RAY : []313 b'51 BOS N
MUNGER, GEORGE : []11 b'51 STL N
RICHMOND, DON : []264 b'51 STL N
ROBINSON, AARON : []142 b'5 DET/BOS A
ROSAR, BUDDY : []236 b'51 BOS A
ROTBLATT, MARV : []303 b'51 CHI A
STARR, DICK : []137 b'51 STL N/WAS
THOMPSON, JOHN : []294 b'51 PHI N

TUCKER, THURMAN : []222 b'51 CLE
WHITMAN, DICK : []221 b'51 PHI N

WYSE, HANK : []192 b'51 PHI A/WAS

1952 Retired

ARFT, HANK : []229 b'52 []284 t'52 STL A
BENTON, AL : []374 b'52 BOS A
CHIPMAN, BOB : []228 b'52 BOS N
COLEMAN, RAY : []201 b'52 []211 t'52 CHI A/STL A
COMBS, MERRILL : []18 t'52 CLE/COA
CUSICK, JOHN : []192 b'52 BOS N
DUBIEL, WALT : []164 t'52 CHI N
DUSAK, ERV : []183 t'52 PIT
FANNIN, CLIFF : []285 t'52 STL A ([]203 b'53 []22 t'53)
FOWLER, DICK : []190 b'52 []210 t'52 PHI A
GOLDSBERRY, GORDON : []46 t'52 STL A
GUMPERT, RANDY : []106 b'52 []247 t'52 BOS /WAS A ([]200 t'53)
HARRIS, MICKEY : []135 b'52 []207 t'52 CLE/WAS
HARTSFIELD, ROY : []28 b'52 []264 t'52 BOS
HARTUNG, CLINT : []141 t'52 NY N
HATTON, JOE : []144 b'52 []194 t'52 CHI N
HAUGSTADT, PHIL : []198 t'52 CIN
HAYNES, JOE : []103 b'52 []145 t'52 WAS ([]223 t'54)
HEINTZELMAN, KEN : []148 t'52 PHI N ([]136 t'53)
HOGUE, BOB : []9 t'52 NY A/STL A
HOWERTON, BILL : []119 b'52 []167 t'52

NY/PIT N
KAZAK, EDDIE : []165 t'52 STL N/CIN ([]194 t'53 DET)
KELL, EVERETT : []242 b'52 PHI A
KLUTTZ, CLYDE : []132 t'52 WAS
MAHONEY, BOB : []58 t'52 STL A
MASI, PHIL : []283 t'52 CHI A
MUIR, JOE : 154 t'52 PIT
OSTROWSKI, JOE : []206 t'52 NY A
OVERMIRE, FRANK : []155 t'52 NY A/STL A
PRAMESA, JOHNNY : []247 b'52 []105 t'52 CHI N
QUEEN, MEL : []171 b'52 PIT
RAMSDELL, WILLARD : []22 b'52 []114 t'52 CHI N
ROBERTSON, SHERRY : []245 t'52 PHI/WAS
ROJEK, STAN : []137 b'52 []163 t'52 PHI A
ROSSI, JOE : []379 t '52 CIN N ([]74 t'53)
SCHMEES, GEORGE : []245 b'52 BOS/STL A
TEBBETTS, BIRDIE : []124 b'52 CLE
UPTON, TOM : []71 t'52 WAS
VAN CUYK, CHRIS : []53 t'52 BKN
WIDMAR, AL : []133 t'52 CHI A
WILSON, AL : []210 b'52 []327 t'52 WAS /BOS/ NYA
ZOLDAK, SAM : []231 t'52 PHI A

1953 Retired

ADDIS, BOB : []94 b'53 []157 t'53 CHI /PIT N
ANTONELLO, BILL : []272 t'53 BKN
BENSON, VERN : []205 t'53 STL N
BERNIER, CARLOS : []243 t'53 PIT ([]171 b'54)
BOKELMAN, DICK : []204 t'53 STL N
BROWN, TOMMY : []42 b'53 CHI N
CAMPOS, FRANK : []51 t'53 WAS
CLARK, ALLIE : []155 b'53 CHI/PHI A
CLARK, MIKE : []193 t'53 STL N
CONNELLY, BILL : []126 t'53 NY N
DiMAGGIO, DOM : []149dp t'53 BOS
EDWARDS, HANK : []90 t'53 STL A
ERAUTT, ED : []226 t'53 STL N/CIN
FUSSELMAN, LES : []218 t'53 STL N
GLAVIANO, TOMMY : []140 t'53 PHI N
HARRIST, EARL : []65 t'53 CHI/DET A
HERMANSKI, GENE : []179 t'53 CHI N ([]228 t'54)

HITCHCOCK, BILLY : []17 t'53 DET
JOHNSON, BILLY : []21 t'53 STL N
KOLLOWAY, DON : []97 t'53 PHI A
KOSHOREK, CLEM : []147 b'53 []8 t'53 PIT
LEONARD, DUTCH : []50 bw'53 []155 t'53 CHI N ([]247 b'55)
LOHRKE, JACK : []47 bw'53 PHI N
MADISON, DAVE : []99 t'53 DET
MAIN, FORREST : []198 t'53 PIT
MULLIN, PAT : []4 bw'53 DET ([]155 t'54)
NEWSOM, BOBO : []15dp t'53 PHI A
NICHOLSON, BILL : []14 bw'53 PHI N
PEDEN, LES : []256 t'53 WAS
PRIDDY, JERRY : []113 t'53 DET
RAMAZZOTTI, BOB : []41 bw'53 CHI N
RIGNEY, BILL : []3 bw'53 NY N
SANDLOCK, MIKE : []247 t'53 PIT ([]104t'54)
SCARBOROUGH, RAY : []213 t'53 DET/NYA
SISLER, DICK : []10 bw'53 STL N

STALLCUP, VIRGIL : []180 t'53 STL N
THOMAS, KEITH : []62 bw'53 []129 t'53
PHI/WAS A
WAUGH, JIM : []178 t'53 PIT

WILKS, TED : []101 t'53 CLE
WOOD, KEN : []109 b'53 WAS
YUHAS, ED : []70 t'53 STL N
ZARRILLA, AL : []181 t'53 BOS

1954 Retired

ALLIE, GAIR : []179 t'54 PIT ([]59 t'55)
BICKFORD, VERN : []176 b'54 BAL
BLYZKA, MICHAEL : []152 t'54 BAL
BRAZLE, AL : []142 b'54 STL ([]230 b'55)
CAIN, BOB : []195 b'54 []61 t'54 CHI/PHI A
CALDERONE, SAM : []68 t'54 MIL
CASTIGLIONE, PETE : []174 b'54 STL
DEAL, ELLIS : []192 t'54 STL
DREWS, KARL : []191 b'54 CIN/PHI N
FOX, HOWIE : []246 t'54 BAL
GLYNN, BILL : []178 t'54 CLE ([]39 t'55)
HETKI, JOHN : []161 t'54 PIT
HODERLEIN, MEL : []120 b'54 WAS
HOGUE, CAL : []134 t'54 PIT
HOSKINS, DAVE : []81 t'54 CLE ([]133 t'55)
HUDSON, SID : []194 b'54 []93 t'54 BOS
([]318 b'55)
KOKOS, DICK : []37 b'54 []106 t'55 BAL
KRESS, CHUCK : []219 t'54 DET
LENHARDT, DON : []53 b'54 BAL/BOS
LIMMER, LOU : []232 t'54 []80 b'54 PHI A
([]54 t'55)
LINDELL, JOHNNY : []159 b'54 []51 t'54 PHI
LIPON, JOHNNY : []19 t'54 CIN
LUNA, MEMO : []222 b'54 STL

LUND, DON : []87 b'54 []167 t'54 DET
MARRERO, CONRADO : []200 b'54 WAS
MICHAELS, CASS : []150 b'54 CHI A ([]85
b'55)
MILLIKEN, BOB : []177 t'54 BKN
MURRAY, RAY : []83 b'54 []49 t'54 BAL
PENSON, PAUL : []236 t'54 PHI N
RAFFENSBERGER, KEN : []92 b'54 []46 t'54
CIN
RICE, HAL : []219 b'54 []95 t'54 CHI/PIT N
RYAN, CONNIE : []136 t'54 CIN ([]52 b'55)
SCHEIB, CARL : []67 b'54 []118 t'54 STL/PHI
SERENA, BILL : []93 b'54 CHI N ([]233 b'55)
SIMA, AL : []216 t'54 CHI A
ST CLAIRE, EBBA : []128 b'54 NY N
TALBOT, BOB : []229 t'54 CHI N ([]137 b'55)
TIPTON, JOE : []180 b'54 WAS
VOLLMER, CLYDE : []136 b'54 WAS ([]13
b'55)
WEIK, DICK : []224 t'54 DET
WERLE, BILL : []144 t'54 BOS
WILBER, DEL : []178 b'54 BOS
WILLIS, JIM : []67 t'54 CHI N
YVARS, SAL : []78 b'54 STL

1955 Retired

BACZEWSKI, FRED : []190 b'55 CIN
BISHOP, CHARLIE : []96 t'55 KC
BOLLWEG, DON : []54 b'55 KC
BORKOWSKI, BOB : []74 t'55 BKN/CIN
BOWMAN, ROGER : []115 b'55 PIT
BOYER, CLOYD : []149 b'55 KC
CHURCH, BUBBA : []273 b'55 CHI N
COLEMAN, JOE : []162 t'55 BAL/DET
CORWIN, AL : []122 b'55 NY N
ELLIOTT, HARRY : []137 t'55 STL
FRICANO, MARION : []316 b'55 KC
GRAY, TED : []86 b'55 BAL/CLE/CHI/NY A
GREENWOOD, BOB : []42 b'55 PHI
HOOPER, BOB : []27 b'55 CIN
JACOBS, ANTHONY : []183 t'55 STL
JOK, STAN : []251 b'55 CHI A
JOOST, EDDIE : []263 b'55 BOS

KERIAZAKOS, GUS : []14 b'55 KC
KIPPER, THORNTON : []62 t'55 PHI
KLINE, BOB : []173 t'55 WAS A
MAJESKI, HANK ; []127 b'55 BAL/CLE
MARSHALL, WILLARD : []131 b'55 CHI A
MAXWELL, CHARLIE : []162 b'55 BAL
McGHEE, ED : []32 t'55 CHI A
MERRIMAN, LLOYD : []135 b'55 CHI /CHI
MILLER, BILL : []245 b'55 BAL
MROZINSKI, RON : []287 b'55 PHI
PEARCE, JIM : []170 t'55 CIN
PERKOWSKI, HARRY : []184 t'55 CHI N
RASCHI, VIC : []185 b'55 KC
ROBERTSON, AL : []5 b'55 []177 t'55 KC
SCHELL, DANNY : []79 t'55 PHI
SHEA, FRANK : []207 b'55 WAS
SMITH, DICK : []288 b'55 PIT

SUDER, PETE : []6 b'55 KC
THIES, JAKE : []12 t'55 PIT
TRICE, BOB : []132 t'55 KC
UMPHLETT, TOM : []45 b'55 WAS

VALENTINE, CORKY : []44 t'55 CIN
WHITE, CHUCK : []103 t'55 MIL
WILSON, BILL : []86 t'55 KC

1956 Retired

ASTROTH, JOE : []106 t'56 KC
ATWELL, TOBY : []232 t'56 MIL/PIT
BRADY, JIM : []126 t'56 DET
DIERING, CHUCK : []19 t'56 BAL
DORISH, HARRY : []167 t'56 BAL/BOS
DYCK, JIM : []303 t'56 BAL/CIN
FRAZIER, JOE : []140 t'56 BAL/STL/CIN
GREENGRASS, JIM : []275 t'56 PHI
HURD, TOM : []256 t'56 BOS
KELLERT, FRANK : []291 t'56 CHI N
LIDDLE, DON : []325 t'56 STL/NY N
MARSH, FRED : []23 t'56 BAL
MINNER, PAUL : []182 t'56 CHI N

ORAVETZ, ERNIE : []51 t'56 WAS
PALICA, ERV : []206 t'56 BAL
PLESS, RANCE : []339 t'56 KC
POLLET, HOWIE : []262 t'56 CHI A/PIT
POPE, DAVE : []154 t'56 BAL/CLE ([]249 t'57)
ROBERTS, CURT : []306 t'56 PIT
SANTIAGO, JOSE : []59 t'56 KC
SARNI, BILL : []247 t'56 STL/NY N ([]86 t'57)
SCHMITZ, JOHNNY : []298 t'56 BAL/BOS
SILVERA, AL: []137 t'56 CIN
TREMEL, BILL : []96 t'56 CHI A
WESTLAKE, WALLY : []81 t'56 PHI

1957 Retired

ABER, AL : []141 t'57 DET/KC
BLAYLOCK, MARV : []224 t'57 PHI
BRIDEWESER, JIM : 382 t'57 BAL
CHAKALES, BOB : []261 t'57 BOS/WAS
COLE, DICK : []234 t'57 MIL
COOPER, WALKER : []380 t'57 STL
CRIMIAN, JACK : []297 t'57 DET
DAVIS, JIM : []273 t'57 STL/NY N
DITTMER, JACK : []282 t'57 DET
GROMEK, STEVE : []258 t'57 DET
HARMON, CHUCK : []299 t'57 STL/PHI ([]48 t'58)
HOUTTEMAN, ART : []385 t'57 BAL/CLE
JOLLY, DAVE : []389 t'57 MIL ([]183 t'58)
KAISER, DON : []134 t'57 CHI N
KINDER, ELLIS : []352 t'57 CHI A
KING, NELSON : []349 t'57 PIT
KUHN, KEN : []266 t'57 CLE

LaPALME, PAUL : []344 t'57 CHI A
LENNON, BOB : []371 t'57 CHI N
LUTTRELL, LYLE : []386 t'57 WAS
MARGONERI, JOE : []191 t'57 NY N
McCALL, WINDY : []291 t'57 NY N
MURFF, JOHN : []321 t'57 MIL
NORTHY, RON : []31 t'57 CHI A/PHI
OLSON, KARL : []153 t'57 DET/WAS
PHILLIPS, JACK : []307 t'57 DET
POHOLSKY, TOM : []235 t'57 CHI N
PYBURN, JIM : []276 t'57 BAL
ROBINSON, EDDIE : []238 t'57 BAL /CLE/DET
ROGOVIN, SAUL : []129 t'57 PHI
SCHOONMAKER, JERRY : []334 t'57 WAS
SURKONT, MAX : []310 t'57 NY N
VALDES, RENE : []337 t'57 BKN

1958 Retired

BAXES, MIKE : []302 t'58 KC ([]381 t'59)
BESSENT, DON : []401 t'58 LA
BOLLING, MILT : []188 t'58 DET
BURK, MACK : []278 t'58 PHI
BURNETTE, WALLY : []69 t'58 KC
CASTLEMAN, FOSTER : []416 t'58 BAL

CRONE, RAY : []272 t'58 SF
FODGE, GENE : []449 t'58 CHI N
FREEMAN, HERSHALL : []27 t'58 CIN/CHI N
GRAFF, MILT : []192 t'58 KC ([]182 t'59)
HAMRIC, BERT : []336 t'58 BAL
HATFIELD, FRED : []339 t'58 CIN/CLE

HAZLE, BOB : []83 t'58 DET/MIL
HOWELL, DIXIE M : []421 t'58 CHI A
HUNTER, BILLY : []98 t'58 CLE /KC
JOHNSON, CONNIE : []266 t'58 BAL ([]21 t'59)
KAZANSKI, TED : []36 t'58 PHI ([]99 t'59)
KEEGAN, BOB : []200 t'58 CHI A
LITTLEFIELD, DICK : []241 t'58 MIL
MAYER, ED : []461 t'58 CHI N
McDANIEL, VON : []65 t'58 STL
MELTON, DAVE : []391 t'58 KC
MIKSIS, EDDIE : []121 t'58 BAL/CIN ([]58 t'59)
MILLER, BOB : []326 t'58 PHI
MORGAN, BOBBY : []144 t'58 CHI N
MOSS, LES : []153 t'58 CHI A

NIXON, WILLARD : []395 t'58 BOS ([]361 t'59)
PAINE, PHIL : []442 t'58 STL
QUALTERS, TOM : []453 t'58 CHI A/PHI
RABE, CHARLEY : []376 t'58 CIN
RAINES, LARRY : []243 t'58 CLE
SLEATER, LOU : []46 t'58 BAL/DET
SMITH, PAUL LESLIE : []269 t'58 CHI/PIT N
TAYLOR, BILL : []389 t'58 DET
THOMPSON, CHUCK : []57 t'58 DET
WALKER, RUBE : []203 t'58 LA
WEHMEIER, HERM : []248 t'58 STL/DET
WIGHT, BILL : []237 t'58 STL/CIN ([]421 t'59)
WILSON, BOB : []213 t'58 DET
WILSON, JIM : []163 t'58 CHI A

1959 Retired

ACKER, TOM : []201 t'59 CIN
ADAMS, BOBBY : []249 t'59 CHI N
ALVAREZ, OSSIE : []504 t'59 DET
ARIAS, RUDOLPH ; []537 t'59 CHI A
AVILA, BOBBY : []363 t'59 BAL/BOS/MIL
BARCLAY, CURT : []307 t'59 SF
BAXES, JIM : []547 t'59 CLE/LA
BELLA, ZEKE : []254 t'59 KC
BLAYLOCK, BOB : []211 t'59 STL
BLAYLOCK, GARY : []539 t'59 STL/NY A
BOLGER, JIM : []29 t'59 CLE/PHI
BOWMAN, BOB : []221 t'59 PHI
BRODOWSKI, DICK : []371 t'59 CLE
CARRASQUEL, CHICO : []264 t'59 BAL
CARROLL, TOMMY : []513 t'59 KC
CLARK, PHIL : []454 t'59 STL
DAVIE, JERRY : []256 t'59 DET
DRAKE, SOLLY : []406 t'59LA/PHI
FINIGAN, JIM : []47 t'59 BAL
FITZGERALD, ED : []33 t'59 CLE/WAS
GORMAN, TOM: []449 t'59 KC
GRIGGS, HAL : []434 t'59 WAS
GRISSOM, MARV : []243 t'59 STL
HEARN, JIM : []63 t'59 PHI
HEMUS, SOLLY : []527 t'59 STL
JACKSON, RANDY : []394 t'59 CLE/CHI N
JEFFCOAT, HAL : []81 t'59 STL/CIN
JOHNSON, ERNIE : []279 t'59 BAL
KELLNER, ALEX : []101 t'59 STL
KING, CHARLES : []538 t'59 STL/CHI N

KORCHECK, STEVE : []284 t'59 WAS
LUMENTI, RALPH : []316 t'59 WAS
MARTIN, MORRIE : []38 t'59 CHI N
MARTYN, BOB : []41 t'59 KC
MEYER, RUSS : []482 t'59 KC
MIRANDA, WILLIE : []540 t'59 BAL
NARLESKI, RAY : []442 t'59 DET
PLEWS, HERB : []373 t'59 BOS/WAS
PORTER, J W : []246 t'59 STL/WAS
PORTERFIELD, BOB : []181 t'59 CHI/PIT N
RENNA, BILL : []72 t'59 BOS
RICKETTS, DICK : []137 t'59 STL
ROMONOSKY, JOHN : []267 t'59 WAS
SAMFORD, RON : []242 t'59 WAS
SCHMIDT, WILLARD : []171 t'59 CIN
SIMPSON, HARRY : []333 t'59 CHI/KC/PIT
SINGLETON, BERT : []548 t'59 CHI N
SKIZAS, LOU : []328 t'59 CHI A
SMITH, BOB G : []83 t'59 DET/PIT
SNYDER, GENE : []522 t'59 LA
SPEAKE, BOB : []526 t'59 SF
SUSCE, GEORGE : []511 t'59 DET
TATE, LEE : []544 t'59 STL
THURMAN, BOB : []541 t'59 CIN
TOMANEK, DICK : []369 t'59 KC
URBAN, JACK : []18 t'59 STL
VALENTINETTI, VITO : []44 t'59 WAS
WARD, PRESTON : []176 t'59 KC
ZAUCHIN, NORM : []311 t'59 WAS
ZUVERINK, GEORGE : []219 t'59 BAL

THERE IS ONE IN EVERY PACK

Every pack, or so it seemed, had one of those cards that you didn't know what to do with. You know the card, the guy who played last year, but didn't play on the team this year. Maybe he was in the service, traded, or just did not play. The card companies may have just speculated he would be playing, but in any case, these players are mirrored on cardboard forever.

t=topps - b=bowman

1949

BLACKBURN, JIM : []160 b /CIN	: not on roster
LaMANNO, RAY : []113 b /CIN	: last game 10-3-48
LUPIEN, TONY : []141 b /CHI A	: last game 10-3-48
McBRIDE, TOM : []74 b /WAS	: last game 9-30-48
McCARTHY, JOHN : []220 b /NY N	: last game 9-26-48
McCORMICK, FRANK : []239 b /BOS N	: last game 10-3-48
McCOSKY, BARNEY : []203 b /PHI A	: not on roster
MOULDER, GLEN : []159 b /CHI A	: last game 9-18-48
OSTERMUELLER, FRITZ : []227 b PIT	: last game 9-30-48
PARTEE, ROY : []149 b'49 STL A	: last game 10-3-48
SINGLETON, BERT : []147 b /PIT	: traded to the Pacific Coast League
WOOTEN, EARL : []189 b /WAS	: last game 9-30-48

1950

GRAHAM, JACK : []145 b'50 STL A	: last game 9-25-49
RESTELLI, DINO : []123 b'50 PIT	: not on roster
VICO, GEORGE : []150 b'50 DET	: last game 10-1-49

1951

FRIEND, OWEN : []101 b'51 STL A	: not on roster
HOUTTEMAN, ART : []45 b'51 DET	: not on roster
KOKOS, DICK : []68 b'51 STL A	: not on roster
LADE, DOYLE : []139 b'51 CHI N	: last game 9-29-50
LAKE, EDDIE : []140 b'51 DET	: last game 9-30-50
LOMBARDI, VIC : []204 b'51 PIT	: last game 9-24-50
MacDONALD, BILL : []239 b'51 PIT	: not on roster
NORTHY, RON : []70 b'51 CHI N	: not on roster
O'CONNELL, DANNY : []93 b'51 PIT	: not on roster
QUINN, FRANK : []276 b'51 BOS A	: last game 4-26-50
ROY, NORMAN : []278 b'51 BOS N	: last game 9-27-50

1952

BASGALL, MONTE : []12 t'52 PIT	: last game 8-11-51
BOLLWEG, DON : []128 t'52 NY A	: not on roster
BUCHA, JOHNNY : []19 t'52 STL N	: not on roster
CHAPMAN, BEN : []391 t'52 CIN	: Coach / last game 5-12-46
COMBS, MERRILL : []18 t'52 CLE	: Coach and played / last game 9-28-52
COOGAN, DALE : []87 t'52 PIT	: last game 7-5-50
DEMPSEY, CON : []44 t'52 PHI N	: last game 5-5-51
ERAUTT, ED : []171 t'52 CIN	: not on roster
EVANS, AL : []152 t'52 BOS A	: last game 8-5-51
FITZSIMMONS, FRED : []234 b'52 NY N	: Coach / last game 7-16-42
FRANKS, HERMAN : []385 t'52 NY N	: Coach / last game 8-28-49
FRIEND, OWEN : []160 t'52 STL A	: not on roster
GILBERT, TOOKIE : []61 t'52 NY N	: not on roster
HOUSE, FRANK : []146 t'52 DET	: not on roster
JONES, SHELDON : []215 b []130 t NY N	: traded 4-8-52 to BOS N / played
KENNEDY, BILL : []102 t'52 STL A	: sold 3-13-52 to CHI A / played
KIELY, LEO : []54 t'52 BOS A	: not on roster
McDONALD, BILL : []138 t'52 PIT	: not on roster
MERRIMAN, LLOYD : []78 b'52 CIN	: not on roster
NICHOLS, CHET : []120 b'52 BOS N	: not on roster
OLSON, KARL : []72 t'52 BOS A	: not on roster
OVERMIRE, FRANK : []155 t'52 NY A	: claimed on waivers 5-12-52 by STL A / played
PALICA, ERV : []273 t'52 BKN	: not on roster
POSEDEL, BILL : []361 t'52 PIT	: Coach / last game 9-13-46
RICKERT, MARV : []50 t'52 CHI A	: last game 9-26-50
ROSS, BOB : []298 t'52 WAS	: not on roster
RUSSELL, JIM : []51 t'52 BKN	: last game 10-1-51
SHEA, FRANK : []230 b'52 []248 t'52 NY A	: traded 5-3-52 to WAS A / played
SILVESTRI, KEN : []200 b'52 PHI N	: last game 7-31-51
SIMA, AL : []93 t'52 WAS	: not on roster
SUKEFORTH, CLYDE : []227 b'52 PIT	: Coach / last game 6-7-45
TERWILLIGER, WAYNE : []7 t'52 BKN N	: not on roster
WELLMAN, BOB : []41 t'52 PHI A	: last game 6-3-50

1953

BARTIROME, TONY : []71 t'53 PIT	: last game 9-28-52
BEVAN, HAL : []43 bw'53 PHI A	: not on roster
BOYER, CLOYD : []115 b []60 t /STL N	: not on roster
BRODOWSKI, DICK : []69 t'53 BOS A	: not on roster
CHITI, HARRY : []7 b'53 CHI N	: not on roster
DANIELS, JACK : []83 b'53 MIL	: last game 9-18-52
DEL GRECO, BOBBY : []48 t'53 PIT	: not on roster
FANNIN, CLIFF : []203 t'53 STL A	: last game 9-27-52
FOX, HOWIE : []158 b'53 []22 t'53 PHI N	: went to minors / picked up by BAL A
FRIDLEY, JIM : []187 t'53 CLE	: claimed on waivers by STL A / did not play
GOLDSBERRY, GORDON : []200 t /STL A	: last game 9-27-52
HEINTZELMAN, KEN : []136 t PHI N	: last game 8-13-52
JOHNSON, DON : []55 bw'53 WAS	: not on roster
KAZAK, EDDIE : []194 t'53 DET	: last game 7-1-52 with CIN N

KLINE, RON : []175 t'53 PIT   : not on roster
MIGGINS, LARRY : []142 b'53 STL N   : last game 9-28-52
MORGAN, TOM : []132 t'53 NY A   : not on roster
NORMAN, BILL : []245 t'53 STL A   : Coach / last game 9-24-32
PORTER, J W : []211 t'53 DET   : not on roster
RIDDLE, JOHN : []274 t'53 STL N   : Coach / last game 9-11-48
RODRIGUEZ, HECTOR : []98 b'53 CHI A   : last game 9-16-52
ROSSI, JOE : []74 t'53 PIT   : not on roster
RUTHERFORD, JOHN : []137 t'53 BKN   : last game 9-23-52
SLEATER, LOU : []224 t'53 WAS   : not on roster
THRONEBERRY, FAYE : []49 t'53 BOS   : not on roster
WALL, MURRAY : []217 t'53 MIL   : not on roster

1954

ALOMA, LUIS : []134 b'54 []57 t'54 CHI A   : last game 8-30-53
BAKER, DEL : []133 t'54 BOS   : Coach / last game 9-30-16
BERNIER, CARLOS : []171 b'54 PIT   : last game 9-22-53
BLADES, RAY : []243 t'54 CHI N   : Coach / last game 9-25-32
BRODOWSKI, DICK : []221 t'54 BOS   : not on roster
BUCHA, JOHNNY : []215 b'54 DET   : last game 9-25-53
CAIN, BOB : []61 t'54 PHI A   : signed by CHI A 8-16-54 played 1 game
CHAMBERS, CLIFF : []126 b'54 STL   : last game 9-22-53
FITZPATRICK, JOHN : []213 t'54 PIT   : Coach / never played
FRIEND, OWEN : []212 b'54 CLE   : not on roster
GALAN, AUGIE : []233 t'54 PHI A   : Coach / last game9-16-49
HAYNES, JOE : []223 t'54 WAS   : Coach / last game 8-30-52
HEMSLEY, ROLLIE : []143 t'54 PHI A   : Coach / last game 4-17-47
HERMANSKI, GENE : []228 t'54 PIT   : last game 9-22-53
KEELY, BOB : []176 t'54 MIL   : Coach / last game 9-29-45
KRESS, RALPH : []160 t'54 CLE   : Coach / last game 7-17-46
MAYO, ED : []247 t'54 PHI N   : Coach / last game 10-3-48
MILLS, BUSTER : []227 t'53 BOS   : Coach / last game 6-1-46
MULLIN, PAT : []151 b'54 DET   : last game 9-21-53
OLIVER, TOM : []207 t'54 BAL   : Coach / last game 9-23-33
QUALTERS, TOM : []174 t'54 PHI N   : not on roster
RIDDLE, JOHN : []147 t'54 STL   : last game 9-11-48
ROGOVIN, SAUL : []140 b'54 CHI A   : traded 12-10-53 to CIN N / not on roster
ROSS, BOB : []189 t'54 WAS   : not on roster
RYBA, MIKE : []237 t'54 STL   : Coach / last game 8-28-46
SANDLOCK, MIKE : []104 t'54 PHI N   : sold 12-19-53 by PIT N / last game 9-27-53
SCHREIBER, PAUL : []217 t'54 BOS   : Coach / last game 9-8-45
SCHULTZ, BOB : []59 b'54 PIT   : not on roster
SCULL, ANGEL : []204 t'54 WAS   : never played
SMITH, PAUL LESLIE : []11 t'54 PIT   : not on roster
SPENCER, DARYL : []185 t'54 NY N   : not on roster
SWIFT, BOB : []65 t'54 DET   : Coach / last game 9-27-53

1955

ALLIE, GAIR : []59 t'55 PIT   : last game 9-26-54
BEARD, RALPH : []206 b'55 STL   : last game 9-9-54
BILKO, STEVE : []88 b'55 []93 t'55 CHI N   : not on roster
BRAZLE, AL : []230 b'55 STL   : last game 9-24-54
CASAGRANDE, TOM : []167 t'55 PHI   : never played
CRAWFORD, RUFUS : []121 b'55 DET   : not on roster
GLYNN, BILL : []39 t'55 CLE   : last game 9-26-54
HALL, BOB : []113 b'55 PIT   : last game 9-26-53
HAWES, ROY LEE : []268 b'55 WAS   : last game 9-30-51
HOSKINS, DAVE : []133 t'55 CLE   : last game 9-21-54
HUDSON, SID : []318 b'55 BOS   : last game 9-25-54
JUDSON, HOWIE : []193 b'55 CIN   : last game 9-25-54
KRALY, STEVE : []139 t'55 NY A   : last game 9-15-53
KRESS, RALPH : []151 t'55 CLE   : Coach / last game 7-17-46
LEHMAN, KEN : []310 b'55 BKN   : not on roster
LENNON, BOB : []119 t'55 NY N   : not on roster
LEONARD, DUTCH : []247 b'55 CHI N   : last game 9-25-53
LIMMER, LOU : []80 b'55 []54 t'55 KC   : last game 9-26-54
LINT, ROYCE : []62 b'55 STL   : last game 8-29-54
MICHAELS, CASS : []85 b'55 CHI A   : last game 8-27-54
MOSES, WALLY : []294 b'55 KC   : last game 9-30-51
O'DELL, BILLY : []57 t'55 BAL   : not on roster
ORTIZ, LOUIS : []114 t'55 PHI   : never played
PARKS, JACK : []23 t'55 MIL   : never played
QUALTERS, TOM : []33 t'55 PHI   : not on roster
RICE, HAL : []52 b'55 CHI N   : last game 9-19-54
RIDDLE, JOHN : []98 t'55 STL   : Coach / last game 9-11-48
ROACH, MEL : []117 t'55 MIL   : not on roster
SAWATSKI, CARL : []122 t'55 CHI A   : not on roster
SCHROLL, AL : []319 b'55 BOS   : not on roster
SERENA, BILL : []233 b'55 CHI N   : last game 8-7-54
TALBOT, BOB : []137 b'55 CHI N   : last game 9-26-54
VOLLMER, CLYDE : []13 b'55 WAS   : last game 9-1-54
WALLS, LEE : []82 b'55 PIT   : not on roster
WYROSTEK, JOHNNY : []237 b'55 PHI   : last game 9-26-54

1956

BURBRINK, NELSON : []27 t'56 STL   : last game 9-21-55
PODBIELAN, BUD : []224 t'56 CIN   : not on roster
POWELL, LEROY : []144 t'56 CHI A   : not on roster
SCHOONMAKER, JERRY : []216 t'56 WAS   : not on roster
SPEAKE, BOB : []66 t'56 CHI N   : not on roster

1957

BURK, MACK : []91 t'57 PHI   : not on roster
CARROLL, TOMMY : []164 t'57 NY A   : not on roster
DRAKE, SOLLY : []159 t'57 CHI N   : not on roster
KRETLOW, LOU : []139 t'57 KC   : last game 9-23-56

NEGRAY, RON : []254 t'57 PHI   : traded 4-5-57 to BKN N / did not play
ORAVETZ, ERNIE : []179 t'57 WAS   : last game 9-30-56
PARNELL, MEL : []313 t'57 BOS   : last game 9-29-56
POPE, DAVE : []249 t'57 CLE   : last game 9-30-56
SARNI, BILL : []86 t'57 NY N   : last game 9-18-56
THOMPSON, HANK : []109 t'57 NY N   : last game 9-30-56
VALDIVIELSO, JOSE : []246 t'57 WAS   : not on roster

1958

BRUNET, GEORGE : []139 t'58 KC   : not on roster
BYRD, HARRY : []154 t'58 DET   : last game 9-27-57
CAFFIE, JOE : []182 t'58 CLE   : last game 9-28-57
CECCARELLI, ART : []191 t'58 BAL   : not on roster
DERRINGTON, JIM : []129 t'58 CHI A   : last game 9-27-57
DOUGLAS, WHAMMY : []306 t'58 PIT   : last game 9-21-57
DURHAM, JOE : []96 t'58 BAL   : not on roster
HARMON, CHUCK : []48 t'58 PHI   : last game 9-15-57
JOLLY, DAVE : []183 t'58 SF   : last game 9-14-57
LANDRUM, DON : []291 t'58 PHI   : not on roster
MERRITT, LLOYD : []231 t'58 STL   : last game 9-28-57
PALYS, STAN : []126 t'58 CIN   : last game 9-25-56
PRITCHARD, BUDDY : []151 t'58 PIT   : last game 9-1-57
RAND, DICK : []218 t'58 PIT   : last game 9-17-57
SCHULT, ART : []58 t'58 WAS   : sold 1-29-58 to BOS A / not on roster
SHEARER, RAY : []283 t'58 MIL   : last game 9-27-57
STRICKLAND, GEORGE : []102 t'58 CLE   : not on roster
USHER, BOB : []124 t'58 WAS   : last game 9-19-57

1959

ABERNATHY, TED : []169 t'59 WAS   : not on roster
BAKER, GENE : []238 t'59 PIT   : not on roster
BAXES, MIKE : []381 t'59 KC   : last game 9-27-58
BEAMON, CHARLIE : []192 t'59 BAL   : last game 9-13-58
BESSENT, DON : []71 t'59 LA   : last game 9-27-58
BILKO, STEVE : []43 t'59 LA   : not on roster
BOROS, STEVE : []331 t'59 DET A   : not on roster
BURTON, ELLIS : []231 t'59 STL N   : not on roster
COLES, CHUCK : []120 t'59 CIN N   : last game 9-28-58
CONLEY, BOB : []121 t'59 PHI N   : not on roster
CONSTABLE, JIMMY : []451 T'59 WAS A   : not on roster
CRADDOCK, WALT : []281 t'59 KC A   : last game 9-28-58
DELSING, JIM : []386 t'59 WAS A   : not on roster
DOUGLAS, WHAMMY : []431 t'59 CIN   : last game 9-21-57 / traded to CIN from PIT 1-30-59
GRAFF, MILT : []182 t'59 KC A   : last game 9-21-58
HAAS, EDDIE : []126 t'59 MIL N   : not on roster
HALL, BILL : []49 t'59 PIT N   : last game 9-26-58
HARRELL, BILLY : []433 t'59 STL N   : claimed on waivers from CLE A / not on roster
HEMAN, RUSS : []283 t'59 CLE A   : not on roster
HERRERA, FRANK : []129 t'59 PHI N   : not on roster
JOHNSON, CONNIE : []21 t'59 BAL A   : last game 9-14-58
KAZANSKI, TED : []99 t'59 PHI N   : last game 9-28-58

LEE, DON : []132 t'59 DET   : not on roster
LEHMAN, KEN : []31 t'59 PHI   : not on roster
McDANIEL, JIM : []134 t'59 PIT   : never played
MIKSIS, EDDIE : []58 t'59 CIN   : last game 9-26-58
MONZANT, RAY : []332 t'59 SF   : not on roster
MOSS, LES : []453 t'59 CHI A   : last game 9-1-58
NICHOLS, DOLAN : 362 t'59 CHI N   : last game 9-26-58
NIXON, WILLARD : 361 t'59 BOS   : last game 7-4-58
QUALTERS, TOM : []341 t'59 CHI A   : last game 9-25-58
RAYDON, CURT : []305 t'59 PIT   : last game 9-14-58
SADOWSKI, ED : []139 t'59 BOS   : not on roster
SECREST, CHARLIE : []140 t'59 KC   : never played
SOLIS, MARCELINO : []214 t'59 CHI N   : last game 9-13-58
STIGMAN, DICK : []142 t'58 CLE   : not on roster
THACKER, MOE : []474 t'59 CHI N   : not on roster
TIEFENAUER, BOB : []501 t'59 CLE   : not on roster
VIRGIL, OZZIE : []203 t'59 DET   : not on roster
WEHMEIER, HERM : []421 DET   : last game 7-23-58
WILL, BOB : []388 t'59 CHI N   : not on roster
ZIMMERMAN, JERRY : []146 t'59 BOS   : not on roster

THEY WERE THE 1ˢᵗ

Here is a list of commons that were the first to do, or be, something no other player can claim. New stadiums opened in the '50's, blacks were added to the rosters, and common players had some individual first time accomplishments.

t=topps - b=bowman

ALSTON, TOM : []257 b'55

Was the 1ˢᵗ black to play for St. Louis Cardinals along with Brooks Lawrence. 1954

BAKER, GENE : []7 b '55
[]142 t'56 []358 t'58 []238 t'59

Was the 1ˢᵗ black (along with *Ernie Banks*) to play for the Chicago Cubs, 1953

BRUTON, BILL : []165 t'59

Hit the 1ˢᵗ home run, triple and had 1ˢᵗ stolen base at Milwaukee County Stadium (Braves) 4/14/53

CARRASQUEL, CHICO : []54 b'53
[]54 b'54 []173 b'55 []230 t'56
[]67 t'57 []55 t'58 []264 t'59

Was the 1ˢᵗ batter and got the 1ˢᵗ hit (single) at Baltimore Memorial Stadium (Orioles). 4/15/54

CIMOLI, GINO : []319 t'57 []286 t'58
[]418 t'59

Was the 1ˢᵗ batter (struck out) at the San Francisco Seals Stadium (Giants). 4/15/58

COAN, GIL : []90 b'49 []54 b'50
[]18 b'51 []51 b'52 []34 b'53
[]40 b'54 []78 b'55 []291 t'52
[]133 t'53

Had the 1ˢᵗ sacrifice at Baltimore Municipal Stadium 4/17/54

COURTNEY, CLINT : []70 b'53
[]69 b'54 []34 b'55 []127dp t'53
[]159 t'56 []51 t'57 []92 t'58
[]483 t'59

Hits the 1ˢᵗ home run and has the 1ˢᵗ rbi at Baltimore Municipal Stadium 4/15/54

CRANDALL, DEL ; []567as t'59

Had the 1ˢᵗ sacrifice at Milwaukee County Stadium 4/15/53

DAVENPORT, JIM ; []413 t'58

Had the 1ˢᵗ RBI and sacrifice fly at San Francisco Seals Stadium 4/15/58 and was 1ˢᵗ batter , 1ˢᵗ hit (single), 1ˢᵗ run scored at Los Angeles Coliseum 4/18/58

DeMAESTRI, JOE : []147 b'54
[]176 b'55 []286 t'52 []161 t'56
[]44 t'57 []62 t'58

Had the 1ˢᵗ RBI at Kansas City Municipal Stadium 4/12/55

DEMETER, DON : []244 t'58
[]324 t'59

Had the 1ˢᵗ inside the park Home Run at Los Angeles Coliseum 4/21/59

FRIEND, BOB : []492as t'58
[]569as t'59

Was the 1ˢᵗ pitcher to win two All-Star games 1956 and 1960

GALAN, AUGIE : []233 t'54

Was the 1ˢᵗ in the National League to Home Run from both sides of the plate, in one game 6/15/37

GOMEZ, RUBEN : []71 t'55
[]9 t'56 []58 t'57 []335 t'58
[]535 t'59

Wins the 1st game at San Francisco Seals Stadium (8-0)
4/15/58

GORDON, SID : []101 b'48 []109 b'50
[]19 b'51 []60 b'52 []5 b'53
[]11 b'54 []117dp t'53

Hit's the 1st Grand Slam, of the season, in the National League
4/19/50

GRISSOM, MARV : []123 b'55
[]301 t'56 []216 t'57 []399 t'58
[]243 t'59

Had the 1st Save at San Francisco Seals Stadium 4/17/58

GUMPERT, RANDY : []87 b'49
[]59 b'51 []106 b'52 []247 t'52

Gave up the 1st of *Mickey Mantle's* 536 Home Runs 5/1/51

HARRIST, EARL : []65 t'53

Struck out *Larry Doby* (1st black in the American League) in
his 1st Major League at bat

HATFIELD, FRED : []153 b'52
[]125 b'53 []119 b'54 []187 b'55
[]163dp t'53 []318 t'56
[]278 t'57 []339 t'58

Had 1st hit (double) at Kansas City Municipal Stadium 4/12/55

HEMUS, SOLLY : []212r b'52
[]85 b'53 []94 b'54 []107 b'55
[]231dp t'53 []117 t'54
[]231 t'57 []207 t'58 []527 t'59

Was the 1st batter (walked) at Milwaukee County Stadium
4/14/53

JABLONSKI, RAY : []189 t'53
[]26 t'54 []56 t'55 []86 t'56
[]218 t'57 []362 t'58 []342 t'59

Had the 1st RBI at Milwaukee County Stadium 4/14/53

JANOWICZ, VIC : []222dp t'53

Was the 1st Heisman Trophy winner (50) to play in Majors

JONES, SAM : []287 t'57

Was the 1st black to pitch a no-hitter 5/12/55

KELLNER, ALEX : []222 b'49
[]14 b'50 []57 b'51 []226 b'52
[]107 b'53 []51 b'54 []53 b'55
[]201 t'52 []176 t'56 []280 t'57
[]3 t'58 []101 t'59

Had the 1st win at Kansas City Municipal Stadium 4/12/55 and
hit the 1st Triple there 4/18/55

KENNEDY, BOB : []33dp t'53

Hit's the 1st Grand Slam for the new Baltimore Orioles
7/30/54

KERR, BUDDY : []186 b'49
[]55 b'50 []171 b'51

Hit a Home Run 1st at-bats in the Majors 9/8/43

KIRKLAND, WILLIE : []128 t'58
[]484 t'59

Had the 1st Stolen Base at San Francisco Seals Stadium
4/17/58 the next day 4/18/58 had the 1st Double at
LA Coliseum

KLINE, RON : []175 t'53 []94 t'56
[]256 t'57 []82 t'58 []265 t'59

Gave up the 1st of *Willie McCovey's* 521 Home Runs 8/2/59

LAWRENCE, BROOKS : []75 b'55 []305 t'56 []66 t'57 []374 t'58 []67 t'59

Was the 1st black to play for the St. Louis Cardinals, along with Tom Alston in 1954

McDERMONT, MICKEY : []97r b'50 []16 b'51 []25 b'52 []35 b'53 []56 b'54 []165 b'55 []55dp t'53 []218 t'57

Gave up Home Runs to Bob Nieman on Bob's 1st two at-bats in the Major Leagues 9/14/51

MICHAELS, CASS : []12 b'49 []91 b'50 []132 b'51 []36 b'52 []130 b'53 []150 b'54 []85 b'55 []178 t'52

Hit the 1st Grand Slam at Baltimore Memorial Stadium 5/28/54

MINNER, PAUL : []211 b'52 []71 b'53 []13 b'54 []127 t'52 []92dp t'53 []182 t'56

Gave up the 1st of *Frank Robinson's* 586 Home Runs 4/28/56

NIEMAN, BOB : []145 b'55 []267 t'56 [][]14 t'57 []165 t'58 []375 t'59

Was the 1st Major Leaguer to hit a Home Run, in his first two at-bats (1st one, on the 1st pitch) 9/14/51

NORTHY, RON : []79 b'49 []81 b'50 []70 b'51 []204 t'52 []31 t'57

Was the 1st player to hit three pinch-hit Grand Slams 9/18/50

O'CONNELL, DANNY : []93 b'51 []160 b'54 []44 b'55 []107dp t'53 []272 t'56 []271 t'57 []166 t'58 []87 t'59

Scored the 1st Run at San Francisco Seals Stadium 4/15/58

PAINE, PHIL : []442 t'58

Is the 1st Major Leaguer to play in Japan 8/23/53

PAULA, CARLOS : []97 t'55

Was 1st black player with Washington Nationals 9/6/54

POLLET, HOWIE : []95r b'49 []72 b'50 []83 b'52 []63 t'52 []83 t'53 []89 t'54 []76 t'55 []262 t'56

Won the 1st game of the 1st ever three game play-off for the Cardinals over the Dodgers 10/1/46

RASCHI, VIC : []185 b'55

Gave up 1st Home Run of *Minnie Minoso's* career 5/1/51
Gave up 1st Home Run of *Hank Aaron's* 755 4/23/54

ROBERTS, CURT : []242 t'54 []107 t'55 []306 t'56

Was 1st black player with Pittsburgh Pirates 1954

RUSSELL, JIM : []235 b'49 []223 b'50 []51 t'52

Was the 1ST Major Leaguer to swith hit Home Runs in a game more than once 7/26/50

SAUER, HANK : []111dp t'53

Hit the 1st Home Run at Los Angeles Coliseum 4/18/58

SCHMIDT, BOB : []468 t'58 []109 t'59

Hit the 1st Triple at the Los Angeles Coliseum 4/18/58

SCHMIDT, WILLARD : []168 t'53 []323 t'56 []206 t'57 []214 t'58 []171 t'59

Was the 1st Major Leaguer to get Hit By a Pitch twice in the same inning 4/26/59

SHEA, FRANK : []230 b'52 []141 b'53 []104 b'54 []207 b'55 []248 t'52 []164dp t'53

Was the 1st Rookie to win an All-Star game 7/8/47

SPENCER, DARYL : []185 b'54 []277 t'56 []49 t'57 []68 t'58 []443 t'59

Hit the 1st Home Run at San Francisco Seals Stadium 4/15/58
Hit the 1st Triple at Los Angeles Coliseum 4/18/58

STALEY, GERRY : []121 b'51 []50 b'52 []17 b'53 []14 b'54 []155 b'55 []79 t'52 []56dp t'53 []227 t'57 []412 t'58

Beat Pittsburgh in the 1st Opening (Day) Night game 4/18/50
Gave up 1st Home Run of *Ernie Bank's* 512 9/20/53

STEPHENS, GENE : []248dp t'53 []313 t'56 []217 t'57 []227 t'58 []261 t'59

Is the 1st American League player to have three hits in the same inning, and he was a rookie 6/18/53

STEPHENS, VERN : []71 b'48 []2 b'50

Had the 1st Triple at Baltimore Memorial Stadium 4/18/54

SURKONT, MAX : []12 b'52 []156 b'53 []75 b'54 []83 b'55 []302 t'52 []209 t'56 []310 t'57

Had the 1st Win for "Milwaukee Braves" (against the Reds) 4/13/53

THOMPSON, HANK : []249 b52 []64 t'54 []109 t'57

Was 1st black along with Willard Brown to play for the St Louis Browns and they are 1st two in same line-up 7/20/47. Hank was also the 1st black batter to face a black pitcher (*Don Newcombe*) 7/8/49

TRICE, BOB : []148 t'54 []132 t'55

Was the 1st black player for Philadelphia Athletics 9/13/53

TRUCKS, VIRGIL : []198 b'54

Has the 1st Loss at Baltimore Memorial Stadium 4/15/54

TURLEY, BOB : []570as t'59

Had the 1st Win at Baltimore Memorial Stadium 4/15/54

VALO, ELMER : []66 b'49 []49 t'50 []206 b'52 []34 t'52 []122 t'53 []145 t'54 []145 t'55 []54 t'57 []323 t'58

Was the 1st American League player to hit two bases loaded Triples in the same game 5/1/49

VIRGIL, OZZIE : []365 t'57 []107 t'58 []203 t'59

Was the 1st black player for the Detroit Tigers 6/6/58

VOLLMER, CLYDE : []53 b'50 []91 b'51 []57 b'52 []152 b'53 []136 b'54 []13 b'55 []255 t'52 []32 t'53

Hit a Home Run on 1st pitch in the Majors 1942

WAKEFIELD, DICK : []91 b'49

Was the 1st "Bonus Baby" ($52'000) Detroit 1941

WILSON, BILL : []222 t'54
[]86 t'55

Scored the 1st Run at KansasnCity Municipal Stadium 4/12/55

WILSON, BOB : []250 t'53
[]58 t'54 []92 t'56 []19 t'57
[]213 t'58 []24 t'59

Hit the 1st Home Run at Kansas City Municipal Stadium 4/12/55

WILSON, JIM : []37 b'53
[]16 b'54 []253 b'55 []276 t'52
[]208 t'53 []171 t'56 []330 t'57
[]163 t'58

Had the 1st No-hitter at Milwaukee County Stadium 6/12/54

WORTHINGTON, AL : []39 t'57
[]427 t'58 []28 t'59

Had the 1st Loss (against *Carl Erskine*) at Los Angeles Coliseum 4/18/58

YOUNG, BOBBY : []193 b'52
[]149 b'54 []147 t52 []160 t'53
[]8 t'54

Had the 1st Double at Baltimore Memorial Stadium 4/15/54

ZUPO, FRANK : []229 t'58

The 1st time a "Z" pitcher and catcher were used in a game 7/1/57

ZUVERINK, GEORGE : []92 b'55
[]199 t'52 []276 t'56 []11 t'57
[]6 t'58 []219 t'59

The 1st time a "Z" pitcher and catcher were used in a game 7/1/57

WE'RE OUTTA HERE!

The Fifties saw five teams abandon their ballparks for new digs. On their way out some common players left a final mark. Even if they went on to have common careers, they will always be in the records of having the last.

t=topps - b=bowman

BURTSCHY, ED : []120 b'55

Was the last pitcher to record a Loss at Philadelphia A's Shibe Park (*Johnny Sain* gets win) 9/19/54

CHAMBERS, CLIFF : []202 b'50 []131 b'51 []14 b'52 []126 b'54 []68 t'52

Had the last no-hitter at Boston Braves Field 5/6/51

CIMOLI, GINO : []319r t'57 []286 t'58 []418 t'59

Scored the last Run at Brooklyn's Ebbets Field 9/24/57

COOPER, WALKER : []9r b'48 9/21/52 []117 b'49 []111 b'50 []135 b'51 []208 b'52 []294 t'52 []273 t'56 []380 t'57

Was the last Batter (fly out) at Boston Braves Field

COX, BILLY : []152 b '52

Had the last Sacrifice Fly at Boston Braves Field 9/21/52

DANIELS, BENNIE : []392 t'58 []122rp t'59

Was the last pitcher to record a Loss at Brooklyn's Ebbets Field (the first game he pitched) 9/24/57

DITMAR, ART : []90 b'55

Had the last Win at Philadelphia A's Shibe Park 9/26/54

DYCK, JIM : []111 b'53 []85 b'54 []177 t'53 []303 t'56

Was the last batter (fly out) at St Louis Browns' Sportsman Park 9/27/53

FONDY, DEE : []231 b'52 []5w b'53 []173 b'54 []224 b'55 []359 t'52 []112 t'56 []42 t'57 []157 t'58

Was the last batter (ground out) at Brooklyn's Ebbets Field 9/24/57

FREESE, GENE : []46 t'56 []293 t'58 []472 t'59

Had the last Stolen Base at New York Giants Polo Grounds 9/29/57

FRIEND, BOB : []492as t'58 []569as t'59

Was to last pitcher to record a Win at New York Giants Polo Grounds 9/29/57

HAMNER, GRANNY : []148 b'51 []35 b'52 []60 b'53 []47 b'54 []221 t'52 []146 t'53 []24 t'54 []197 t'56 []335 t'57 []268 t'58 []436 t'59

Had the last Triple at Brooklyn's Ebbets Field 9/20/57

HARRIS, GAIL : []91 t'56 []281 t'57 []309 t'58 []378 t'59

Was the last Giant player to hit a Home Run at New York Giants' Polo Grounds 9/21/5

HUNTER, BILLY : []5 b'54
[]166 t'53 []207 t'57 []98 t'58

Was the last player to hit a Home Run wearing a St Louis Browns uniform 9/26/53

KATT, RAY : []121 b'54
[]183 b'55 []331 t'57 []284 t'58

Had the last Single at the New York Giants Polo Grounds 9/29/57

LIMMER, LOU : []80 b'55
[]232 t'54 []54 t'55

Had the last Stolen Base at Philadelphia A's Shibe Park 9/19/54

LOPATA, STAN : []207 b'54
[]18 b'55 []119 t'57 []353 t'58
[]412 t'59

Had the last Sacrifice Fly at Brooklyn's Ebbetts Field 9/20/57

MARSH, FRED : []8 t'52
[]240 t'53 []218 t'54 []13 t'55
[]23 t'56

Had the last Single, and scored the last Run, at St Louis Browns' Sportsman Park 9/27/53

McCAHAN, BILL : []31 b'48
[]80 b'49

Had the last No-hitter at Philadelphia A's Shibe Park 9/3/47

McDEVITT, DANNY : []357 t'58
[]364 t'59

Was the last Winning pitcher (shut-out) at Brooklyn's Ebbetts Field 9/24/57

O'CONNELL, DANNY : []93 b'51
[]160 b'54 []44 b'55 []107dp t'53
[]272 t'56 []271 t'57 []166 t'58
[]87 t'59

Had the Last Sacrifice at New York Giants Polo Grounds 9/28/57

PAFKO, ANDY : []57w b'53

Had the last Put-out at Boston Braves Field 9/21/52

PILLETTE, DUANE : []316 b'51
[]59w b'53 []133 b'54 []244 b'55
[]82 t'52 []269 t'53 []107 t'54
[]168 t'55

Had the last Loss at St Louis Browns Sportsman Park 9/27/53

POWERS, JOHN : []432 t'58
[]489 t'59

Had the last Hit, Run, RBI, and Home Run At New York Giants' Polo Grounds

RIVERA, JIM : []156dp t'53
[]34 t'54 []58 t'55 []70 t'56
[]107 t'57 []11 t'58

Had the last Triple at St Louis Browns Sportsman Park 9/27/53

SEMINICK, ANDY : []51 b'51
[]7w b'53 []172 b'54 []93 b'55
[]297 t'52 []153dp t'53 []296 t'56

Had the last inside the park Home Run at Boston Braves Field 9/1/50

WERTZ, VIC : []244 t'52

Hit the last Grand Slam at St louis Browns Sportsman Park 9/4/53

WILSON, BOB : []250 t'53
[]58 t'54 []92 t'56 []19 t'57
[]213 t'58 []24 t'59

Hit the last Grand Slam at Philadelphia A's Shibe Park 7/9/54

LEAGUE LEADERS

Baseball keeps statistics on everything that happens on the field. At the end of the year they are compiled to give us the league leaders in a number of categories, both complimentary and embarrassing. Many common players have had the distinction of being the "uncommon" hero, or the goat, for a year or more.

t=topps - b=bowman

ADAMS, BOBBY : []288 b'51
[]166 b'52 []249 t'52 []108 b'53 []152 t'53
[]123 t'54[]118 b'55 []178 t'55 []287 t'56
[]99 t'58[]249 t'59

Led NL in at-bats (637) in '52

ADDIS, BOB : []259 b'52
[]94 b'53 []157 t'53

Led NL in pinch-hits (12) in '51

ANDERSON, HARRY : []404 t'57
[]171 t'58 []85 t'59

Led NL in striking out (95) in '58

AVILA, BOBBY : []132 t'56 []195 t'57
[]276 t'58 []363 t'59

Led AL in batting average (341) in '54

BARRETT, RED : []213 b'49

Led NL in wins (23) - complete games (24)
innings pitched (284.2) - hits given (287) in '45

BAUMHOLTZ, FRANK : []195 b'52
[]225 t'52 []221 b'54 []60 t'54
[]227 b'55 []172 t'55 []274 t'56

Led NL in pinch-hit hits (15) in '55
Led NL in pinch-hit hits (14) in '56

BEARDEN, GENE : []173 b'52 []229 t'52

Led AL in earned run average (2.43) in '48

BECQUER, JULIO : []458 t'58 []93 t'59

Led AL in pinch-hit at-bats (65) and hits (18) in '57
Led AL in pinch-hit at-bats (56) and hits (12) in '59

BELL, GUS : []118dp t'53

Led NL in triples (12) in '51

BENTON, AL : []374 t'52

Led AL in relief wins (10) and saves (17) in '40

BOLGER, JIM : []179 t'55 []289 t'57
[]201 t'58 []29 t'59

Led NL in pinch-hit at-bats (48) and hits (17) in '57

BONHAM, ERNIE : []77 b'49

Led AL in winning % (.808) - complete games (22) -
shut-outs (6) '42

BOONE, RAY : []214 b'52

Led AL in runs batted in (116) in '55

BRUTON, BILL : []165 t'59

Led NL in stolen bases (26) '53
Led NL in stolen bases (34) '54
Led NL in at-bats (636) - stolen bases (25) '55
Led NL in triples (15) '56

BUHL, BOB : []347 t'59

Led NL in shut-outs (4) in '59

BYRD, HARRY : []38 b'52 []131dp t'53   Led AL in losses (20) in '53
[]49 b'54 []159 b'55 []154 t'58

CHAPMAN, BEN : []391er b'52   Led AL in stolen bases (61) in '31
                                               Led AL in stolen bases (38) in '32
                                               Led AL in stolen bases (27) in '33
                                               Led AL in triples (13) in '34
                                               Led AL in stolen bases (35) in '37

CHAPMAN, SAM : []104 b'50 []9 b'51   Led AL in striking out (96) in '40

CONSUEGRA, SANDY : []96 b'51 []143 b'52   Led AL in winning % (.842) in '54
[]89 b'53 []166 b'54 []116 b'55 []265 t'56

CROWE, GEORGE : []254 t'56 []73 t'57   Led NL in pinch-hit at-bats (63) and hits (17) in '59
[]12 t'58 []337 t'59

DILLINGER, BOB : []105 b'50 []63 b'51   Led AL in stolen bases (34) in '47
                                               Led AL in hits (207) - stolen bases (28) in '48
                                               Led AL in stolen bases (20) in '49

DiMAGGIO, DOM : []149dp t'53   Led AL in at-bats (648) in '48
                                               Led AL in triples (11) runs (131) stolen bases (15) in '50
                                               Led AL in at-bats (639) - runs (113) in '51

DITMAR, ART : []48 b'54 []212 b'55   Led AL in losses (22) in '56

DONOVAN, DICK : []146r t'55 []18 t'56   Led AL in winning % (.727) - complete games (16) in '57
[]181 t'57 []290 t'59

DROPO, WALT : []235 t'52 []257 t'57   Led AL in runs batted in (144) in '50
[]158 t'59

EASTER, LUKE : []2dp t'53   Led AL in home run % (7.1) in '52

EDWARDS, HANK : []136 b'49 []169 b'50   Led AL in triples (16) in '46
[]141 b'52 []176 t'52 []90dp t'53   Led NL in pinch-hit at-bats (37) in '51

FACE, ROY : []246dp t'53   Led NL in games pitched (68) relief losses (12) in '56
                                               Led NL in saves (20) '58
                                               Led NL in relief wins (19) - winning % (.947) in '59

FARRELL, DICK : []76 t'58   Led NL in relief wins (10) - relief losses (9) in '57

FERRISS, BOO : []211 b'49   Led AL in hits given (263) in '45
                                               Led AL in winning % (.806) in '46

FOWLER, DICK : []171 b'49 []214 b'50   Led AL in losses (16) in '46
[]190 b'52 []210 t'52

FOX, HOWIE : []80 b'50 []180 b'51   Led NL in losses (19) in '49
[]125 b'52 []209 t'52 []158 b'53 []22 t'53
[]246 t'54

FOYTACK, PAUL : []77 t'57 []282 t'58   Led AL in walks given (142) in '56
[]233 t'59   Led AL in games started (37) in '59

FRAZIER, JOE : []141 t'56   Led NL in pinch-hit at-bats (62) and hits (20) in '54

FREEMAN, HERSHALL : []290 b'55   Led NL in relief wins (16) in '56
[]24 t'56 []32 t'57 []27 t'58

FRIEND, BOB : []492as t'58 []569as t'59   Led NL in earned run average (2.83) in '55
                                               Led NL in games started (42) - innings (314.1) in '56
                                               Led NL in games started (38) innings (277) hits (273) '57
                                               Led NL in wins (22) starts (38) hits (299) in '58
                                               Led NL in losses (19) in '59

GALAN, AUGIE : []39 b'48 []233 t'54   Led NL in runs (133) and stolen bases (22) in '35
                                               Led NL in stolen bases (23) in '37
                                               Led NL in walks (103) in '43
                                               Led NL in walks (101) in '44

GARDNER, BILLY : []17 t'57 []105 t'58   Led AL in at-bats (644) and doubles (36) in '57
[]89 t'59

GARVER, NED : []15 b'49 []51 b'50   Led AL in losses (17) in '49
[]172 b'51 []29 b'52 []212 t'52 []47 b'53   Led AL in complete games (22) in '50
[]112dp '53 []39 b'54 []44 t'54 []188 b'55   Led AL in complete games (24) in '51
[]189 t'56 []285 t'57 []292 t'58 []245 t'59   Led AL in hits given (251) in '55

GOLDSBERRY, GORDON : []46 b'52   Led AL in pinch-hit at-bats (39) and hits (12) in '50
[]200 t'53

GOMEZ, RUBEN : []71 t'55 []9 t'56   Led NL in walks given (109) in '54
[]58 t'57 []335 t'58 []535 t'59

GRAY, TED : []10 b'49 []210 b'50   Led AL in losses (14) in '51
[]178 b'51 []199 b'52 []86 t'52 []72 b'53
[]52dp t'53 []71 b'54 []86 b'55

GRIM, BOB : []36 t'57   Led AL in relief winning % (1.000) in '54
                                               Led AL in relief wins (12) losses (8) saves (19) in '57

HACKER, WARREN : []318 b'51 []324 t'52   Led NL in losses (19) in '53
[]144 b'53 []125 b'54 []8 b'55 []282 t'56
[]370 t'57 []251 t'58

HADDIX, HARVEY : []265dp t'57   Led NL in shut-outs (6) in '53

HAMNER, GRANNY : []148 b'51 []35 b'52   Led NL in at-bats (662) in '49
[]221 t'52 []60 b'53 []146 t'53 []47 b'54
[]24 t'54 []197 t'56 []335 t'57 []268 t'58
[]436 t'59

HARRIS, MICKEY : []151 b'49 []160 b'50   Led AL in games (53) relief losses (9) saves (15) in '50
[]311 b'51 []135 b'52 []207 t'52   Led AL in relief losses (8) in '51

HAYNES, JOE : []191 b'49 []240 b'51   Led AL in games (40) in '42
[]103 b'52 []145 t'52 []223 t'54

58

HEMUS, SOLLY : []212r b'52 []85 b'53   Led NL in runs (105) in '52
[]231dp t'53 []94 b'54 []117 t'54
[]107 b'55 []231 t'57 []207 t'58 []527 t'59

HENRY, BILL : []264 b'55 []46 t'59   Led NL in games (65) in '59

HOAK, DON : []21 b'55 []274 t'57   Led NL in doubles (39) in '57

HOEFT, BILLY : []165 t'53 []167 b'54   Led AL in shut-outs (7) in '55
[]13 t'58 []343 t'59

HOUTTEMAN, ART : []42 b'50 []45 b'51   Led AL in shut-outs (4) in '50
[]238 t'52 []4 b'53 []20 b'54 []144 b'55   Led AL in losses (20) '52
[]281 t'56 []385 t'57

HOWELL, DIXIE M : []149 t'56 []221 t'57   Led AL in relief wins (8) in '55
[]421 t'58

HUDSON, SID : []17 b'50 []169 b'51   Led AL in losses (17) in '49
[]123 b'52 []60 t'52 []29 b'53 []251 t'53
[]194 b'54 []93 t'54 []318 b'55

HUGHES, JIM : []216 t'53   Led NL in games (60) - saves (24) in '54

HUGHSON, TEX : []199 b'49   Led AL in wins (22) complete games (22) innings (281)
strike-outs (113) in '42
Led AL in complete games (20) in '43
Led AL in winning % (.783) in '44

HURD, TOM : []116 t'55 []256 t'56   Led AL in relief wins (8) '55

HYDE, DICK : []403 t'57 []156 t'58   Led AL in relief wins (10) in '58
[]498 t'59

JANSEN, LARRY : []40w b'53   Led NL in winning % (.808) in '47
Led AL in shut-outs (5) in'50
Led AL in wins (23) in '51

JOHNSON, EARL : []231 b'49 []188 b'50   Led AL in relief wins (9) in '48
[]321 b'51

JONES, SAM : []287 t'57   Led NL in losses (20) walks (185) strike-outs (198) in '55
Led NL in walks (115) strike-outs (176) in '56
Led NL in walks (107) strike-outs (225) in '58
Led NL in wins (21) earned run average (2.83) walks
(109) shut-outs (4) in '59

JOOST, EDDIE : []15 b'48 []55 b'49   Led AL in striking out (110) in '47
[]103 b'50 []119 b'51 []26 b'52 []45 t'52
[]105 b'53 []35 b'54 []263 b'55

KAZAK, EDDIE : []85 b'51 []165 t'52   Led NL in pinch-hit at-bats (42) in '50
[]194 t'53

KELLNER, ALEX : []222 b'49 []14 b'50
[]57 b'51 []226 b'52 []201 t'52 []107 b'53
[]51 b'54 []53 b'55 []176 t'56 []280 t'57
[]3 t'58 []101 t'59

Led AL in losses (20) in '50
Led AL in losses (14) in '51

KENNEDY, BILL : []105 b'49 []102 t'52
[]94dp t'53

Led AL in games (47) in '52

KENNEDY, MONTE : []237 b'49 []175 b'50
[]163 b'51 []213 b'52 []124 t'52

Led NL in walks given (116) in '46

KINDER, ELLIS : []152r b'50 []128 b'51
[]78 t'52 []98 b'54 []47 t'54 []115 t'55
[]336 t'56 []352 t'57

Led AL in winning % (.793) shut-outs (6) in '49
Led AL in games (63) relief wins (10) saves (14) in '51
Led AL in games (69) relief wins (10) saves (27) in '53
Led AL in relief losses (8) in '54

KING, CLYDE : []299 b'51

Led NL in relief wins (13) in '51

KLINE, RON : []175 t'52 []94 t'56
[]82 t'58 []265 t'59

Led NL in losses (18) in '56
Led NL in losses (16) in '58

KOKOS, DICK : []31 b'49 []50 b'50
[]68 b'51 []232 t'53 []106 t'54

Led AL in striking out (91) in '49

KOLLOWAY, DON : []28 b'49 []133 b'50
[]105 b'51 []91 b'52 []104 t'52 []97dp t'53

Led AL in doubles (40) in '42

KOSLO, DAVE : []34 b'49 []65 b'50
[]90 b'51 []182 b'52 []336 t'52

Led NL in losses (19) game starts (35) hits (251) in '46
Led NL in earned run average (2.50) in '49

LABINE, CLEM : []14dp t'53

Led NL in relief wins (10) in '53
Led NL in games (60) relief wins (10) in '55
Led NL in saves (19) in '56
Led NL in relief losses (7) saves (17) in '57
Led NL in relief losses (10) in '59

LEMON, JIM : []103r t'54 []262 b'55

Led AL in triples (11) strike-outs (138) in '56
Led AL in strike-outs (94) in '57
Led AL in strike-outs (120) in '58

LEONARD, DUTCH : []115 b'49 []170 b'50
[]102 b'51 []159 b'52 []110 t'52 []
[]50w b'53 []155 t'53 []247 b'55

Led NL in saves (8) in '35
Led NL in hits given (273) in '39
Led NL in losses (19) hits given (328) in '40
Led NL in losses (18) in '48

LINDELL, JOHNNY : []209 b'50 []230dp t'53
[]159 b'54 []51 t'54

Led AL in triples (12) in '43
Led AL in triples (16) in '44

LOES, BILLY : []240r b'52

Led NL in relief losses (7) in '59

LOGAN, JOHNNY : []80 b'54

Led NL in doubles (37) in '55

LOWN, TURK : []16 b'52 []154 b'53
[]130dp t'53 []157 b'54 []247 t'57
[]261 t'58

Led NL in games (67) relief losses (7) in '57
Led NL in relief wins (9) saves (15) in '59

LOWREY, PEANUTS : []22 b'49 []172 b'50
[]194 b'51 []102 b'52 []16dp t'53
[]158 t'54

Led NL in pinch-hit hits (13) in '51
Led NL in pinch-hit at-bats (59) pinch-hit hits (22) in '52

MALZONE, FRANK : []558as t'59

Led AL in at-bats (627) in '58

MARCHILDON, PHIL : []187 b'49

Led AL in walks given (140) in '42
Led AL in losses (16) in '46
Led AL in walks given (141) in '47

McCARTHY, JOHN : []220 b'49

Led NL in pinch-hit at-bats (43) pinch hits (11) in '40
Led NL in pinch-hit at-bats (45) pinch hits (13) in '48

McCORMICK, FRANK : []239 b'49

Led NL in at-bats (640) hits (209) in '38
Led NL in hits (209) runs batted in (128) in '39
Led NL in at-bats (618) hits (191) doubles (44) in '40
Led NL in pinch-hit hits (13) in '47

McCOSKY, BARNEY : []25 b'48 []203 b'49
[]84 b'51

Led AL in hits (200) triples (19) in '40

McLISH, CAL : []208 t'58 []445 t'59

Led AL in hits given (253) in '59

McMAHON, DON : []147r t'58

Led NL in saves (15) in '59

MELE, SAM : []118 b'49 []52 b'50
[]168 b'51 []15 b'52 []94 t'52
[]22 b'54 []147 b'55

Led AL in doubles (36) in '51

MEYER, JACK : []269 t'56 []162 t'57
[]186 t'58 []269 t'59

Led NL in relief losses (7) saves (16) in '55

MINNER, PAUL : []211 b'52 []127 t'52
[]71 b'53 []92dp t'53 []13 b'54 []182 t'56

Led NL in losses (17) in '51

MITCHELL, DALE : []239 b'52 []26dp t'53

Led AL in at-bats (640) hits (203) triples (23) in '49
Led AL in pinch-hit at-bats (45) in '55

MIZELL, WILMER : []128dp t'53

Led NL in walks given (103) in '52

MOORE, RAY : []43 t'56 []106 t'57
[]249 t'58 []293 t'59

Led AL in relief losses (7) in '55
Led AL in walks given (112) in '57

MORGAN, TOM : []132 t'53 []100 b'55
[]239 t'57 []365 t'58 []545 t'59

Led AL in relief losses (7) in '56

MOSES, WALLY : []294 b'55

Led AL in triples (12) in '43
Led AL in doubles (35) in '45

NARLESKI, RAY : []96r b'55 []160r t'55
[]133 t'56 []144 t'57 []439 t'58 []442 t'59

Led AL in games (60) relief wins (8) saves (19) in '55

NEWSOM, BOBO : []15dp t'53

Led AL in losses (20) walks given (149) in '34
Led AL in losses (18) in '35
Led AL in games started (38) in '36
Led AL in games started (37) walks given (167) in '37

Led AL in games started (40) complete games (31)
innings (329.2) hits given (334) in '38
Led AL in games started (37) complete games (31) in '39
Led AL in strike-outs (134) in '42
Led AL in losses (20) in '45

NICHOLSON, BILL : []113 b'51 []14w b'53   Led NL in home runs (29) home run % (4.8) Runs batted
in (128) in '43
Led NL in home runs (33) runs (116) and runs batted in
 (122) in '44
Led NL in striking out (83) in '47

NORTHY, RON : []79 b'49 []81 b'50   Led AL in pinch-hit hits (15) in '56
[]70 b'51 []204 t'52 []31 t'57

OLIVER, TOM : []207 t'54   Led AL in at-bats (646) in '30

ORAVETZ, ERNIE : []51 t'56 []179 t'57   Led AL in pinch-hit at-bats (49) in '56

PARNELL, MEL : []241 b'52 []19dp t'53   Led AL in wins (25) earned run average (2.77) complete
[]313 t'57   games (27) innings (295.1) in '49
Led AL in walks given (166) in '53

PECK, HAL : []182 b'49   Led AL in pinch-hit hits (8) in '48

PHILLEY, DAVE : []44 b'49 []127 b'50   Led NL in pinch-hit hits (18) in '58
[]297 b'51 []226 t'52 []64 t'53 []159 t'54
[]222 t'56 []124 t'57 []92 t'59

PILLETTE, DUANE : []316 b'51 []82 t'52   Led AL in losses (14) in '51
[]59w b'53 []269 t'53 []133 b'54 []107 t'54
[]244 b'55 []168 t'55

PLATT, MIZELL : []89 b'49   Led AL in pinch-hit at-bats (34) in '49

POLLET, HOWIE : []95r b'49 []72 b'50   Led NL in earned run average (1.75) in '43
[]83 b'52 []63 t'52 []83 t'53 []89 t'54   Led NL in wins (21) earned run average (2.10)
innings (266) in '46

PORTERFIELD, BOB : []216 b'50 []194 b'52   Led AL in wins (22) complete games (24) shut-outs
[]301 t'52 []22 b'53 []108dp t'53 []24 b'54   (9) in '53
[]104 b'55 []248 t'56 []118 t'57 []344 t'58   Led AL in complete games (21) hits given (249) in '54
[]98 t'59

RAFFENSBERGER, KEN : []176 b'49   Led NL in losses (20) in '44
[]48 b'51[]55 b'52 []118 t'52 []106 b'53   Led NL in saves (6) in '46
[]276 t'53[]92 b'54 []46 t'54   Led NL in starts (38) hits given (289) shut-outs (5) in '49
Led NL in shut-outs (6) in '52

RAMOS, PEDRO : []49 t'56 []326 t'57   Led AL in losses (18) starts (37) hits given (277) in '58
[]331 t'58 []78 t'59   Led AL in losses (19) in '59

RASCHI, VIC : []185 b'55   Led AL in games started (37) in '49
Led AL in winning % (.724) in '50
Led AL in games started (34) strike-outs (164) in '51

REYNOLDS, ALLIE : []141dp '53

Led AL in strike-outs (151) in '43
Led AL in walks given (130) in '45
Led AL in winning % (.704) in '47
Led AL in shut-outs (7) in '51
Led AL in earned run average (2.06) strike-outs (160)
shut-outs (6) in '52

RIVERA, JIM : []156dp t'53 []34 t'54
[]58 t'55 []70 t'56 []107 t'57 []11 t'58

Led AL in triples (16) in '53
Led AL in stolen bases (25) in '55

ROBINSON, EDDIE : []18 b'50 []88 b'51
[]77 b'52 []32 t'52 []20w b'53 []73 t'53
[]193 b'54 []62 t'54 []153 b'55 []302 t'56
[]238 t'57

Led AL in pinch-hit at-bats (49) pinch hits (15) in '54

ROE, PREACHER : []254dp t'53

Led NL in strike-outs (148) in '45
Led NL in winning % (.714) in '49
Led NL in winning % (.880) in '51

ROGOVIN, SAUL : []165 b'52 []159 t'52
[]75 b'53 []140 b'54 []129 t'57

Led AL in earned run average (2.78) in '51

ROJEK, STAN : []135 b'49 []86 b'50
[]166 b'51 []137 b'52 []163 t'52

Led NL in at bats (641) in '48

ROLFE, RED : []296 t'52

Led AL in triples (15) in '36
Led AL in hits (213) doubles (46) runs (139) in '39

ROSEN, AL : []135dp t'53

Led AL in home runs (37) home run % (6.7) in '50
Led AL in runs batted in (105) in '52
Led AL in slugging average (.613) home runs (43)
runs (115) runs batted in (145) in '53

RUSH, BOB : []61 b'50 []212 b'51
[]153 t'52 []110 b'53 []77 b'54 []182 b'55
[]214 t'56 []137 t'57 []313 t'58 []396 t'59

Led NL in losses (20) in '50

SANFORD, FRED : []236 b'49

Led AL in losses (21) in '48

SAUER, HANK : []111dp t'53

Led NL in striking out (85) in '48
Led NL in home runs (37) runs batted in (121) in '52

SCHEIB, CARL : []25 b'49 []213 b'50
[]83 b'51 []46 b'52 []116 t'52 []150 b'53
[]57 t'53 []67 b'54 []118 t'54

Led AL in relief losses (9) in '50

SCHMITZ, JOHNNY : []52 b'49 []24 b'50
[]69 b'51 []224 b'52 []33 t'54 []105 b'55
[]159 t'55 []298 t'56

Led NL in strike-outs (135) in '46
Led NL in losses (18) in '47

SEWELL, RIP : []234 b'49

Led NL in losses (17) in '41
Led NL in wins (21) complete games (25) in '43

SHAW, BOB : []206r t'58

Led Al in winning % (.750) in '59

SIEVERS, ROY : []67dp t'53   Led AL in home runs (42) runs batted in (114) in '57

SIMPSON, HARRY : []223 b'52 []86 b'53   Led AL in triples (11) in '56
[]150dp t'53 []239 t'56 []225 t'57   Led AL in triples (9) in '57
[]299 t'58 []333 t'59

SMALLEY, ROY : []115 b'50 []44 b'51   Led NL in striking out (114) in '50
[]173 t'52 []56w b'53 []109 b'54 []231 t'54
[]252 b'55 []397 t'57

SMITH, AL : []105 t'56 []145 t'57   Led AL in runs (123) in '55
[]177 t'58

SMITH, FRANK : []186 b'52 []179 t'52   Led NL in relief losses (9) in '52
[]116dp t'53 []188 b'54 []71 t'54 []204 t'55 Led NL in relief losses (8) in '54

SOUTHWORTH, BILLY : []207 b'51   Led NL in triples (14) in '19

SPENCE, STAN : []102 b'49   Led AL in triples (15) in '42

STALEY, GERRY : []121 b'51 []50 b'52   Led AL in games (67) in '59
[]17 b'53 []56dp t'53 []14 b'54 []155 b'55
[]227 t'57 []412 t'58

STEPHENS, VERN : []71 b'49 []2 b'50   Led AL in runs batted in (109) in '44
                                              Led AL in home runs (24) home run % (4.2) in '45
                                              Led AL in runs batted in (159) in '49
                                              Led AL in runs batted in (144) in '50

STEWART, ED : []173 b'49 []143 b'50   Led NL in pinch-hit hits (10) in '41
[]159 b'51 []185 b'52 []279 t'52   Led AL in pinch-hit hits (9) in '51

STURDIVANT, TOM : []471 t'59   Led AL in winning % (.727) in '57

SULLIVAN, FRANK : []15 b'55 []106 t'55   Led AL in wins(18) starts (35) innings (260) in '55
[]71 t'56 []21 t'57 []18 t'58 []323 t'59

TAYLOR, BILL : []74 t'54 []53 t'55   Led NL in pinch-hit at-bats (60) pinch hits (15) in '55
[]389 t'58

TEMPLE, JOHNNY : []212 t'56 []478as t'58   Led NL in at bats (632) in '56
                                              Led NL in walks (94) in '57

TORGESON, EARL : []17 b'49 []163 b'50   Led NL in runs (120) in '50
[]99 b'51 []72 b'52 []97 t'52 []63 b'54
[]210 b'55 []147 t'56 []357 t'57 []138 t'58
[]351 t'59

TRINKLE, KEN : []193 b'49   Led NL in games (48) in '46
                                              Led NL in games (62) in '47

TROUT, DIZZY : 134 b'50   Led AL in wins (20) shut-outs (5) in '43
                                              Led AL in earned run average (2.12) games started (40)
                                              complete games (33) innings (352.1) shut-outs (7) in '44
                                              Led AL in losses (14) in '51

TRUCKS, VIRGIL : []198 b'54

Led AL in strike-outs (153) shut-outs (6) in '49
Led AL in shut-outs (5) in'54

TURLEY, BOB : []570as t'59

Led AL in walks given (181) strike-outs (185) in '54
Led AL in walks given (177) in '55
Led AL in wins (21) winning % (.750) complete games
(19) walks given (128) in '58

WAKEFIELD, DICK : []91 b'49

Led AL in at-bats (633) hits (200) doubles (38) in '43

WALKER, HARRY : []130 b'49

Led NL in batting average (.363) triples (16) in '47

WALL, MURRAY : []217 t'53 []410 t'58

Led AL in relief losses (8) in '52

WEHMEIER, HERM : []46 b'48 []51 b'49
[]27 b'50 []144 b'51 []150 b'52 []23 b'53
[]110dp t'53 []162 t'54 []29 t'55 []78 t'56
[]81 t'57 []248 t'58 []421 t'59

Led NL in walks given (117) in '49
Led NL in walks given (135) in '50
Led NL in walks given (103) in '52

WHITE, HAL : []320 b'51

Led AL in relief losses (8) in '52

WHITMAN, DICK : []221 b'51

Led NL in pinch-hit hits (12) in '50

WIGHT, BILL : []164 b'51 []117 b'52
[]177 t'52 []100 b'53 []312 b'55 []286 t'56
[]340 t'57 []237 t'58

Led AL in walks given (135) in '48

WILKS, TED : 137 b'49 []193 b'51
[]138 b'52 []109 t'52 []101 t'53

Led NL in winning % (.810) in '44
Led NL in games (59) relief wins (10) saves (9) in '49
Led NL in games (65) saves (13) in '51

WILLEY, CARL : []95 t'59

Led NL in shut-outs (4) in '58

WILSON, JIM : []276 t'52 []37 b'53
[]208 t'53 []16 b'54 []253 b'253 []171 t'56
[]330 t'57 []163 t'58

Led AL in losses (18) in '55
Led AL in shut-outs (5) in '57

WRIGHT, TOMMY : []271 b'50 []140 t'54
[]141 t'55

Led AL in pinch-hit hits (10) in '52

WYSE, HANK : []192 b'51

Led NL in hits given (277) in '44

YOST, EDDIE : []173 t'58

Led AL in walks (141) in '50
Led AL in doubles (36) in '51
Led AL in walks (129) in '52
Led AL in walks (123) in '53
Led AL in walks (156) in '56
Led AL in runs (115) walks (135) in '59

YUHAS, ED : []70 t'53

Led NL in relief winning % (.917) in '52

ZAUCHIN, NORM : []176 t'55 []89 t'56
[]372 t'57 []422 t'58 []311 t'59

Led AL in striking out (105) in '55

ZERNIAL, GUS : []42dp t'53

Led AL in striking out (110) in '50
Led AL in home runs (33) runs batted in (129)
striking out (101) in '51
Led AL in home run % (7.6) in '53
Led AL in home run % (7.3) in '55
Led AL in pinch-hit hits (115) in '58

ZUVERINK, GEORGE : []199 t'52 []92 b'55
[]276 t'56 []11 t'57 []9 t'58 []219 t'59

Led AL in games (62) saves (16) in '56
Led AL in games (56) in '57

THEY DIDN'T DECK THE HALL

The BBWAA (BaseBall Writers Association of America) elects players into the Hall of Fame. These un-common players have received at least one vote into this star-studded fraternity. Voting in 2008 included the enshrinement of SOUTHWORTH, BILLY (1951 Bowman card # 207). I've already collected one, but still need a few of the following.

ro = runoff

NAME	YEAR(S)	NAME	YEAR(S)
[] ADAMS, BOBBY	66	[] McMILLAN, ROY	72-3-4
[] BLADES, RAY	58-60	[] MIKSIS, EDDIE	64
[] BRUTON, BILL	71	[] MOSES, WALLY	58-60-8-9-70-1
[] CARRASQUEL, CHICO	66	[] NEWSOM, BOBO.	60-2-4-4ro-6-7-7ro-8-970-1-2-3
[] CHAPMAN, SAM	58		
[] COOPER, WALKER	68-9-70-1-2-3-4-5-6-7	[] NICHOLSON, BILL	60
		[] NORTHY, RON	64
[] COURTNEY, CLINT	67	[] O'NEILL, STEVE	48-9-50-1-2-3-8
[] COX, BILLY	62	[] PAFKO, ANDY	66-7
[] CRANDALL, DEL	76-7-8-9	[] PORTERFIELD, BOB	66
[] DiMAGGIO, DOM	60-2-4-8-9-70-1-2-3	[] RASCHI, VIC	62-4-8-9-71-2-3-4-5
[] DROPO, WALT	67	[] REYNOLDS, ALLIE	56-60-2-4-4ro-6-7-7ro8-9-70-1-2-3-4
[] DYKES, JIMMY	48-9-50-1-2-3-5-6-8-60-2		
[] EDWARDS, HANK	60	[] RICE, DEL	66
[] FITZSIMMONS, FRED	48-9-50-8-60-2	[] ROE, PREACHER	60-2-8-70-1-2
[] GALAN, AUGIE	68-70	[] ROLFE, RED	50-1-2-3-8-60-2
[] GARVER, NED	67	[] SAUER, HANK	66
[] GRISSOM, MARV	66	[] SEWELL, RIP	58-62-4
[] GROMEK, STEVE	64	[] SIEVERS, ROY	71-2
[] GUSTINE, FRANK	58	[] SISTI, SIBBY	60
[] HADDIX, HARVEY	71-2-3-4-5-6-7-8-9-85	[] SMALLEY, ROY	64
		[] SOUTHWORTH, BILLY	INDUCTED '08
[] HATTON, GRADY	66-7	[] SUKEFORTH, CLYDE	58
[] HEARN, JIM	66-7	[] TEBBETTS, BIRDIE	58-60
[] HEMUS, SOLLY	66	[] TORGESON, EARL	67
[] HOUTTEMAN, ART	64	[] TROUT, DIZZY	64
[] KINDER, ELLIS	64	[] TRUCKS, VIRGIL	64
[] KRESS, RALPH	58-60	[] VALO, ELMER	67
[] KUZAVA, BOB	64	[] WALKER, HARRY	58
[] LEONARD, DUTCH	60-8-9-70-1-2-3	[] WERTZ, VIC	70-1-2-3-4-5-6-7-8
[] MARTIN, MORRIE	66		
[] McCORMICK, FRANK	56-62-4-8	[] WESTRUM, WES	64
[] McMAHON, DON	80	[] WILSON, JIM	64

THE SUMMER CLASSIC

Every year Major League Baseball puts on a game to showcase their Premier players (or at least the players the fans want to see). The following list of "common" players were voted to play in this Midsummer Nights/day Dream. Along with this list are the Star players that didn't get picked, or didn't play if they were picked.

t=topps - b=bowman

1948 Sportsman Park St. Louis

COOPER, WALKER : []9r b'48   Was the starting NL catcher : went 0 for 2

RIGNEY, BILL : []32r b '48   Replaced *Ed Stanky* NL: went 0 for 1 w/walk

ROSAR, BUDDY : []10 b'48   Starting catcher AL : went 0 for 1

Roy Campanella, Jackie Robinson weren't picked ; Yogi Berra didn't play

1949 Ebbetts Field Brooklyn

POLLET, HOWIE : []95r b'49   Pitched 1.0 ins. NL : gave up 4 hits, 3 earned runs

MICHAELS, CASS : []12 b'49   Was the starting 2b AL : went 0 for 2 w/walk

MUNGER, GEORGE : []40 b'49   Pitched 1.0 ins. NL : gave up 0 hits, 0 - K, 1 - BB

BRISSIE, LOU : []41 b'49   Pitched 3.0 ins. AL : gave up a HR to *Ralph Kiner*

MARSHALL, WILLARD : []48 b'49   Starting rf NL : went 0 for 1, 2/walks, 1 run scored

JOOST, EDDIE : []55 b'49   Starting ss AL : went 1 for 2 (single),1/walk

STEPHENS, VERN : []71 b'49   Did Not Start : SS AL : went 0 for 2, 1/K

GORDON, SID : []101 b'49   Did Not Start : 3b NL : went 1 for 2 (double), 1/walk

COOPER, WALKER : []117 b'49   Did Not Play : catcher NL

KELLNER, ALEX : []222 b'49   Did Not Play : pitcher AL

Robin Roberts, Johnny Sain, Bobby Doerr, Early Wynn, Richie Ashburn, Phil Rizzuto,
Luke Appling, Bob Feller, and Hal Newhouser weren't picked

1950 Comisky Park Chicago

EVERS, HOOT: []41 b'50   Starting rf AL : went 0 for 2, 1/K, 1/BB

STEPHENS, VERN : []2 b'50   Did Not Play : SS AL

HOUTTEMAN, ART : []42 b'50	Pitched 3.0 ins AL : gave up a HR to *Ralph Kiner*
RUSH, BOB: []61 b'50	Did Not Play : pitcher NL
MICHAELS, CASS : []91 b'50	Did Not Start 2b AL : 1 for 1 (double) 1 run scored
SCARBOROUGH, RAY : []108 b'50	Did Not Play : pitcher AL
COOPER, WALKER : []111 b'50	Did Not Play : catcher NL
WYROSTEK, JOHNNY : []197 b'50	Did Not Start : rf NL 0 for 2
GRAY, TED : []178 b'50	Pitched 1.1 ins AL : (LOSS) gave up HR to *Red Schoendienst*

Hank Bauer, Lou Boudreau, Early Wynn, Johnny Sain, Nellie Fox, Mel Parnell,
Richie Ashburn, and Hal Newhouser weren't picked

1951 Briggs Stadium Detroit

GUMPERT, RANDY: []59 b'51	Did Not Play : pitcher AL
ROBINSON, EDDIE : []88 b'51	Did Not Start : 1b AL 0 for 1
LEONARD, DUTCH : []102 b'51	Did Not Play : pitcher AL
JONES, WILLIE : []112 b'51	Did Not Start : 3b NL 0 for 2 1/K, 1/walk
EDWARDS, BRUCE : []116 b'51	Did Not Play : catcher NL
GARVER, NED : []172 b'51	Starting pitcher : 3.0 ins gave up 1 run
MARRERO, CONRADO : []206 b'51	Did Not Play : pitcher AL
BUSBY, JIM : []302 b'51	Did Not Start : lf AL 0 at bats
WYROSTEK, JOHNNY : []107 b'51	Did Not Start : rf NL went 0 for 1

Early Wynn, Mickey Vernon, Bob Feller, Mike Garcia, Hal Newhouser, Hank Bauer,
and Willie Mays weren't picked

1952 Shibe Park Philadelphia

JOOST, EDDIE : []26 b'52 []45 t'52	Did Not Play : ss AL
ROBINSON, EDDIE : []77 b'52 []32 t'52	Starting 1b AL : 1 for 2 (single), 1 RBI
HAMNER, GRANNY : []35 b'52 []221 t'52	Starting ss NL : 0 for 1 1/walk

STALEY, GERRY : []50 b'52 []79 t'52	Did Not Play : pitcher NL
RUSH, BOB : []153 t'52	Starting pitcher 2.0 ins NL : Got the WIN
MITCHELL, DALE : []239 b'52	Starting lf AL : 0 for 1 1/K
WERTZ, VIC : []244 t'52	Did Not Play : rf AL
HEARN, JIM : []49 b'52	Replaced Preacher Roe, Did Not Play : pitcher NL

Ted Kluszewski, Johnny Sain, Bob Feller, Johnny Mize, Richie Ashburn, Willie Mays,
And Eddie Mathews weren't picked

1953 Crosley Field Cincinnati

WHITE, SAMMY : []41 b'53 []139 t'53	Did Not Play : catcher AL
ZERNIAL, GUS : []42dp t'53	Starting lf AL : 1 for 2 (single) 1/K
RICE, DEL : []53 b'53 []68 t'53	Injured : replaced by Wes Westrum
CARRASQUEL, CHICO: []54 b'53	Starting ss AL : went 0 for 2
HAMNER, GRANNY : []60 b'53 []146 t'53	Did Not Start : 0 at bats
BELL, GUS : []118dp t'53	Starting cf NL : 0 for3
ROSEN, AL : []135dp t'53	Starting 3b AL : 0 for 4
REYNOLDS, ALLIE : []141dp t'53	Did Not Start : pitcher AL 2.0 ins got the LOSS
HUNTER, BILLY : []166 t'53	Did Not Start : ss AL
STALEY, GERRY : []17 b'53 []56dp t'53	Did Not Play : pitcher AL
ROBINSON, EDDIE : []20bw b'53 []73 t'53	Did Not Start : 1b AL 0 for 1

Early Wynn, Bob Feller, Whitey Ford, and Willie Mays weren't picked

1954 Municipal Stadium Cleveland

WILSON, JIM : []16 b'54	Replaced Harvey Haddix: pitcher NL 1.0 ins no decision
PORTERFIELD, BOB : []24 b'54	Did Not Start : pitcher AL 3.0 ins gave up HR to *Ted Kluszewski*

HAMNER, GRANNY : []41 b'54   Starting 2b NL : 0 for 3
[]24 t'54

JABLONSKI, RAY : []26 t'54   Starting 3b NL : 1 for 3 (single) 1/RUN 1/RBI

STONE, DEAN : []114 t'54   Replaced *Ferris Fain* : pitcher AL got the Win
                                    (didn't throw a pitch)

JACKSON, RANDY : []189 b'54   Did Not Start : 3b NL went 0 for 2

TRUCKS, VIRGIL : []198 b'54   Did Not Start : pitcher AL 1.0 ins got a SAVE

CARRASQUEL, CHICO : []54 b'54   Starting ss AL : went 1 for 5 (single) 1/RUN 2/K

KEEGAN, BOB : []100 t'54   Did Not Start : pitcher AL 0.2 ins gave up HR to BELL, GUS

CONSUEGRA, SANDY : []166 b'54   Replaced *Mike Garcia* : pitcher AL 0.1 ins gave up 5 RUNS

Ernie Banks, Hank Aaron, Al Kaline, and Bill Skowron weren't picked

1955 County Stadium Milwaukee

BAKER, GENE : []7 b'55   Did Not Start : 2b NL went 0 for 1

SULLIVAN, FRANK : []15 b'55   Did Not Start : pitcher AL 3.1 in LOSS gave up HR to *Musial*
[]106 t'55

LOPATA, STAN : []18 b'55   Did Not Start replaced *Campanella* : catcher NL went 0 for 3

JACKSON, RANDY : []87 b'55   Did Not Start : 3b NL went 1 for 3 (single) 1/RUN 1/RBI 1/K

CARRASQUEL, CHICO : []173 b'55   Did Not Start : ss AL went 2 for 3 (singles)

WILSON, JIM : []253 b'55   Did Not Play : pitcher AL

DONOVAN, DICK : []146r t'55   Did Not Play : pitcher AL

FINIGAN, JIM : []14 t'55   Starting 3b AL : went 0 for 3 1/K

*Bill Skowron, Jackie Robinson, Sandy Koufax, Harmon Killebrew, Roberto Clemente,
and Phil Rizzuto weren't picked*

1956 Griffith Stadium Washington D.C.

NARLESKI, RAY : []133 t'56   Injured pitcher AL : replaced by *Herb Score*

WILSON, JIM : []171 t'56   Did Not Start : pitcher AL 1.0 ins

SIMPSON, HARRY : []239 t'56   Did Not Start : of AL went 0 for 1 1/K

SULLIVAN, FRANK : []71 t'56   Did Not Play : pitcher AL

REPULSKI, RIP : []201 t'56   Did Not Start : of NL went 0 for 1

TEMPLE, JOHNNY : []212 t'56   Starting 2b NL : went 2 for 4 (singles) 1/RUN 1/RBI

LAWRENCE, BROOKS : []305 t'56   Did Not Play : pitcher NL

BREWER, TOM : []34 t'56   Did Not Start : pitcher AL 2.0 ins gave up HR to *Stan Musial*

*Jackie Robinson, Roberto Clemente, Sandy Koufax, Phil Rizzuto, Richie Ashburn, Harmon
Killebrew, Bob Feller, Pee Wee Reese, and Luis Aparicio weren't picked*

1957 Sportsman's Park St. Louis

GRIM, BOB : []36 t'57   Did Not Start : pitcher AL 0.1 ins faced 1 batter SAVE

FOILES, HANK : []104 t'57   Did Not Start : catcher NL went 1 for 1 (single) 1/RUN

SMITH, HAL R : []111 t'57   Did Not Play : catcher NL

DeMAESTRI, JOE : []44 t'57   Did Not Play : ss AL

CIMOLI, GINO : []319r t'57   Did Not Start : of NL went 0 for 1 1/K

*Don Drysdale, Pee Wee Reese, Roberto Clemente, Roy Campanella, Rocky Colovito, Sandy
Koufax, Brooks Robinson, and Luis Aparicio weren't picked*

1958 Memorial Stadium Baltimore

CROWE, GEORGE : []12 t'58   Did Not Play : 1b NL

MORYN, WALT : []122 t'58   Did Not Play : of NL

McMAHON, DON : []147r t'58   Did Not Play : pitcher NL

O'DELL, BILLY : []84 t'58   Did Not Start : pitcher AL 3.0 ins got the SAVE

JACKSON, LARRY : []97 t'58   Did Not Start : pitcher NL 0.2 ins no decision

BLASINGAME, DON : []199 t'58   Did Not Start : 2b NL went 0 for 1

PURKEY, BOB : []311 t'58   Did Not Play : pitcher NL

LOLLAR, SHERM : []491as t'58   Did Not Play : catcher AL

FRIEND, BOB : []492as t'58   Did Not Start : pitcher NL 2.1 ins got the LOSS

FARRELL, DICK : []76 t'58   Did Not Start : pitcher NL 2.0 ins no decision

SCHMIDT, BOB : []468 t'58   Did Not Play : catcher NL

WALLS, LEE : []66 t'58   Did Not Start : lf NL went 0 for 1

BRIDGES, ROCKY : []274 t'58   Did Not Play : SS AL

NARLESKI, RAY : []439 t'58   Did Not Start : pitcher AL 3.1 ins no decision
                                 (went 1 for 1 at the plate)

*Don Drysdale, Roger Maris, Roberto Clemente, Duke Snider, Enos Slaughter, Gil Hodges,
Ted Kluszewski, Sandy Koufax, Frank Robinson, Brooks Robinson, Harmon Killebrew,
Orlando Cepeda, and Pee Wee Reese weren' picked*

1959 Forbes Field Pittsburgh
Game 1

TRIANDOS, GUS : []568as t'59   Starting catcher AL : went 1 for 4 2/RBI

DALEY, BUD : []263 t'59   Did Not Start : pitcher AL 0.2 ins 1/K

MALZONE, FRANK : []558as t'59   Did Not Start : 3b AL went 0 for 2

SIEVERS, ROY : []566as t'59   Did Not Start : of AL pinch-hit walk

CUNNINGHAM, JOE : []285 t'59   Did Not Play : of NL

SMITH, HAL R : []497 t'59   Did Not Play : catcher NL

CRANDALL, DEL : []567as t'59   Starting catcher NL : went 1 for 3 1/RUN 1/RBI

ELSTON, DON : []520 t'59   Replaced Wilmer Mizell : pitcher NL 1.0 ins got the SAVE

*Roger Maris, Duke Snider, Bobby Richardson, Herb Score, Felipe Alou, Enos Slaughter,
Gil Hodges, Richie Ashburn, Sandy Koufax, Brooks Robinson, Roberto Clemente,
Norm Cash, and Bob Gibson weren't picked*

1959 Memorial Coliseum Los Angeles
Game 2

DALEY, BUD : []263 t'59   Did Not Play : pitcher AL

MALZONE, FRANK : []558as t'59   Starting 3b AL : went 1 for 4 HR off *Don Drysdale*

McLISH, CAL : []445 t'59   Did Not Start : pitcher AL 2.0 ins got the SAVE

O'DELL, BILLY : []250 t'59   Did Not Start : pitcher AL 1.0 ins gave up HR to *Jim Gilliam*

RAMOS, PEDRO : []78 t'59   Replaced *Camilo Pascual* : pitcher AL Did Not Play

SIEVERS, ROY : []566as t'59   Did Not Play : of AL

WALKER, JERRY : []144rp t'59   Starting pitcher AL : 3.0 ins got the WIN

CRANDALL, DEL : []567as t'59   Starting catcher NL : went 1 for 2

CUNNINGHAM, JOE : []285 t'59   Did Not Start : of NL went 0 for 1

SMITH, HAL R : []497 t'59   Did Not Start : catcher NL went 0 for 2 1/K

Roger Maris, Duke Snider, Herb Score, Felipe Alou, Enos Slaughter, Gil Hodges,
Richie Ashburn, Sandy Koufax, Brooks Robinson, Roberto Clemente,
and Bob Gibson weren't picked

THE FALL CLASSIC

Another "classic" in baseball is the World Series. Although a teams super-stars might have played a major role in getting there, they couldn't do it alone. Some of the best players in the game have played their whole career and have never been in the World Series, Ernie Banks comes to mind. The following list of un-commons (in the year they won) have something that 99.9 something % of the world doesn't have, a World Series "RING". Along with the ring bearers, the commons that came up short are also listed.

t=topps - b=bowman

1948 Cleveland Indians 4 - Boston Braves 2

No common 1948 cards are listed

1949 New York Yankees 4 - Brooklyn Dodgers 1

Yankees
KRYHOSKI, DICK : []218 b'49   Did not play
NIARHOS, GUS : []181 b'49   1 game 0 ab
PORTERFIELD, BOB : []3 b'49   Did not play
SANFORD, FRED : []236 b'49   Did not play

Dodgers
EDWARDS, BRUCE : []206 b'49   2 games ph 1-2 1k
HATTON, JOE : []116 '49   2 games p 1.2 innings 3 er
HERMANSKI, GENE : []20 b'49   4 games of 4-13 1triple 1r 2rbi 3bb 3k
McCORMICK, MIKE : []146 b'49   1 game of 0-0

1950 New York Yankees 4 - Philadelphia Phillies 0

Yankees
LINDELL, JOHNNY : []209 b'50   Did not play
NIARHOS, GUS : []154 b'50   Did not play
PORTERFIELD, BOB : []216 b'50   Did not play

Phillies
BOROWY, HANK : []177 b'50   Did not play
DONNELLY, BLIX : []176 b'50   Did not play
GOLIAT, MIKE : []205 b'50   4 games 2b 3-14 1r 1bb 1k
HEINTZELMAN, KEN : []85 b'50   1 game p 7.2 innings 1er 6bb 3k
THOMPSON, JOHN : []120 b'50   Did not play

1951 New York Yankees 4 - New York Giants 2

Yankees
BYRNE, TOMMY : []73 b'51   Did not play
FERRICK, TOM : []182 b'51   Did not play
KRAMER, JACK : []200 b'51   Was released 8/30/51
KUZAVA, BOB : []97 b'51   1 game p 1.0 innings 1 Save
OVERMIRE, FRANK : []280 b'51   Did not play

Giants
GETTELL, AL : []304 b'51   Did not play
JONES, SHELDON : []199 b'51   2 games p 4.1 innings 1 Save gave up HR to Woodling
KENNEDY, MONTE : []163 b'51   2 games p 3.0 innings gave up HR to *Phil Rizzuto*
KOSLO, DAVE : []90 b'51   2 games p 15.0 innings 1 Win - 1 Loss 7bb 6k
KRAMER, JACK : []200 b'51   Was released 5/19/51
LOHRKE, JACK : []235 b'51   4 games ph 1-4 1k
NOBLE, RAY : []269 b'51   2 games 0-2 1k
WESTRUM, WES : []161 b'51   6 games 4-17 1 double 1r 5bb 3

1952 New York Yankees 4 - Brooklyn Dodgers 3

Yankees
KUZAVA, BOB : []140 b'52   1 game p 2.2 innings 1 Save 2k
NOREN, IRV : []63 b'52   4 games of-3b 3-10 1rbi 1bb 1k
SCARBOROUGH, RAY : []140 b'52   1 game p 1.0 inning 1er 1k gave up HR to *Pee WeeReese*
[]43 t'52
SILVERA, CHARLIE : []197r b'52   Did not play

Dodgers
COX, BILLY : []52 b'52   7 games 3b 2-27 2 doubles 4r 3bb 4k
LOES, BILLY : []240r b'52   2 games 0 Wins - 1 Loss 10.1 innings 5er 5bb 5k
             Gave up HR's to *Yogi Berra, Mickey Mantle, Billy Martin*
PODBIELAN, BUD : []188 t'52   Did not play
WALKER, RUBE : []319 t'52   Did not play

1953 New York Yankees 4 - Brooklyn Dodgers 2

Yankees
BRIDEWESER, JIM : []136 b'53   Did not play
GORMAN, TOM : []61 bw'53   1 game p 3.0 innings 1er 1k
KUZAVA, BOB : []33 bw'53   1 game p .2 innings 1 er 1k gave up HR to *Jim Gilliam*
MILLER, BILL : []54 bw'53   Did not play
[]100 t'53
MIRANDA, WILLIE : []278 t'53   Did not play acquired from St Louis Browns 6/12/53
NOREN, IRV : []45 bw'53   2 games ph 0-1 1bb
[]35 t'53
REYNOLDS, ALLIE : []141dp t'53 3 games p 8.0 innings 1 Win - 1 Save 6er 4 bb 9k
             Gave up HR's to *Gilliam, Hodges, Shuba, Furillo*

SCHULT, ART : []167 t'53	Did not play
WOODLING, GENE : []264dp t'53	6 games of 6-20 1hr 5r 3rbi 6bb 2k
	Hit HR off of *Johnny Podres*

Dodgers

ANTONELLO, BILL : []272 t'53	Did not play (played his last game 9/27/53)
DRESSEN, CHUCK : []50 t'53	Manager
HOWELL, DIXIE H : []255 t'53	Did not play
HUGHES, JIM : []216 t'53	1 game p 4.0 innings 1er 3k 1bb gave up HR to *Berra*
LABINE, CLEM : []14dp t'53	3 games 5.0 innings 2 Losses 1 Save 2er 3k 1bb
	Gave up HR to *Joe Collins*
MEYER, RUSS : []129 b'53	1 game p 4.1 innings 3er 5k 1bb
	Gave up HR's to *Mickey Mantle, Billy Martin*
MILLIKEN, BOB : []221 t'53	1 game p 2.0 innings 1bb
MORGAN, BOBBY : []135 b'53	1 game ph 0-1
[]85 t'53	
ROE, PREACHER : []254dp t'53	1 game p 8.0 innings 1 Loss 4er 4k 4bb
	Gave up HR's to *Mickey Mantle, Billy Martin*
WADE, BEN : []4 t'53	2 games p 2.1 innings 4er 2k 1bb

1954 New York Giants 4 - Cleveland Indians 0

Giants

CORWIN, AL : []137 b'54	Did not play
EVERS, HOOT : []18 b'54	Claimed on waivers by the Tigers 7/29/54
HOFMAN, BOBBY : []99 b'54	Did not play
KATT, RAY : []121 b'54	Did not play
LIDDLE, DON : []225 t'54	2 games 7.0 innings 1 Win 1er 2k 1bb
	Gave up HR to Hank Majeski
TAYLOR, BILL : []74 t'54	Did not play
THOMPSON, HANK : []64 t'54	4 games 3b 4-11 1double 6r 2rbi 1k 7bb
WILLIAMS, DAVE : []9 b'54	4 games 2b 0-11 1rbi 2k 2bb

Indians

DYCK, JIM : []85 b'54	Did not play
GINSBERG, JOE : []52 b'54	Did not play
GLYNN, BILL : []178 t'54	2 games 1b-1 1-2 1double 1r 1k
GRASSO, MICKEY : []184 b'54	1 game 0-0
HOOPER, BOB : []4 b'54	Did not play
HOSKINS, DAVE : []81 t'54	Did not play
HOUTTEMAN, ART : []20 b'54	1 game p 2.0 innings 1er 1k 1bb
PHILLEY, DAVE : []159 t'54	4 games of-2 1-8 3k 1bb
STRICKLAND, GEORGE : []36 b'54	3 games ss 0-9 2k
WESTLAKE, WALLY : []92 t'54	2 games of 1-7 3k 1bb
KRESS, RALPH : []160 t'54	Coach

1955 Brooklyn Dodgers 4 - New York Yankees 3

Dodgers

BORKOWSKI, BOB : []74 t'55	Did not play
HOAK, DON : []21 b'55	3 games 3b-1 1-3 2bb

YANKEES

LEJA, FRANK : []99 t'55	Did not play
MORGAN, TOM : []100 b'55	2 games 3.2 innings 2er 1k 3bb
ROBINSON, EDDIE : []153 b'55	4 games 1b-1 2-3 1rbi 1k 2bb
SILVERA, CHARLIE : []188 t'55	Did not play

1956 New York Yankees 4 - Brooklyn Dodgers 3

Yankees

RENNA, BILL : []82 t'56	Did not play

Dodgers

JACKSON, RANDY : []223 t'56	3 games ph 0-3 2k
WALKER, RUBE : []333 t'56	2 games ph 0-2

1957 Milwaukee Braves 4 - New York Yankees 3

Braves

COVINGTON, WES : []283 t'57	7 games OF 5-24 1double 1r 1rbi 6k 2bb
JOHNSON, ERNIE : []333 t'57	3 games p 7.0 innings 1 Loss 1er 8k 1bb
	Gave up HR to *Hank Bauer*
JOLLY, DAVE : []389 t'57	Did not play : played his last game 9/14/57
PHILLIPS, TAYLOR : []343 t'57	Did not play
PIZARRO, JUAN : []383 t'57	1 game p 1.2 innings 2er 1k 2bb
RICE, DEL : []193 t'57	2 games c 1-6 2k 1bb

Yankees

DEL GRECO, BOBBY : []94 t'57	Did not play : joined team 9/10/57
GRIM, BOB : []36 t'57	2 games p 2.1 innings 1 Loss 2er 2k
	Gave up HR to *Eddie Mathews*
JOHNSON, DARRELL : []306 t'57	Did not play
SIMPSON, HARRY : []225 t'57	5 games 1b-4 1-12 1rbi 4k

1958 New York Yankees 4 - Milwaukee Braves 3

Yankees

DICKSON, MURRY : []349 t'58	2 games p 4.0 innings 2er 1k
JOHNSON, DARRELL : []61 t'58	Did not play
KUCKS, JOHNNY : []87 t'58	2 games p 4.1 innings 1er 1bb
LUMPE, JERRY : []193 t'58	6 games 3b-3 ss-2 2-12 2k 1bb
MAAS, DUKE : []228 t'58	1 game p .1 inning 3er 1bb
	Gave up HR to *Lew Burdette*

Braves

HANEBRINK, HARRY : []454 t'58   2 games ph 0-2
MANTILLA, FELIX : []17 t'58   4 games ss-1 0-0 1r
McMAHON, DON : []147 t'58   3 games p 3.1 innings 2er 5k 3bb
    Gave up HR to *Hank Bauer*

RICE, DEL : []51 t'58   Did not play
RUSH, BOB : []313 t'58   1 game p 6.0 innings 1Loss 2er 5k 5bb
TAYLOR, BOB : []164 t'58   Did not play
TROWBRIDGE, BOB : []252 t'58   Did not play
WISE, CASEY : []247 t'58   2 games ph 0-1 1k

1959 Los Angeles Dodgers 4 - Chicago White Sox 2

Dodgers

DEMETER, DON : []324 t'59   6 games of 3-12 2r 3k 1bb
ESSEGIAN, CHUCK : []278 t'59   4 games ph 2-3 2hr 2r 2rbi 1k 1bb
    Hit HR's off of Bob Shaw, Ray Moore

FOWLER, ART : []508 t'59   Did not play
KIPP, FRED : []258 t'59   Did not play
KLIPPSTEIN, JOHNNY : []152 t'59   1 game p 2.0 innings 2k
LILLIS, BOB : []133 t'59   Did not play
PIGNATANO, JOE : []16 t'59   1 game c 0-0
REPULSKI, RIP : []195 t'59   1 game of 0-0 1bb
SNYDER, GENE : []522 t'59   Did not play

White Sox

ARIAS, RUDOLPH : []537 t'59   Did not play (last game was 8/26/59)
ESPOSITO, SAMMY : []438 t'59   2 games 3b 0-2 1k
LATMAN, BARRY : []477 t'59   Did not play
MOORE, RAY : []293 t'59   1 game p 1.0 innings 1er 1k
    Gave up HR to Chuck Essegian

ROMANO, JOHN : []138 t'59   1 game ph 0-1
TORGESON, EARL : []351 t'59   3 games 1b-1 0-1 1r 1bb

A LIST OF RING BEARERS WITH COMMON CARDS

AMALFITANO, JOE 54
BARRETT, RED 40-6
BEARDEN, GENE 48
BENTON, AL 45
BESSENT, DON 55
BLADES, RAY 31
BOLLWEG, DON 53
BONHAM, ERNIE 41-3
BOONE, RAY 48
BORKOWSKI, BOB 55
BOROWY, HANK 43
BRAZLE, AL 46
BRIDEWESER, JIM 52-53
BUHL, BOB 57

BYERLY, BUD 44
BYRNE, TOMMY 43-7-9-50-6
CARROLL, TOMMY 56
CASTLEMAN, FOSTER 54
CHAPMAN, BEN 32-6
CLARK, ALLIE 47-8
COOPER, WALKER 42-4
CORWIN, AL 54
COURTNEY, CLINT 51
COVINGTON, WES 57
CRANDALL, DEL 57
DEMETER, DON 59
DICKSON, MURRY 46-58

DITMAR, ART 58
DIXON, SONNY 56
DONNELLY, BLIX 44-46
DRESSEN, CHUCK 33
DREWS, KARL 47
DUSAK, ERV 46
ESSEGIAN, CHUCK 59
FERRICK, TOM 50
FITZSIMMONS, FRED 33
FOWLER, ART 59
GARDNER, BILLY 54
GOMEZ, RUBEN 54
GORMAN, TOM 52-3
GRIM, BOB 56

GRISSOM, MARV 54
GROMEK, STEVE 48
GUMBERT, HARRY 37-42
GUMPERT, RANDY 44-7
HAMRIC, BERT 55
HAZLE, BOB 57
HEARN, JIM 54
HEMSLEY, ROLLIE 43
HILLER, FRANK 49
HOAK, DON 55
HOFMAN, BOBBY 54
HOGUE, BOB 51-2
HOPP, JOHNNY 42-4-50-1
HOUTTEMAN, ART 45
HOWELL, DIXIE H 55
HUGHES, JIM 55
HUNTER, BILLY 56
JANSEN, LARRY 54
JOHNSON, BILLY 43-7-9-
50
JOHNSON, DARRELL 58
JOHNSON, DON 47
JOHNSON, ERNIE 57
JONES, NIPPY 46
JOOST, EDDIE 40
KATT, RAY 54
KEELY, BOB 44
KELLERT, FRANK 55
KENNEDY, BILL 48
KENNEDY, BOB 48
KLIPPSTEIN, JOHNNY 59
KLUTTZ, CLYDE 46
KRALY, STEVE 53
KRAMER, JACK 51
KRYHOSKI, DICK 49
KUCKS, JOHNNY 56-8
KUZAVA, BOB 51-2-3
LABINE, CLEM 55-9
LANIER, MAX 42-4-6
LENNON, BOB 54
LIDDLE, DON 54
LINDELL, JOHNNY 43-7
-9-50
LITWHILER, DANNY 44

LOES, BILLY 55
LOGAN, JOHNNY 57
LOLLAR, SHERM 47
LUMPE, JERRY 58
MAAS, DUKE 58
MADISON, DAVE 50
MAPES, CLIFF 49-50
MAYO, ED 45
McCALL, WINDY 54
McCORMICK, FRANK 40
McCORMICK, MIKE 40
McDERMOTT, MICKEY 56
McDEVITT, DANNY 59
McDONALD, JIM 53
McMAHON, DON 57
MEYER, RUSS 55
MILLER, BILL 52-3
MILLS, BUSTER 34
MIRANDA, WILLIE 53
MITCHELL, DALE 48
MONZANT, RAY 54
MORGAN, TOM 51-6
MORYN, WALT 55
MUNCRIEF, BOB 48
MUNGER, GEORGE 44-6
MURRAY, RAY 48
NEWSOM, BOBO 47
NIARHOS, GUS 49-50
NOREN, IRV 52-3-6
OSTROWSKI, JOE 50-1-2
OVERMIRE, FRANK 45-51
PAFKO, ANDY 57
PECK, HAL 48
PHILLIPS, JACK 47
PIGNATANO, JOE 59
PILLETTE, DUANE 49
PIZARRO, JUAN 57
POLLET, HOWIE 42-46
PORTERFIELD, BOB 49-50
PRIDDY, JERRY 41
RASCHI, VIC 47-9-50-1-2-3
REPULSKI, RIP 59
REYNOLDS, ALLIE 44-7-9
-50-1-2-3

RICE, DEL 46-57
RICHARDS, PAUL 33-45
ROBINSON, AARON 43-7
ROBINSON, EDDIE 48
ROLFE, RED 36-7-8-9-41
ROSAR, BUDDY 39-41
ROSEN, AL 48
SANFORD, FRED 49-50
SAWATSKI, CARL 57
SCARBOROUGH, RAY 52
SCHMITZ, JOHNNY 52
SCHULT, ART 53
SHEA, FRANK 47-51
SIEBERN, NORM 56-58
SILVERA, CHARLIE 49-51
-2-6
SILVESTRI, KEN 41-7
SISLER, DICK 46
SNYDER, GENE 59
SPENCER, GEORGE 54
ST CLAIRE, EBBA 54
STARR, DICK 47
SWIFT, BOB 45
TAYLOR, BILL 54
THOMPSON, HANK 54
TIPTON, JOE 48
TROUT, DIZZY 45
TROWBRIDGE, BOB 57
TRUCKS, VIRGIL 45
TUCKER, THURMAN 48
TURLEY, BOB 56-58
VERBAN, EMIL 44
WALKER, HARRY 42-6
WALKER, RUBE 55
WIESLER, BOB 51
WIGHT, BILL 47
WILKS, TED 44-46
WILLIAMS, DAVE 54
WILSON, AL 52
WOODLING, GENE 49-50 -
1-2-3
WORTHINGTON, AL 54
ZOLDAK, SAM 48

A GAME THE FAMILY CAN PLAY

The athletic ability of one family member does not necessarily mean baseball can become the family business. In the list of commons below you will find family members from, one at bats, to members of the Hall of Fame.

t=topps - b=bowman

ADAMS, BOBBY : []288 b'51 []166 b'52 []249 t'52 []108 b'53 []152 t'53 []123 t'54 []118 b'55 []178 t'55 []287 t'56 []99 t'58 []249 t'59

Brother Dick : 1947 A's 37 games
Son Mike : 1972-3-6-7-8 Twins - Cubs - A's 100 games

ASPROMONTE, KEN : []405 t '58 []424 t'59

Brother Bob : 1956, 1960-71 Dodgers/Colt 45's/Astros Braves/ Mets 13 years

AVERILL, EARL : []301 t'59

Father Earl : 1929-41 Indians /Tigers/Braves HOF(1975)

BAILEY, ED : []184 t'54 []490as t'58 []210 t'59

Brother Jim : 1959 Reds 3 games

BAXES, JIM :[]547 t'59

Brother Mike : 1956, 1958 A's 146 games

BAXES, MIKE : []302 t'58 []381 t'59

Brother Jim : 1959 Dodgers/Indians 88 games

BEAMON, CHARLIE : []192 t'59

Son Charlie : 1978, 79, 81 Mariners/Blue Jays 45 games

BELL, GUS : []118dp'53

Son Buddy : 1978-89 Indians/Reds/Astros/Rangers

BOLLING, FRANK : []325 t'57 []95 t'58 []280 t'59

Brother Milt : 1952-58 Red Sox/Senators /Tigers 7 years

BOLLING, MILT : []130 'b'54 []82 t'54 []91 t'55 []315 t'57 []131 t'57 []188er t'59

Brother Frank : 1954, 1956-66 Tigers/Braves 12 years

BOONE, RAY : []214 b'52

Son Bob : 1972-90 Phillies - Angels - Royals 19 years
Grandson Bret : 1992-05 Mariners/Reds/Braves/Padres Twins 14 years
Grandson Aaron : 1997-? Reds/Yankees/Indians /Marlins Nationals ? years

BOYER, CLOYD : []115 b'53 []60dp t'53 []149 b'55

Brother Ken : 1955-69 Cards/Mets/White Sox/Dodgers
Brother Clete : 1955-57, 1959-71 A's/Yankees/Braves

BROWN, DICK : []456 t'58 []61 t'59

Brother Larry : 1963-74 Indians/A's/Orioles/Rangers

DiMAGGIO, DOM : []149dp t'53

Brother Joe : 1936-51 Yankees HOF(1955)
Brother Vince : 1937-46 Bees/Reds/Pirates/Phillies/Giants

DRAKE, SOLLY : []159 t'57 []406 t'59

Brother Sammy : 1960-62 Cubs/Mets, 53 games

FRANCONA, TITO : []184r t'57 []268 t'59

Son Terry : 1981-90 Expos/Cubs/Reds/Indians/Brewers

GILBERT, TOOKIE : []235 b'50 []61 t'52   Brother Charlie : 1940-43,46,47 Dodgers/Cubs/Phillies

GRAHAM, JACK : []145 b'50   Father Peaches : 1902-3,08-12, 7 years 373 games

HAMNER, GRANNY : []148 b'51 []35 b'52   Brother Garvin : 1945 Phillies 32 games
[]221 t'52 []60 b'53 []146 t'53 []47 b'54
[]24 t'54 []197 t'56 []335 t'57 []268 t'58
[]436 t'59

HEINTZELMAN, KEN : []108 b'49 []85 b'50   Son Tom : 1973-4, 77-8 Cards/Giants 90 games
[]147 b'51 []148 b'52 []136dp t'53

HITCHCOCK, BILLY : []191 b'51 []89 b'52   Brother Jim : 1938 Bees 38 games
[]182 t'52 []17 t'53

JEFFCOAT, HAL : []211 b'51 []104 b'52   Brother George : 1936-7, 39,43 Dodgers/Braves 70 games
[]37 bw'53 []29 t'53 []205 b'54 []223 b'55
[]289 t'56 []93 t'57 []294 t'58 []81 t'59

JOHNSON, EARL : []231 b'49 []188 b'50   Brother Chet : 1946 Browns 5 games
[]321 b'51

KELL, EVERETT : []242 b'52   Brother George : 1943-57 A's/Tigers/Red Sox/White Sox/
                                                 Orioles 15 years HOF (1983)

KELLNER, ALEX : []222 b'49   Brother Walt : 1952-3 A's 3 games
[]14 b'50 []57 b'51 []226 b'52
[]107 b'53 []51 b'54 []53 b'55
[]201 t'52 []176 t'56 []280 t'57
[]3 t'58 []101 t'59

KENNEDY, BOB : []33dp t'53   Son Terry : 1978-91 Cards/Padres/Orioles/Giants

KEOUGH, MARTY : []371 t'58 []303 t'59   Son Matt : 1977-83, 85-86A's/Yankees /Cards/
                                                 Cubs/Astros

KLAUS, BILLY : []150 b'55 []217 t'56   Brother Bobby : 1964-65 Reds/Mets 215 games
[]292 t'57 []89 t'58 []299 t'59

KRSNICH, ROCKY : []229 t'53   Brother Mike : 1960, 62 Braves 15 games

LANIER, MAX : []207 b'50 []230 b'51   Son Hal : 1964-73 Giants/Yankees 10 years
[]110 b'52 []101 t'52

LEE, DON : []379 t'57 []132rp t'59   Father Thorton : 1933-48 Indians - White Sox - Giants

McDANIEL, VON : []65r t'58   Brother Lindy : 1955-75Cards/Cubs/ Giants/
                                                 Yankees/Royals

NARLESKI, RAY : []96r b'55 []160r t'55   Father Bill : 1929-30 Red Sox 135 games
[]133 t'56 []144 t'57 []439 t'58 []442 t'59

NICHOLS, CHET : []120 b'52 []72 b'55   Father Chet : 1926-28, 30-32 Pirates/Giants/Phillies
[]278 t'56

NORTHY, RON : []79 b'49
[]81 b'50 []70 b'51 []204 t'52
[]31 t'57

Son Scott : 1969 Royals 20 games

O'BRIEN, EDDIE : []249dp'53 []116 t'56
[]259 t'57

Twin Johnny : 1953, 1955-59 Pirates/Cards/Braves

O'BRIEN, JOHNNY : []223dp t'53

Twin Eddie : 1953, 1955-58 Pirates

O'NEILL, STEVE : []201 b'51 []127 t'54

Brother Jack : 1902-06 Cards/Cubs/Beaneaters 303 games
Brother Jim : 1920, 1923 Senators 109 games
Brother Mike : 1901-04, 1907 Cards - Reds 137 games

OSBORNE, LARRY : []524 t'59

Father Earnest "Tiny" : 1922-25 Cubs/Robins 142 games

O'TOOLE, JIM : []136rp t'59

Brother Denny : 1969-73 White Sox 5 years 15 games

PILLETTE, DUANE : []316 b'51 []82 t'52
[]59 bw'53 []269 t'53 []133 b'54 []107 t'54
[]244 b'55 []168 t'55

Father Herman : 1917, 1922-24 Reds/Tigers 107 games

QUEEN, MEL : []309 b'51 []171 b'52

Son Mel : 1964-72 Reds/Angels 269 games

RICKETTS, DICK : []137rp t'59

Brother Dave : 1963, 65, 67-70 Cards/Pirates 130 games

RIDDLE, JOHN : []274 t'53 147 t'54
[]98 t'55

Brother Elmer : 1939-45, 47-49 Reds/Pirates 190 games

SADOWSKI, ED : []139rp t'59

Brother Bob : 1963-66 Braves/Red Sox 115 games
Brother Ted : 1960-62 Senators/Twins 43 games

SHANTZ, WILMER : []175 b'55

Brother Bobby : 1949-64 A's/Yankees/Pirates /Colt 45's
Cards/Cubs/Phillies 578 games 16 years

SISLER, DAVE : []56 t'57 []59 t'58
[]384 t'59

Brother Dick : 1946-53 Cards/Phillies/Reds 190 games
Father George : 1915-22 24-30 HOF (1939)

SISLER, DICK : []127 b'52 []10 bw'53

Brother Dave : 1956-62 Red Sox/Tigers/Senators/Reds
Father George : 1915-22 24-30 HOF (1939)

SMALLEY, ROY : []115 b'50 []44 b'51
[]173 t'52 []56 bw'53 []109 b'54 []231 t'54
[]252 b'55 []397 t'57

Son Roy : 1975-87 Rangers/Twins/Yankees/White Sox

ST CLAIRE, EBBA : []172 b'52 []34 bw'54
[]91dp t'53 []128 b'54

Son Randy : 1984-89,91,92,94 Expos/Reds/Twins/Braves
Blue Jays, 9 years 162 games

SUSCE, GEORGE : []93 t'56 []229 t'57
[]189 t'58 []511 t'59

Father George : 1929,32, 39-40 Phillies/Tigers/Pirates
Browns/Indians, 146 games 8 years

THRONEBERRY, FAYE : []376 t'52
[]49dp t'53[]163 t'55 []356 t'57 []534 t'59

Brother Marv : 1955, 58-63 Yankees/A's/Orioles-Mets

TRESH, MIKE : []166 b'49

Son Tom : 1961-69 Yankees/Tigers 9 years 1192 games

TROUT, DIZZY : []134 b'50

Son Steve : 1978-89 White Sox/Cubs/Yankees/Mariners

VAN CUYK, CHRIS : []53 t'52

Brother Johnny : 1947-49 Dodgers 7 games

VIRGIL, OZZIE : []365 t'57 []107 t'58
[]203 t'59

Son Ozzie : 1980-90 Phillies/Braves/Blue Jays 739 games

WADE, BEN : []4 t'53 []126 t'54

Brother Jake : 1936-39,42-44,46 Tigers/Red Sox/Browns
White Sox/Yankees/Senators, 171 games

WALKER, HARRY : []130 b'49

Father "Dixie" Ewart : 1909-12 Senators 76 games
Brother "Dixie" Fred : 1931, 33-49 Yankees/White Sox
Tigers/Dodgers/Pirates 18 years

WESTLAKE, WALLY : []45 b'49
[]69 b'50 []38 t'52 []192 t'53
[]92 t'54 []102 t'55[]81 t'56

Brother Jim : 1955 Phillies 1 game 1 at-bat (struck out)

NICKNAMES

Baseball players love giving nicknames to their team-mates. Some of these monikers stick ("Babe" Ruth) and some don't ("Biscuit Pants" Gehrig). The list of commons below have some descriptive and some "uncommon" nicknames. Like the Babe, a few of these players are widely known by their nickname.

ABER, AL	LEFTY	CHAKALES, BOB	CHICK
ABRAMS, CAL	ABIE	CHAMBERS, CLIFF	LEFTY
ACKER, TOM	SHOULDERS	CHAPMAN, BEN	CHAPPY
ALOMA, LUIS	WITTO	CHAPMAN, SAM	TIBURON TERROR
ALTMAN, GEORGE	DADDY LONG LEGS	CHIPMAN, BOB	MR CHIPS
ANDERSON, BOB	HAMMONDHUMMER	CHRISTMAN, MARK	IRISH
ANDERSON, HARRY	THE HORSE	CHURCH, EMORY	BUBBA
ARFT, HANK	BOW WOW	CICOTTE, AL	BOZO
ARROYO, LUIS	YO-YO	CLEVENGER, TRUMAN	TEX
ASPROMONTE, KEN	CHIP	CONNELLY, BILL	WILD BILL
AVILA, BOBBY	BETO	CONSTABLE, JIMMY	SHERIFF
BACZEWSKI, FRED	LEFTY	CONSUEGRA, SANDY	PORTRERILLO
BAKER, FLOYD	GLOVE MAN	COOPER, WALKER	COOP
BARRETT, CHARLES	RED	COURTNEY, CLINT	SCRAP IRON
BAUMAN, FRANK	BEAU	CRAWFORD, RUFUS	JAKE
BEARDEN, GENE	ARK. TRAVELER	CROWE, GEORGE	BIG GEORGE
BELARDI, WAYNE	FOOTSIE	CUNNINGHAM, JOE	JERSEY JOE
BELL, GARY	DING	DALEY, LEAVITT	BUD
BERNIER, CARLOS	COMET	DANIELS, JACK	SOUR MASH
BESSENT, DON	THE WEASEL	DAVENPORT, JIM	PEANUT
BILKO, STEVE	HUMPHREY	DEAL, ELLIS	COT/COTTON TOP
BIRRER, WERNER	BABE	DEL GRECO, BOBBY	THE GREEK
BLACKBURN, JIM	BONES	DELOCK, IVAN	IKE
BLACKBURN, RON	BLACKIE	DeMAESTRI, JOE	OATS
BLASINGAME, DON	BLAZER	DEMARS, BILLY	KID
BLATNICK, JOHNNY	CHIEF	DEMPSEY, CORNELIUS	CON
BOLGER, JIM	DUTCH	DENTE, SAM	BLACKIE
BOLLING, MILT	SCOOPS/ROWDIE	DERRINGTON, JIM	BLACKIE
BONHAM, ERNIE	TINY	DICKSON, MURRY	EDISON OF THE MOUND
BOONE, RAY	IKE	DILLINGER, BOB	DUKE
BORKOWSKI, BOB	BUSH	DIXON, JOHN	SONNY
BOYD, BOB	THE ROPE	DOBERNIC, ANDREW	JESS
BOYER, CLOYD	JUNIOR	DOBSON, JOE	BURRHEAD
BRADY, JIM	DIAMOND JIM	DONNELLY, SYLVESTER	BLIX
BRANDT, JACKIE	FLAKEY	DONOVAN, DICK	TRICKY DICK
BRAZLE, AL	COTTON	DOTTERER, HENRY	DUTCH
BRIDGES, EVERETT	ROCKY	DROPO, WALT	MOOSE
BROWN, HECTOR	SKINNY	DROTT, DICK	HUMMER
BROWN, TOMMY	BUCKSHOT	DUBIEL, WALT	MONK
BRUNET, GEORGE	LEFTY	DURHAM, JOE	POP
BRUTON, BILL	BULLET BILL	DUSAK, ERV	FOUR SACK
BURTSCHY, ED	MOLASSESS FOOT	EASTER, LUKE	BIG LUKE
BYERLY, ELDRED	BUD	EDWARDS, BRUCE	BULL
BYRNE, TOMMY	THE WILDMAN	EVERS, WALTER	HOOT
CAFFIE, JOE	RABBIT	FANNIN, CLIFF	MULE
CAIN, BOB	SUGAR	FARRELL, DICK	TURK
CANDINI, MARIO	MILO	FERNANDEZ, HUMBERT	CHICO
CARRASQUEL, ALFONSO	CHICO	FERRARESE, DON	MIDGET
CECCARELLI, ART	CHIC	FERRISS, DAVE	BOO

FITZSIMMONS, FRED	FAT FREDDIE	KINDALL, JERRY	SLIM
FODGE, GENE	SUDS	KINDER, ELLIS	OLD FOLKS
FOWLER, ART	KING ARTHUR	KING, CHARLES	CHICK
FRAZIER, JOE	COBRA JOE	KIRKLAND, WILLIE	BOOM BOOM
FRANCONA, JOHN	TITO	KOLLOWAY, DON	BUTCH/CAB
FREEMAN, HERSHALL	BUSTER	KORCHECK, STEVE	HOSS
FREESE, GENE	AUGIE	KOSHOREK, CLEM	SCOOTER
FREESE, GEORGE	BUD	KRALY, STEVE	LEFTY
FRIDLEY, JIM	BIG JIM	KRAVITZ, DANNY	DUSTY/BEAK
FRIEND, BOB	WARRIOR	KRETLOW, LOU	LENA
FRIEND, OWEN	RED	KUZAVA, BOB	SARGE
GARDNER, BILLY	SHOTGUN	LADE, DOYLE	PORKY
GILBERT, HAROLD	TOOKIE	LAKE, EDDIE	INKY/SPARKY
GLAVIANO, TOMMY	RABBIT	LaPALME, PAUL	LEFTY
GOLDSBERRY, GORDON	GOLDIE	LATMAN, BARRY	SHOULDERS
GOMEZ, RUBEN	EL DIVINO LOCO	LAWRENCE, BROOKS	BULL
GRANT, JIM	MUDCAT	LEHNER, PAUL	GULLIVER
GREENWOOD, BOB	GREENIE	LENHARDT, DON	FOOTSIE
GUMBERT, HARRY	GUNBOAT	LENNON, BOB	ARCH
HADDIX, HARVEY	THE KITTEN	LEONARD, EMIL	DUTCH
HALL, BOB	TARZAN	LILLIS, BOB	FLEA
HALL, DICK	TURKEY	LIPON, JOHNNY	SKIDS
HAMNER, GRANVILLE	HAM	LOGAN, JOHNNY	YATCHA
HAMNER, RALPH	BRUZ	LOHRKE, JACK	LUCKY
HANEY, FRED	PUDGE	LOPATA, STAN	STASH
HANSEN, ANDY	SWEDE	LOWREY, HARRY	PEANUTS
HARRIST, EARL	IRISH	LOWN, OMAR	TURK
DORISH, HARRY	FRITZ	LUMENTI, RALPH	COMMUTER
HARTSFIELD, ROY	SPEC	LUNA, GUILLERMO	MEMO
HARTUNG, CLINT	FLOPPY	MAAS, DUANE	DUKE
HATFIELD, FRED	SCRAP IRON	MADDERN, CLARENCE	MADDY
HAZLE, BOB	HURRICANE	MAIN, FORREST	WOODY
HIGGINS, MIKE	PINKY	MAJESKI, HANK	HEENEY
HILLER, FRANK	DUTCH	MANTILLA, FELIX	THE CAT
HOAK, DON	TIGER	MAPES, CLIFF	TIGER
HOPP, JOHNNY	HIPPITY	MARCHILDON, PHIL	BABE
HOUSE, FRANK	PIG	MARTIN, BORIS	BABE
HOWELL, HOMER	DIXIE	MARTIN, PAUL	JAKE
HOWELL, MILLARD	DIXIE	MAXWELL, CHARLIE	SMOKEY
HUGHSON, CECIL	TEX	McCALL, JOHN	WINDY
HURD, TOM	WHITEY	McCORMICK, FRANK	BUCK
JABLONSKI, RAY	JABO	McCORMICK, MYRON	MIKE
JACKSON, LARRY	HOT POTATO	McDONALD, JIM	HOT ROD
JACKSON, RANDY	HANDSOME RANSOM	McLISH, CAL	BUSTER
JACOBS, FORREST	SPOOK	MELE, SAM	SABOO
JANOWICZ, VIC	CRASH	MERRIMAN, LLOYD	CITATION
JOHNSON, BILLY	BILLY THE BULL	METKOVICH, GEORGE	CATFISH
JOHNSON, EARL	LEFTY	MEYER, RUSS	THE MAD MONK
JOHNSON, KEN	HOOK	MIGGINS, LARRY	IRISH
JOK, STAN	TUCKER	MILLER, BILL	HOOKS
JOLLY, DAVE	GABBY	MILLIKEN, BOB	BOBO
JONES, SAM	SAD SAM	MILLS, COLONEL	BUSTER
JONES, SHELDON	AVAILABLE	MINARCIN, RUDY	BUSTER
JONES, VERNAL	NIPPY	MINNER, PAUL	LEFTY
JONES, WILLIE	PUDDIN' HEAD	MIZELL, WILMER	VINEGAR BEND
KAISER, DON	TIGER	MONZANT, RAY	THE GAY RELIEVER
KEEGAN, BOB	SMILEY	MOORE, RAY	FARMER
KELL, EVERETT	SKEETER	MOREHEAD, SETH	MOE
KEMMERER, RUSS	DUTCH	MORGAN, TOM	PLOWBOY
KENNEDY, BILL	LEFTY	MORYN, WALT	MOOSE
KERR, JOHN	BUDDY	MOSES, WALLY	PEEPSIGHT
KIELY, LEO	KIKI	MUELLER, RAY	IRON MAN

MUFFETT, BILLY	MUFF	SCHMEES, GEORGE	ROCKY
MUNGER, GEORGE	RED	SCHMITZ, JOHNNY	BEAR TRACKS
MURFF, JOHN	RED	SCHROLL, AL	BULL
MURRAY, RAY	DEACON	SCHULT, ART	DUTCH
NELSON, BOB	TEX/BABE	SEMPROCH, ROMAN	BABY
NELSON, GLEN	ROCKY	SHEA, FRANK	SPEC
NEWSOM, LOUIS	BOBO/BUCK	SHIPLEY, JOE	MOSES
NICHOLS, DOLAN	NICK	SIEVERS, ROY	SQUIRREL
NICHOLSON, BILL	SWISH	SILVERA, CHARLIE	SWEDE
NUXHALL, JOE	OL' LEFTHANDER	SILVESTRI, KEN	HAWK
O'DELL, BILLY	DIGGER	SIMPSON, HARRY	SUITCASE
OLIVER, GENE	BEEF/BEEFALO	SINGLETON, BERT	SMOKY
OLIVER, TOM	REBEL	SISTI, SEBASTIAN	SIBBY
OLSON, KARL	OLE	SKIZAS, LOU	NERVOUS GREEK
ORAVETZ, ERNIE	MOOSE	SMITH, AL	FUZZY
OSBORNE, LARRY	BOBO	SMITH, BOB	RIVERBOAT
OSTERMUELLER, FRITZ	OLD FOLKS	SMITH, FRANK	FIREBALL
OSTROWSKI, JOE	PROFESSER	SMITH, HAL R	CURA
OVERMIRE, FRANK	STUBBY	SOUCHOCK, STEVE	BUD
OWENS, JIM	BEAR	SOUTHWORTH, BILLY	BILLY THE KID
PAFKO, ANDY	HANDY ANDY	SPEAKE, BOB	SPOOK
PAINE, PHIL	FLIP	SPENCER, DARYL	BIG DEE
PARNELL, MEL	DUSTY	STALLCUP, VIRGIL	RED
PEDEN, LES	GOOCH	STEPHENS, VERN	BUSTER/JUNIOR
PHILLEY, DAVE	DURABLE DAVE	STEWART, ED	BUD
PHILLIPS, JACK	STRETCH	STEWART, VESTON	BUNKY
PHILLIPS, JOHN	BUBBA	STRICKLAND, GEORGE	BO
PHILLIPS, TAYLOR	T-BONE	STURDIVANT, TOM	SNAKE
PIERETTI, MARINO	CHICK	SUDER, PETE	PECKY
PILLETTE, DUANE	DEE	SUKEFORTH, CLYDE	SUKEY
PLATT, MIZELL	WHITEY	SURKONT, MATTHEW	MAX
PODBIELAN, CLARENCE	BUD	SWANSON, ART	RED
POSEDEL, BILL	SAILOR BILL	TATE, LEE	SKEETER
PRESKO, JOE	LITTLE JOE	TAYLOR, BILL	CASH
PRITCHARD, HAROLD	BUDDY	TAYLOR, BOB	HAWK
RAMOS, PEDRO	PETE	TAYLOR, JOE	MOOSE
RAMSDELL, WILLARD	WILLIE THE KNUCK	TEBBETTS, GEORGE	BIRDIE
RASCHI, VIC	SPRINGFIELD RIFLE	TERWILLIGER, WAYNE	TWIG
RENNA, BILL	BIG BILL	THIES, VERNON	JAKE
REPULSKI, ELDON	RIP	THOMAS, KEITH	KITE
RESTELLI, DINO	DINGO	THOMPSON, CHARLIE	TIM
REYNOLDS, ALLIE	SUPERCHIEF	THOMPSON, JOHN	JOCKO
RICE, HAL	HOOT	TOMANEK, DICK	BONES
RICKERT, MARV	TWITCH	TORGESON, EARL	EARLOF SNOHOMISH
RIDDLE, JOHN	MUTT	TREMEL, BILL	MUMBLES
RIGNEY, BILL	THE CRICKETT	TROUT, PAUL	DIZZY
RIVERA, JIM	JUNGLE JIM	TRUCKS, VIRGIL	FIRE
ROTBLATT, MARV	ROTTY	TUCKER, THURMAN	JOE E
RODGERS, ANDRE	ANDY	TURLEY, BOB	BULLET BOB
ROJEK, STAN	HAPPY RABBIT	UPTON, TOM	MUSCLES
ROLFE, ROBERT	PRIDE OFPENACOOK	VALDES, RENE	LATIGO
ROMANO, JOHN	HONEY	VALENTINE, HAROLD	CORKY
ROSAR, WARREN	BUDDY	VALO, ELMER	WALL CRUSHER
ROSEN, AL	FLIP	VEAL, ORVILLE	COOT
ROY, NORMAN	JUMBO	VERBAN, EMIL	THE ANTELOPE
RUNNELS, JAMES	PETE	VICO, GEORGE	SAM
RUSH, BOB	BIG BOB	VOLLMER, CLYDE	BIG-UN
RUTHERFORD, JOHN	DOC	WALKER, ALBERT	RUBE
SANTIAGO, JOSE	PANTALONES	WALKER, HARRY	THE HAT
SAUER, HANK	HAMMERIN' HANK	WALL, MURRAY	TEX
SAVAGE, BOB	RABBIT	WALLS, LEE	CAPTAIN MIDNIGHT
SAWATSKI, CARL	SWATS	WEIK, DICK	LEGS

WERLE, BILL	BUGS	WORTHINGTON, AL	RED
WIGHT, BILL	LEFTY	WRIGHT, TAFT	TAFFY
WILBER, DEL	BABE	WYSE, HANK	HOOKS
WILKS, TED	CORK	YOST, EDDIE	THE WALKING MAN
WILL, BOB	BUTCH	ZARRILLA, AL	ZEKE
WILSON, AL	ARCHIE	ZERNIAL, GUS	OZARK IKE
WILSON, BOB	RED	ZOLDAK, SAM	SAD SAM
WOODLING, GENE	ROCK	ZUPO, FRANK	NOODLES
WOOTEN, EARL	JUNIOR		

THAT NUMBER HAS BEEN RETIRED

In 1997 Major League Baseball retired number 42 through-out the league. This was to honor Jackie Robinson, the first Black in the major leagues. We all know Babe Ruth's (3), Mickey Mantle's (7), Hank Greenberg's (5), but did you know "uncommon" Cliff Mapes wore all three of these Hall of Fame numbers? Cliff was wearing Babe's # 3 in the same year it was retired (1948). The list below shows the commons that wore, eventually retired, uniform numbers from 1948 - 1959.

t=topps - b=bowman

Jackie Robinson's (42)

Orioles
ZUPO, FRANK 57

Red Sox
BRODOWSKI, DICK 55
MOFORD, HERB 59

Boston Braves
ST CLAIRE, EBBA 52

Milwaukee Braves
ST CLAIRE, EBBA 53
CALDERONE, SAM 1954

White Sox
JACKSON, RON 54-5-6

Cubs
BROSNAN, JIM 56-7
SINGLETON, BERT 58-9
JACKSON, LOU 59

Reds (Redlegs)
STALEY, GERRY 55
JEFFCOAT, HAL 56-7-8-9
BROSNAN, JIM 59

Tigers
STUART, MARLIN 51
AGUIRRE, HANK 58

Yankees
STEWART, ED 48

Philadelphia A's
MARTIN, MORRIE 51

Phillies
MEYER, JACK 55-6-7-8-9

Cardinals
HADDIX, HARVEY 52-3-4-5-6
MORGAN, BOBBY 56
GRISSOM, MARV 59

N Y Giants
LANIER, MAX 52
HILLER, FRANK 53
GRISSOM, MARV 54-5-6-7

S F Giants
GRISSOM, MARV 58
SHIPLEY, JOE 59

Senators (Nationals)
MICHAELS, CASS 50

Baltimore Orioles - St. Louis Browns
4 - Earl Weaver 5 - Brooks Robinson 8 - Cal Ripken Jr. 20 - Frank Robinson
22 - Jim Palmer 33 - Eddie Murray

4
PELLAGRINI, EDDIE []174 b'49
NIEMAN, BOB []267 t'56

PHILLEY, DAVE []222 t'56
NIEMAN, BOB []14 t'57

NIEMAN, BOB []165 t'58
NIEMAN, BOB []375 t'59

5
PLATT, MIZELL []89 b'49
YOUNG, BOBB Y []193 b'52
YOUNG, BOBBY []147 t'52

YOUNG, BOBBY []160 t'53
YOUNG, BOBBY []149 b'54
YOUNG, BOBBY []8 t'54

MAJESKI, HANK []127 b'55
ADAMS, BOBBY []287 t'56
HATTON, GRADY []26 t'56

8
SPENCE, STAN []102 b'49
GOLDSBERRY, GORDON []46t'52
DYCK, JIM : []111 b'53

DYCK, JIM []177 t'53
KRYHOSKI, DICK []117 b'54
KRYHOSKI, DICK []150 t'54
PYBURN, JIM []276 t'57

CASTLEMAN, FOSTER []416 t'58
AVILA, BOBBY []363 t'59

20

DREWS, KARL []188 b'49
WIDMAR, AL []281 b'51
FANNIN, CLIFF []285 t'52

WERTZ, VIC []244 t'52
CONSUEGRA, SANDY []265
t'56

HAMRIC, BERT []336 t'58

22

KRETLOW, LOU []50 b'53
SMITH, HAL W []8 t'55

GINSBERG, JOE []236 t'57
GINSBERG, JOE []67 t'58

GINSBERG, JOE []66 t'59

33

CAIN, BOB []19 b'52
CAIN, BOB []56 b'53

CAIN, BOB []266 t'53
BUSBY, JIM []28 t'58

FINIGAN, JIM []47 t'59

Boston - Milwaukee - Atlanta Braves
3 - Dale Murphy 21 - Warren Spahn 35 - Phil Niekro
41 - Eddie Mathews 44 - Hank Aaron

3

PENDLETON, JIM []185 t'53

PENDLETON, JIM []165 t'54

PENDLETON, JIM []15 t'55

Boston Red Sox
1 - Bobby Doer 4 - Joe Cronin 6 - Johnny Pesky 8 - Carl Yastrzemski
9 - Ted Williams 27 - Carlton Fisk

1

HATFIELD, FRED []153 b'52
HATTON, GRADY []208 t'54
HATTON, GRADY []131 t'55

HATTON, GRADY []26 t'56
CONSOLO, BILLY []399 t'57
CONSOLO, BILLY []148 t'58

CONSOLO, BILLY []112 t'59
PLEWS, HERB []373 t'59

4

MELE, SAM []118 b'49

6

LIPON, JOHNNY []163 b'52
LIPON, JOHNNY []89 t'52

LIPON, JOHNNY []123 b'53

LIPON, JOHNNY []40 t'53

8

ROBINSON, AARON []142
b'51
GUERRA, MIKE []202 b'51

WRIGHT, TOMMY []271 b'51
CONSOLO, BILLY []195 t'54
WHITE, SAMMY []47 b'55

DALEY, PETE []388 t'57
DALEY, PETE []73 t'58
DALEY, PETE []276 t'59

27

STRINGER, LOU []183 b'49
STRINGER, LOU []187 b'50
BENTON, AL []374 t'52
BROWN, HECTOR []184 t'53

BROWN, HECTOR []172 t'54
BROWN, HECTOR []221 b'55
BROWN, HECTOR []148 b'55
SUSCE, GEORGE []93 t'56

SUSCE, GEORGE []229 t'57
SUSCE, GEORGE []189 t'58

Brooklyn - Los Angeles Dodgers
1 - Pee Wee Reese 2 - Tommy Lasorda 4 - Duke Snider 19 - Jim Gilliam
20 Don Sutton 24 - Walt Alston 32 - Sandy Koufax 39 Roy Campanella
42 Jackie Robinson 53 - Don Drysdale

2

MORGAN, BOBBY []222 b'50	MORGAN, BOBBY []85 b'53	JACKSON, RANDY []301 t'58
MORGAN, BOBBY []108 b'52	JACKSON, RANDY []223 t'56	DEMETER, DON []244 t'58
MORGAN, BOBBY []135 b'53	JACKSON, RANDY []190 t'57	DEMETER, DON []324 t'59

19

HATTON, JOE []116 b'49	HATTON, JOE []190 b'51	SCHMITZ, JOHNNY []224b'52
HATTON, JOE []166 b'50	SCHMITZ, JOHNNY []69 b'51	

20

REPULSKI, RIP []195 t'59

24

ANTONELLO, BILL []272 t'53

32

ABRAMS, CAL []86 b'52	ANTONELLO, BILL []272t'53

Chicago Cubs
10 - Ron Santo 14 - Ernie Banks 23 - Ryne Sandberg 26 - Billy Williams

10

SCHEFFING, BOB []83 b'49	NORTHY, RON []81 b'50	TALBOT, BOB []229 t'54
SCHEFFING, BOB []168 b'50	NORTHY, RON []204 t'52	TAPPE, ELVIN []184 t'58

23

LADE, DOYLE []235 b'49	CHURCH, BUBBA []273 b'55	KINDALL, JERRY []221 t'58
LADE, DOYLE []196 b'50		

26

BOROWY, HANK []134 b'49	DUBIEL, WALT []283 b'51	DUBIEL, WALT []164 t'52

Chicago White Sox
2 - Nellie Fox 3 - Harold Baines 4 - Luke Appling 9 - Minnie Minoso
16 - Ted Lyons 19 - Billy Pierce 72 - Carlton Fisk

2

KOZAR, AL []15 b'50	ZARRILLA, AL []113 b'52	ZARRILLA, AL []70 t'52
ZARRILLA, AL []35 b'51		

3

BUSBY, JIM []302 b'51	HATTON, GRADY []208 t'54	HATFIELD, FRED []318 t'56
BUSBY, JIM []68 b'52	BRIDEWESER, JIM []151b'55	HATFIELD, FRED []278 t'57
RYAN, CONNIE []102 t'53	BRIDEWESER, JIM []382 t'56	SKIZAS, LOU []328 t'59

4

JACKSON, RON []26 t'58

9

PHILLEY, DAVE []44 b'49
PHILLEY, DAVE []127 b'50

PHILLEY, DAVE []297 b'51

SMITH, AL []177 t'58

11

COURTNEY, CLINT []34b'55

16

FORNIELES, MIKE []154 t'54

FORNIELES, MIKE []266b'55

SMITH, AL []177 t'58

Cincinnati Reds / Redlegs
1 - Fred Hutchinson 5 - Johnny Bench 8 - Joe Morgan 10 - Sparky Anderson
13 - Dave Concepcion 18 - Ted Kluszewski 20 - Frank Robinson
24 Tony Perez 41 - NUXHALL, JOE

5

HOWELL, DIXIE H []252b'51

LANDRITH, HOBIE []220b'54

LANDRITH, HOBIE []50 b'55

8

PAVLETICH, DON []494 t'59

10

STALLCUP, VIRGIL []81 b'49
STALLCUP, VIRGIL []116 b'50
STALLCUP, VIRGIL []108 b'51
STALLCUP, VIRGIL []6 b'52

STALLCUP, VIRGIL []69 t'52
KAZAK, EDDIE []165 t'52
HARMON, CHUCK []182 t'54
HARMON, CHUCK []82 t'55
HARMON, CHUCK []308 t'56

GRAMMAS, ALEX []37 t'56
GRAMMAS, ALEX []222 t'57
GRAMMAS, ALEX []254 t'58
KASKO, EDDIE []232 t'59

18

BILKO, STEVE []346 t'58

DROPO, WALT []158 t'59

20

MERRIMAN, LLOYD []173b'50

MERRIMAN, LLOYD []72b'51

24

USHER, BOB []286 b'51
BORKOWSKI, BOB []7 t'53

BORKOWSKI, BOB []138t'54
BORKOWSKI, BOB []74 t'55

MELE, SAM []147 b'55

41

GUMBERT, HARRY []152b'49
HILLER, FRANK []114 b'52

HILLER, FRANK []156 t'52

KELLNER, ALEX []3 t'58

Cleveland Indians
3 – Earl Averill 5 - Lou Boudreau 14 - Larry Doby 18 Mel Harder
19 - Bob Feller 21 - Bob Lemon

3

MITCHELL, DALE []239 b'52
MITCHELL, DALE []26 t'53

STRICKLAND, GEORGE
[]263t'57

HELD, WOODY []202 t'58
HELD, WOODY []266 t'59

5

MAJESKI, HANK []58 b'52
MAJESKI, HANK []112 t'52

MAJESKI, HANK []127 b'55

WEBSTER, RAY []531 t'59

14

GLYNN, BILL []171 t'53

HOUTTEMAN, ART []4 b'53

FRANCONA, TITO []268 t'59

18

PIERETTI, MARINO []181b'50
TIPTON, JOE []134 t'52
TIPTON, JOE []13 bw'53

WIGHT, BILL []100 b'53
NARAGON, HAL []129 b'55
NARAGON, HAL []311 t'56

NARAGON, HAL []22 t'58
NARAGON, HAL []376 t'59
MORAN, BILLY []196 t'59

Detroit Tigers
2 - Charlie Gehringer 5 - Hank Greenberg 6 - Al Kaline
16 - Hal Newhouser 23 - Willie Horton

2

LIPON, JOHNNY []285 b'51
HATFIELD, FRED []153 b'52
LIPON, JOHNNY []163 b'52
LIPON, JOHNNY []89 t'52

ABER, AL []233 t'53
GINSBERG, JOE []6 b'53
HOUSE, FRANK []87 t'55
HOUSE, FRANK []32 t'56

HOUSE, FRANK []223 t'57
BOLLING, FRANK []95 t'58
BOLLING, FRANK []280 t'59

5

VICO, GEORGE []122 b'49
MAPES, CLIFF []13 b'52
MAPES, CLIFF []102 t'52

TUTTLE, BILL []35 b'55
TUTTLE, BILL []203 t'56
FINIGAN, JIM []248 t'57

HARRIS, GAIL []309 t'58
HARRIS, GAIL []378 t'59

6

MULLIN, PAT []56 b'49
MULLIN, PAT []135 b'50

MULLIN, PAT []106 b'51
MULLIN, PAT []183 b'52

MULLIN, PAT []275 t'53
MULLIN, PAT []4 bw'53

16

BERTOIA, RENO []94 t'55
BERTOIA, RENO []390 t'57

BERTOIA, RENO []232 t'58

NARLESKI, RAY []442 t'59

23

CAIN, BOB []197 b'51
MAAS, DUKE []405 t'57

BOLLING, MILT []188 t'58

VEAL, COOT []52 t'59

Minnesota Twins - Washington Senators / Nationals
3 - Harmon Killebrew 6 - Bobby Oliva 14 - Kent Hrbek
29 - Rod Carew 34 - Kirby Puckett

3

COAN, GIL []90 b'49

OLSON, KARL []322 t'56

OLSON, KARL []153 t'57

6

STEWART, ED []173 b'49
BAKER, FLOYD []292 t'52

SNYDER, JERRY []216 b'54
SNYDER, JERRY []74 b'55

SNYDER, JERRY []22 t'57
CONSOLO, BILLY []112 t'59

14

HARRIS, MICKEY []151 b'49	BUSBY, JIM []68 b'52	COURTNEY, CLINT []159t'56
MELE, SAM []168 b'51	LEMON, JIM []103 t'54	COURTNEY, CLINT []51 t'57
MELE, SAM []15 b'52	LEMON, JIM []262 b'55	COURTNEY, CLINT []92 t'58
MELE, SAM [] 94 t'52	COURTNEY, CLINT []34 b'54	COURTNEY, CLINT []483t'59

29

WRIGHT, TOMMY []140 t'54	[]334 t'57	BECQUER, JULIO []93 t'5
SCHOONMAKER, JERRY	BECQUER, JULIO []458 t'58	

34

STEWART, ED []143 b'50	CHRISLEY, NEIL []320 t'57	ROMONOSKY, JOHN []267 t'59
SLEATER, LOU []306 t'52		

New York - San Francisco Giants
3 - Ralph Terry 4 - Mel Ott 11 - Carl Hubbard 24 - Willie Mays
27 - Juan Marichal 30 - Orlando Cepeda 36 - Gaylord Perry
44 Willie McCovey

27

MARSHALL, WILLARD []48 b'49	CORWIN, AL []126 b'53	TAYLOR, BILL []53 t'55
	TAYLOR, BILL []74 t'54	SCHMIDT, BOB []468 t'58

30

POAT, RAY []42 b'48	SPENCER, GEORGE []356 t'52	LENNON, BOB []104 t'56
HIGBE, KIRBY []215 b'49	SPENCER, GEORGE []115 t'53	

36

HARTUNG, CLINT []118 b'50	SURKONT, MAX []209 t'56	MUFFETT, BILLY []241 t'59
LENNON, BOB []104 t'56	SURKONT, MAX []310 t'57	

44

GETTELL, AL []304 b'51	RIDZIK, STEVE []123 t'57	CRONE, RAY []272 t'58
CRONE, RAY []68 t'57		

New York Yankees
1 - Billy Martin 3 - Babe Ruth 4 - Lou Gehrig 5 - Joe DiMaggio 7 - Mickey Mantle
8 - Bill Dickey - Yogi Berra 9 - Roger Maris 10 - Phil Rizzuto 15 - Thurman Munson
16 Whitey Ford 23 - Don Mattingly 32 - Elston Howard 37 - Casey Stengel
44 - Reggie Jackson - 49 - Ron Guidry

15

WILSON, AL []210 b;52	WILSON, AL [] 327 t'52	PISONI, JIM []259 t'59

23

KRYHOSKI, DICK []218 b'49	MILLER, BILL []100 t'53	DICKSON, MURRY []349 t'58
MILLER, BILL []54 bw'53		

Philadelphia - Kansas City - Oakland Athletics
9 - Reggie Jackson 27 Catfish Hunter 34 - Rollie Fingers 43 - Dennis Eckersley

9

GUERRA, MIKE []155 b'49
ASTROTH, JOE []298 b'51
ASTROTH, JOE []170 b'52
ASTROTH, JOE []290 t'52

ASTROTH, JOE []82 b'53
ASTROTH, JOE []103 t'53
ASTROTH, JOE []131 b'54
SMITH, HAL W []41 t'57

SMITH, HAL W []257 t'58
SMITH, HAL W []227 t'59

27

BURTSCHY, ED []120 b'55

KERIAZAKOS, GUS []14 b'55

34

KELLNER, ALEX []14 b'50
RENNA, BILL []121 t'55

RENNA, BILL []82 t'56
SANTIAGO, JOSE []59 t'56

MAAS, DUKE []228 t'58

Philadelphia Phillies
1 - Richie Ashburn 14 - Jim Bunning 20 - Mike Schmidt
32 - Steve Carlton 36 - Robin Roberts

14

REPULSKI, RIP []245 t'57

20

BOROWY, HANK []134 b'49
BOROWY, HANK []177 b'50
HANSEN, ANDY []74 t'52

DICKSON, MURRY []111 b'54
DICKSON, MURRY []236 b'55

DICKSON, MURRY []211 t'56
HADDIX, HARVEY []265 t'57

Pittsburgh Pirates
1 - MEYER, BILLY 4 - Ralph Kiner 8 - Willie Stargell 9 - Bill Mazeroski
11 - Paul Waner 20 - Pie Traynor 21 - Roberto Clemente
33 - Honus Wagner 40 - Danny Murtaugh

1

MEYER, BILLY []272 b'51

MEYER, BILLY []155 b'52

MEYER, BILLY []387 t'52

4

GORDON, SID []11 b'54

8

McCULLOUGH, CLYDE []163 b49
McCULLOUGH, CLYDE []124 b50
McCULLOUGH, CLYDE []94

b51
HOWERTON, BILL []229 b'51
HOWERTON, BILL []119 b'52
HOWERTON, BILL []167 t'52
ALLIE, GAIR []179 t'54

FREESE, GENE []46 t'56
FREESE, GENE []293 t'58
BRIGHT, HARRY []523 t'59

9

FITZGERALD, ED []109 b'49
FITZGERALD, ED []178 b'50

FITZGERALD, ED []180 b'52
FITZGERALD, ED []236 t'52

ROBERTS, CURT []306 t'56

11

METKOVICH, GEORGE []214 b51
POLLET, HOWIE []83 b'52
POLLET, HOWIE []63 t'52

ATWELL, TOBY []123 b'54
ATWELL, TOBY []164 b'55
ATWELL, TOBY []232 t'56
POLLET, HOWIE []262 t'56

SMITH, PAUL LESLIE []345 t'57
SMITH, PAUL LESLIE []269 t'58

20

FOILES, HANK []104 t'57   FOILES, HANK []4 t'58   FOILES, HANK []294 t'59

21

DICKSON, MURRY []167 b'51   BEARD, TED []150 t'52

St. Louis Cardinals
1 - Ozzie Smith 2 - Red Schoendienst 6 - Stan Musial 9 - Enos Slaughter
14 - Ken Boyer 17 - Dizzy Dean 20 - Lou Brock
42 - Bruce Sutter 45 - Bob Gibson

1

KAZAK, EDDIE []85 b'51
JOHNSON, BILLY []122
b'52
JOHNSON, BILLY []83 t'52

JOHNSON, BILLY []21
t'53
CASTIGLIONE, PETE []174
b'54

JACOBS, ANTHONY []183
t'55
GREEN, GENE []37 t'59

2

SMITH, HAL R []497 t'59

14

STALEY, GERRY []121
b'51

STALEY, GERRY []50 b'52
STALEY, GERRY []79 t'52

STALEY, GERRY []17 b'53
STALEY, GERRY []56 t'53

17

 WESTLAKE, WALLY []38
t'52

FUSSELMAN, LES []218
t'53

YVARS, SAL []11 t'53

20

MUNGER, GEORGE []40
b49
MUNGER, GEORGE []89
b'50

MUNGER, GEORGE []11
b'51
MUNGER, GEORGE []243
b'52

MUNGER, GEORGE []115
t'52
WERLE, BILL []248 b'52
WERLE, BILL []73 t'52

42

MORGAN, BOBBY : []337
t'56

GRISSOM, MARV : []243
t'59

45

JONES, GORDON []78 t'55
McDANIEL, VON []65 t'58

WIGHT, BILL []237 t'58

STONE, DEAN []286 t'59

TRADED FOR.......

    In the real world, some of these trades seemed like the right thing to do at the time. Some of these teams were trading over-the-hill stars for young up-starts, or maybe didn't see the Hall of Fame potential of others. How many *Sandy Koufax* rookie cards were traded for a Rip Repulski? (at least one that I know of). In the list below are trades that you probably wouldn't make, card for card.

t=topps b=bowman +=with other players

McCOSKY, BARNEY : to PHI A	*George Kell* : to DET	5/18/46
WOODLING, GENE : to PIT	*Al Lopez* : to CLE	12/7/46
ROBINSON, AARON : to DET	*Billy Pierce* $: to CHI A	11/10/48
HAYNES, JOE + : to WAS	*Early Wynn* + : to CLE	12/14/48
ROBINSON, EDDIE + : to WAS	*Early Wynn* + : to CLE	12/14/48
TIPTON, JOE []103 b'49 : to PHI A	*Nellie Fox* : to CHI A	10/19/49
EDWARDS, HANK $ []169 b'50 : to BKN	*Chuck Conners* : to CHI N	10/10/50
BRISSIE, LOU []155 b'51 : to CLE	*Minnie Minoso* + : to PHI A	4/30/51
PHILLEY, DAVE + []297 b'51 : to PHI A	*Minnie Minoso* + : to CHI A	4/30/51
ZERNIAL, GUS + : to PHI A	*Minnie Minoso* + : to CHI A	4/30/51
DROPO, WALT + []235 t'52 : to DET	*George Kell* + : to BOS A	6/3/52
HATFIELD, FRED + []153 b'52 : to DET	*George Kell* + : to BOS A	6/3/52
LENHARDT, DON + []4 t'52 : to DET	*George Kell* + : to BOS A	6/3/52
WIGHT, BILL []117 b'52 []177 t'52 : DET	*George Kell* + : to BOS A	6/3/52
ATWELL, TOBY + []112 b'53 []23 t'53 : to PIT	*Ralph Kiner* + : to CHI N	6/4/53
FREESE, GEORGE + : to PIT	*Ralph Kiner* + : to CHI N	6/4/53
HERMANSKI, GENE + []179 t'53 : to PIT	*Ralph Kiner* + : to CHI N	6/4/53
SCHULTZ, BOB + []144dp t'53 : to PIT	*Ralph Kiner* + : to CHI N	6/4/53
WARD, PRESTON + []173 t'53 : to PIT	*Ralph Kiner* + : to CHI N	6/4/53
WADE, GALE + : to PIT	*Ralph Kiner* + : to CHI N	6/4/53
DIXON, SONNY []211 b'55 : to NY A	*Johnny Sain/Enos Saughter* : to KC 5/11/55	

BUSBY, JIM + []166 b'55 : to CLE	*Larry Doby* : to CHI A	10/25/55
CARRASQUEL, CHICO + []173 b'55 : to CLE	*Larry Doby* : to CHI A	10/25/55
PHILLEY, DAVE +[]222 t'56 : to CHI A	*George Kell* : to BAL	5/21/56
WILSON, JIM []171 t'56 : to CHI A	*George Kell* : to BAL	5/21/56
KATT, RAY + : to STL N	*Red Schoendienst* : to NY N	6/14/56
LIDDLE, DON + []325 t'56 : to STL N	*Red Schoendienst* : to NY N	6/14/56
LITTLEFIELD, DICK : to BKN	*Jackie Robinson* : to NY N	12/13/56
O'CONNELL, DANNY + []271 t'57 : to NY N	*Red Schoendienst* : to MIL	6/15/57
CRONE, RAY + []68 t'57 : to NY N	*Red Schoendienst* : to MIL	6/15/57
FRANCONA, TITO + []184r t'57 : to CHI A	*Larry Doby* : to BAL	12/3/57
MOORE, RAY + []106 t'57 : to CHI A	*Larry Doby*: to BAL	12/3/57
HATFIELD, FRED + []278 t'57 : to CLE	*Early Wynn* + : to CHI A	12/4/57
SMITH, AL + []145 t'57 : to CHI A	*Minnie Minoso* + : to CLE	12/4/57
SCHMIDT, WILLARD + []206 t'57 : to CIN	*Curt Flood* + : to STL N	12/5/57
FONDY, DEE []42 t'57 : to CIN	*Ted Kluszewski* : to PIT	12/28/57
DALEY, BUD + []222 t'58 : to BAL	*Larry Doby* : to CLE	4/1/58
WOODLING, GENE + : to BAL	*Larry Doby* + : to CLE	4/1/58
BILKO, STEVE + []346 t'58 : to LA N	*Don Newcombe* : to CIN	6/15/58
KLIPPSTEIN, JOHNNY + []242 t'58 : to LA N	*Don Newcombe* : to CIN	6/15/58
HELD, WOODY + []202r t'58 : to CLE	*Roger Maris* + : to KC	6/15/58
GEIGER, GARY + : to BOS	*Jimmy Piersall* : to CLE	12/2/58
WERTZ, VIC + : to BOS	*Jimmy Piersall* : to CLE	12/2/58
REPULSKI, RIP []14 t'58 : to LA N	*Sparky Anderson* : to PHI	12/23/58
SNYDER, GENE + : to LA N	*Sparky Anderson* : to PHI	12/23/58
FRANCONA, TITO []268 t'59 : to CLE	*Larry Doby* : to DET	3/21/59
SIMPSON, HARRY + []333 t'59 : to PIT	*Ted Kluszewski* : to CHI A	8/25/59
PHILLIPS, BUBBA + : to CLE	*Minnie Minoso* + : to CHI A	12/6/59
ROMANO, JOHN + []138 t'59 : to CLE	*Minnie Minoso* + : to CHI A	12/6/59

HADLEY, KENT + []127 t'59 : to NY A   *Hank Bauer* + : to KC   12/11/59

SIEBERN, NORM + []308 t'59 : to KC   *Roger Maris* + : to NY A   12/11/59

MY FAVORITE TEAM

Growing up in the Chicago area you had to commit to either the Cubs or the White Sox. As I recall, once you made your choice you couldn't change your mind. My brother chose the Cubs, so I was forced into the White Sox. This explains the wear and tear of my collection of these two teams. Although I have moved 1200 miles away, and have become a fan of a few other teams, the Chicago teams have been a focal point in my collection. Below is a list of common players that helped make up your favorite team. Some of these players were traded to, or from, a team after their picture hit the cardboard.

b=bowman / t=topps / dnp=did not play

Boston / Milwaukee Braves

1949
(all bowman)

[] 213 BARRETT, RED
[] 153 MASI, PHIL
[] 239 McCORMICK, FRANK dnp
[] 235 RUSSELL, JIM

[] 88 SALKELD, BILL
[] 201 SISTI, SIBBY
[] 17 TORGESON, EARL

1950
(all bowman)

[] 57 BICKFORD, VERN
[] 192 CHIPMAN, BOB
[] 111 COOPER, WALKER
[] 19 GORDON, SID
[] 183 HAEFNER, MICKEY

[] 55 KERR, BUDDY
[] 73 MARSHALL, WILLARD
[] 164 SISTI, SIBBY
[] 163 TORGESON, EARL

1951
(all bowman)

[] 42 BICKFORD, VERN
[] 135 COOPER, WALKER
[] 208 DONNELLY, BLIX
[] 19 GORDON, SID
[] 277 HARTSFIELD, ROY
[] 171 KERR, BUDDY

[] 98 MARSHALL, WILLARD
[] 313 MUELLER, RAY
[] 278 NORMAN, ROY dnp
[] 170 SISTI, SIBBY
[] 207 SOUTHWORTH, BILLY
[] 99 TORGESON, EARL

1952

[] b48 BICKFORD, VERN
[] t252 BICKFORD, VERN
[] b228 CHIPMAN, BOB
[] b132 COLE, DAVE
[] b208 COOPER, WALKER
[] t294 COOPER, WALKER
[] b192 CUSICK, JOHN
[] b28 HARTSFIELD, ROY
[] t264 HARTSFIELD, ROY
[] b215 JONES, SHELDON
[] t130 JONES, SHELDON

[] b97 MARSHALL, WILLARD
[] t96 MARSHALL, WILLARD
[] b120 NICHOLS, CHET dnp
[] b100 SISTI, SIBBY
[] t293 SISTI, SIBBY
[] b172 ST CLAIRE, EBBA
[] b12 SURKONT, MAX
[] t302 SURKONT, MAX
[] b72 TORGESON, EARL
[] t97 TORGESON, EARL
[] t276 WILSON, JIM

1953

[] t161 BICKFORD, VERN
[] bw38 COLE, DAVE
[] bw30 COOPER, WALKER
[] b83 DANIELS, JACK dnp
[] t212 DITTMER, JACK
[] b5 GORDON, SID
[] t117 GORDON, SID
[] bw57 PAFKO, ANDY

[] t185 PENDLETON, JIM
[] t124 SISTI, SIBBY
[] bw34 ST CLAIRE, EBBA
[] t91 ST CLAIRE, EBBA
[] b156 SURKONT, MAX
[] t217 WALL, MURRAY dnp
[] b37 WILSON, JIM
[] t208 WILSON, JIM

1954

[] t68 CALDERONE, SAM
[] t206 CRONE, RAY
[] b48 DITTMER, JACK
[] t188 JOLLY, DAVE
[] t176 KEELY, BOB
[] b80 LOGAN, JOHNNY

[] b160 O'CONNELL, DANNY
[] t165 PENDLETON, JIM
[] t181 ROACH, MEL
[] b109 SMALLEY, ROY
[] t231 SMALLEY, ROY
[] b16 WILSON, JIM

1955

[] t149 CRONE, RAY
[] b212 DITTMER, JACK
[] b71 JOLLY, DAVE
[] t35 JOLLY, DAVE
[] b72 NICHOLS, CHET
[] b44 O'CONNELL, DANNY

[] t23 PARKS, JACK np
[] t15 PENDLETON, JIM
[] b106 RICE, DEL
[] t117 ROACH, MEL dnp
[] t182 ROBINSON, HUMBERTO
[] t103 WHITE, CHUCK

1956
(all topps)

[] 232 ATWELL, TOBY
[] 76 CRONE, RAY
[] 254 CROWE, GEORGE dnp

[] 278 NICHOLS, CHET
[] 272 O'CONNELL, DANNY
[] 131 ROSELLI, BOB

1957

(all topps)

[] 234 COLE, DICK
[] 283 COVINGTON, WES
[] 68 CRONE, RAY
[] 333 JOHNSON, ERNIE
[] 389 JOLLY, DAVE

[] 321 MURFF, JOHN
[] 272 O'CONNELL, DANNY
[] 343 PHILLIPS, TAYLOR
[] 383 PIZARRO, JUAN
[] 193 RICE, DEL

1958

(all topps)

[] 454 HANEBRINK, HARRY
[] 83 HAZLE, BOB
[] 241 LITTLEFIELD, DICK
[] 17 MANTILLA, FELIX
[] 147 McMAHON, DON
[] 51 RICE, DEL

[] 313 RUSH, BOB
[] 234 SAWATSKI, CARL
[] 283 SHEARER, RAY dnp
[] 164 TAYLOR, BOB
[] 252 TROWBRIDGE, BOB
[] 247 WISE, CASEY

1959

(all topps)

[] 363 AVILA, BOBBY
[] 165 BRUTON, BILL
[] 347 BUHL, BOB
[] 290 COVINGTON, WES
[] 126 HAAS, EDDIE dnp
[] 128 HARTMAN, BOB
[] 412 LOPATA, STAN
[] 157 MANTILLA, FELIX

[] 259 PISONI, JIM
[] 188 PIZARRO, JUAN
[] 54 ROACH, MEL
[] 396 RUSH, BOB
[] 239 TROWBRIDGE, BOB
[] 95 WILLEY, CARL
[] 204 WISE, CASEY

Boston Red Sox

1949

(all bowman)

[] 7 DOBSON, JOE
[] 211 FERRISS, BOO
[] 199 HUGHSON, TEX
[] 231 JOHNSON, EARL
[] 53 KRAMER, JACK

[] 167 MARTIN, BABE
[] 157 MASTERSON, WALT
[] 71 STEPHENS, VERN
[] 183 STRINGER, LOU
[] 156 ZARRILLA, AL

1950

(all bowman)

[] 44 DOBSON, JOE
[] 188 JOHNSON, EARL
[] 152 KINDER, ELLIS
[] 153 MASTERSON, WALT
[] 19 McDERMONT, MICKEY
[] 245 PAPAI, AL

[] 136 ROSAR, BUDDY
[] 2 STEPHENS, VERN
[] 187 STRINGER, LOU
[] 53 VOLLMER, CLYDE
[] 45 ZARRILLA, AL

1951

(all bowman)

[] 129 BATTS, MATT
[] 38 EVANS, AL
[] 202 GUERRA, MIKE
[] 128 KINDER, ELLIS
[] 307 MASTERSON, WALT
[] 16 McDERMONT, MICKEY
[] 210 MOSS, LES
[] 270 NIXON, WILLARD

[] 201 O'NEILL, STEVE
[] 276 QUINN, FRANK dnp
[] 95 ROBINSON, AARON
[] 236 ROSAR, BUDDY
[] 39 SCARBOROUGH, RAY
[] 91 VOLLMER, CLYDE
[] 164 WIGHT, BILL
[] 271 WRIGHT, TOMMY

1952

[] t374 BENTON, AL
[] b250 DELOCK, IKE
[] b157 DELSING, JIM
[] t235 DROPO, WALT
[] t152 EVANS, AL dnp
[] b111 EVERS, HOOT
[] t222 EVERS, HOOT
[] t343 GERNERT, DICK
[] b106 GUMPERT, RANDY
[] t247 GUMPERT, RANDY
[] b153 HATFIELD, FRED
[] b123 HUDSON, SID
[] t60 HUDSON, SID
[] t54 KIELY, LEO
[] t78 KINDER, ELLIS
[] t4 LENHARDT, DON
[] t335 LEPCIO, TED
[] b163 LIPON, JOHNNY
[] t89 LIPON, JOHNNY
[] b205 MASTERSON, WALT
[] t186 MASTERSON, WALT
[] b25 McDERMONT, MICKEY

[] b129 NIARHOS, GUS
[] t121 NIARHOS, GUS
[] bw2 NIXON, WILLARD
[] t269 NIXON, WILLARD
[] t72 OLSON, KARL dnp
[] b241 PARNELL, MEL
[] b140 SCARBOROUGH, RAY
[] t43 SCARBOROUGH, RAY
[] b245 SCHMEES, GEORGE
[] t376 THRONEBERRY, FAYE
[] b57 VOLLMER, CLYDE
[] t255 VOLLMER, CLYDE
[] t345 WHITE, SAMMY
[] b117 WIGHT, BILL
[] t177 WIGHT, BILL
[] b225 WILBER, DEL
[] t383 WILBER, DEL
[] b210 WILSON, AL
[] t327 WILSON, AL
[] t139 WOOD, KEN
[] b113 ZARRILLA, AL
[] t10 ZARRILLA, AL

1953

[] bw49 BAKER, FLOYD
[] t69 BRODOWSKI, DICK dnp
[] t184 BROWN, HECTOR
[] tdp149 DiMAGGIO, DOM
[] b25 EVERS, HOOT
[] bw11 GERNERT, DICK
[] bw29 HUDSON, SID
[] t251 HUDSON, SID
[] t94 KENNEDY, BILL
[] t18 LEPCIO, TED
[] b123 LIPON, JOHNNY
[] t40 LIPON, JOHNNY
[] b35 McDERMONT, MICKEY

[] t55 McDERMONT, MICKEY
[] t63 NIARHOS, GUS
[] bw2 NIXON, WILLARD
[] t30 NIXON, WILLARD
[] tdp19 PARNELL, MEL
[] t248 STEPHENS, GENE
[] t49 THRONEBERRY, FAYE dnp
[] t32 VOLLMER, CLYDE
[] t170 WERLE, BILL
[] b41 WHITE, SAMMY
[] t139 WHITE, SAMMY
[] bw24 WILBER, DEL
[] t181 ZARRILLA, AL

1954

[] t133 BAKER, DEL
[] b13 BOLLING, MILT
[] t82 BOLLING, MILT
[] t221 BRODOWSKI, DICK dnp
[] t172 BROWN, HECTOR
[] t195 CONSOLO, BILLY
[] b18 EVERS, HOOT
[] b146 GERNERT, DICK
[] t208 HATTON, GRADY
[] b194 HUDSON, SID
[] t93 HUDSON, SID
[] t171 KIELY, LEO
[] b98 KINDER, ELLIS

[] t47 KINDER, ELLIS
[] b53 LENHARDT, DON
[] b162 LEPCIO, TED
[] t66 LEPCIO, TED
[] b22 MELE, SAM
[] t227 MILLS, BUSTER
[] b114 NIXON, WILLARD
[] t186 OLSON, KARL
[] t217 SCHREIBER, PAUL
[] t144 WERLE, BILL
[] b34 WHITE, SAMMY
[] b178 WILBER, DEL

1955

[] t91 BOLLING, MILT
[] b178 BREWER, TOM
[] t83 BREWER, TOM
[] t171 BRODOWSKI, DICK
[] b221 BROWN, HECTOR
[] t148 BROWN, HECTOR
[] t207 CONSOLO, BILLY
[] t206 DALEY, PETE
[] b276 DELOCK, IKE
[] b256 FRIEND, OWEN
[] t131 HATTON, GRADY
[] b264 HENRY, BILL
[] t150 HIGGINS, MIKE
[] b318 HUDSON, SID
[] t116 HURD, TOM
[] b263 JOOST, EDDIE

[] b222 KEMMERER, RUSS
[] t18 KEMMERER, RUSS
[] t36 KIELY, LEO
[] t115 KINDER, ELLIS
[] b150 KLAUS, BILLY
[] t128 LEPCIO, TED
[] b147 MELE, SAM
[] b177 NIXON, WILLARD
[] t72 OLSON, KARL
[] b319 SCHROLL, AL dnp
[] b15 SULLIVAN, FRANK
[] t106 SULLIVAN, FRANK
[] t163 THRONEBERRY, FAYE
[] b47 WHITE, SAMMY
[] t176 ZAUCHIN, NORM

1956

(all topps)

[] 315 BOLLING, MILT
[] 34 BREWER, TOM
[] 284 DELOCK, IKE
[] 167 DORISH, HARRY
[] 26 HATTON, GRADY
[] 256 HURD, TOM
[] 217 KLAUS, BILLY
[] 122 NIXON, WILLARD

[] 322 OLSON, KARL
[] 248 PORTERFIELD, BOB
[] 298 SCHMITZ, JOHNNY
[] 313 STEPHENS, GENE
[] 71 SULLIVAN, FRANK
[] 93 SUSCE, GEORGE
[] 168 WHITE, SAMMY
[] 89 ZAUCHIN, NORM

1957

(all topps)

[] 131 BOLLING, MILT
[] 112 BREWER, TOM
[] 261 CHAKALES, BOB
[] 399 CONSOLO, BILLY
[] 288 DALEY, PETE
[] 63 DELOCK, IKE
[] 116 FORNIELES, MIKE
[] 202 GERNERT, DICK
[] 292 KLAUS, BILLY
[] 288 LEPCIO, TED
[] 189 NIXON, WILLARD

[] 313 PARNELL, MEL dnp
[] 118 PORTERFIELD, BOB
[] 56 SISLER, DAVE
[] 217 STEPHENS, GENE
[] 381 STONE, DEAN
[] 21 SULLIVAN, FRANK
[] 229 SUSCE, GEORGE
[] 356 THRONEBERRY, FAYE
[] 163 WHITE, SAMMY
[] 372 ZAUCHIN, NORM

1958

(all topps)

[] 405 ASPROMONTE, KEN
[] 167 BAUMAN, FRANK
[] 383 BERBERET, LOU
[] 220 BREWER, TOM
[] 297 BUDDIN, DON
[] 72 BYERLY, BUD
[] 148 CONSOLO, BILLY
[] 73 DALEY, PETE
[] 328 DELOCK, IKE
[] 361 FORNIELES, MIKE
[] 38 GERNERT, DICK
[] 371 KEOUGH, MARTY
[] 204 KIELY, LEO

[] 89 KLAUS, BILLY
[] 29 LEPCIO, TED
[] 395 NIXON, WILLARD
[] 344 PORTERFIELD, BOB
[] 473 RENNA, BILL
[] 59 SISLER, DAVE
[] 445 SMITH, BOB W
[] 227 STEPHENS, GENE
[] 18 SULLIVAN, FRANK
[] 189 SUSCE, GEORGE
[] 410 WALL, MURRAY
[] 414 WHITE, SAMMY

1959

(all topps)

[] 363 AVILA, BOBBY
[] 161 BAUMAN, FRANK
[] 236 BOWSFIELD, TED

[] 55 BREWER, TOM
[] 32 BUDDIN, DON
[] 185 BUSBY, JIM

[] 456 CASALE, JERRY
[] 112 CONSOLO, BILLY
[] 276 DALEY, PETE
[] 437 DELOCK, IKE
[] 476 FORNIELES, MIKE
[] 521 GEIGER, GARY
[] 475 HARSHMAN, JACK
[] 343 HOEFT, BILLY
[] 303 KEOUGH, MARTY
[] 199 KIELY, LEO
[] 348 LEPCIO, TED
[] 91 MOFORD, HERB

[] 361 NIXON, WILLARD dnp
[] 373 PLEWS, HERB
[] 72 RENNA, BILL
[] 139 SADOWSKI, ED dnp
[] 546 SCHROLL, AL
[] 384 SISLER, DAVE
[] 384 SISLER / BREWER
[] 261 STEPHENS, GENE
[] 323 SULLIVAN, FRANK
[] 486 WHITE, SAMMY
[] 146 ZIMMERMAN, JERRY dnp

Brooklyn / Los Angeles Dodgers

1949
(all bowman)

[] 206 EDWARDS, BRUCE
[] 116 HATTON, JOE

[] 20 HERMANSKI, GENE
[] 146 McCORMICK, MIKE

1950
(all bowman)

[] 224 BANTA, JACK
[] 165 EDWARDS, BRUCE
[] 166 HATTON, JOE

[] 113 HERMANSKI, GENE
[] 222 MORGAN, BOBBY
[] 223 RUSSELL, JIM

1951
(all bowman)

[] 152 ABRAMS, CAL
[] 116 EDWARDS, BRUCE
[] 190 HATTON, JOE
[] 55 HERMANSKI, GENE
[] 299 KING, CLYDE

[] 117 MIKSIS, EDDIE
[] 189 PALICA, ERV
[] 69 SCHMITZ, JOHNNY
[] 175 TERWILLIGER, WAYNE

1952

[] b86 ABRAMS, CAL
[] b152 COX, BILLY
[] b240 LOES, BILLY
[] b108 MORGAN, BOBBY
[] t273 PALICA, ERV dnp
[] t188 PODBIELAN, BUD

[] t51 RUSSELL, JIM dnp
[] b224 SCHMITZ, JOHNNY
[] t7 TERWILLIGER, WAYNE dnp
[] t53 VAN CUYK, CHRIS
[] t319 WALKER, RUBE

1953

[] t272 ANTONELLO, BILL
[] t50 DRESSEN, CHUCK
[] t255 HOWELL, DIXIE H
[] t216 HUGHES, JIM
[] tdp14 LABINE, CLEM
[] b129 MEYER, RUSS

[] t221 MILLIKEN, BOB
[] b135 MORGAN, BOBBY
[] t85 MORGAN, BOBBY
[] tdp254 ROE, PREACHER
[] t137 RUTHERFORD, JOHN
[] t4 WADE, BEN

1954

[] b186 MEYER, RUSS
[] t177 MILLIKEN, BOB

[] t209 THOMPSON, CHUCK
[] t126 WADE, BEN

1955

[] t74 BORKOWSKI, BOB
[] b21 HOAK, DON

[] b310 LEHMAN, KEN dnp

1956
(all topps)

[] 223 JACKSON, RANDY

[] 333 WALKER, RUBE

1957
(all topps)

[] 178 BESSENT, DON
[] 319 CIMOLI, GINO
[] 268 COLLUM, JACK
[] 376 ELSTON, DON
[] 190 JACKSON, RANDY

[] 366 LEHMAN, KEN
[] 337 VALDES, RENE
[] 54 VALO, ELMER
[] 147 WALKER, RUBE

1958
(all topps)

[] 401 BESSENT, DON
[] 346 BILKO, STEVE
[] 286 CIMOLI, GINO
[] 244 DEMETER, DON
[] 146 GRAY, DICK
[] 301 JACKSON, RANDY

[] 242 KLIPPSTEIN, JOHNNY
[] 257 McDEVITT, DANNY
[] 373 PIGNATANO, JOE
[] 323 VALO, ELMER
[] 203 WALKER, RUBE

1959
(all topps)

[] 547 BAXES, JIM
[] 71 BESSENT, DON dnp

[] 43 BILKO, STEVE dnp
[] 324 DEMETER, DON

[] 406 DRAKE, SOLLY
[] 278 ESSEGIAN, CHUCK
[] 508 FOWLER, ART
[] 244 GRAY, DICK
[] 258 KIPP, FRED
[] 152 KLIPPSTEIN, JOHNNY

[] 133 LILLIS, BOB
[] 364 McDEVITT, DANNY
[] 16 PIGNATANO, JOE
[] 195 REPULSKI, RIP
[] 522 SNYDER, GENE

Chicago Cubs

1949
(all bowman)

[] 184 CHIPMAN, BOB
[] 200 DOBERNIC, JESS
[] 136 EDWARDS, HANK
[] 99 GUSTINE, FRANK
[] 212 HAMNER, RALPH
[] 168 LADE, DOYLE
[] 115 LEONARD, DUTCH

[] 152 MADDERN, CLARENCE
[] 221 MUNCRIEF, BOB
[] 83 SCHEFFING, BOB
[] 52 SCHMITZ, JOHNNY
[] 38 VERBAN, EMIL
[] 130 WALKER, HARRY

1950
(all bowman)

[] 169 EDWARDS, HANK
[] 196 LADE, DOYLE
[] 170 LEONARD, DUTCH
[] 81 NORTHY, RON
[] 61 RUSH, BOB
[] 168 SCHEFFING, BOB

[] 24 SCHMITZ, JOHNNY
[] 230 SERENA, BILL
[] 115 SMALLEY, ROY
[] 114 TERWILLIGER, WAYNE
[] 231 WARD, PRESTON

1951
(all bowman)

[] 283 DUBIEL, WALT
[] 116 EDWARDS, BRUCE
[] 318 HACKER, WARREN
[] 190 HATTON, JOE
[] 55 HERMANSKI, GENE
[] 211 JEFFCOAT, HAL
[] 248 KLIPPSTEIN, JOHNNY
[] 139 LADE, DOYLE dnp
[] 102 LEONARD, DUTCH

[] 117 MIKSIS, EDDIE
[] 70 NORTHY, RON dnp
[] 247 RAMAZZOTTI, BOB
[] 212 RUSH, BOB
[] 69 SCHMITZ, JOHNNY
[] 246 SERENA, BILL
[] 44 SMALLEY, ROY
[] 175 TERWILLIGER, WAYNE

1952

[] t259 ADDIS, BOB
[] b236 BAUMHOLTZ, FRANK

[] t225 BAUMHOLTZ, FRANK
[] b 236 BROWN, TOMMY

[] t164 DUBIEL, WALT
[] b88 EDWARDS, BRUCE
[] t224 EDWARDS, BRUCE
[] b231 FONDY, DEE
[] t359 FONDY, DEE
[] t324 HACKER, WARREN
[] b144 HATTON, JOE
[] t194 HATTON, JOE
[] b136 HERMANSKI, GENE
[] t16 HERMANSKI, GENE
[] b 175 JACKSON, RANDY
[] b104 JEFFCOAT, HAL
[] t348 KELLY, ROBERT
[] t148 KLIPPSTEIN, JOHNNY
[] b159 LEONARD, DUTCH

[] t110 LEONARD, DUTCH
[] b16 LOWN, TURK
[] b32 MIKSIS, EDDIE
[] t172 MIKSIS, EDDIE
[] b211 MINNER, PAUL
[] t127 MINNER, PAUL
[] t204 NORTHY, RON
[] b247 PRAMESA, JOHNNY
[] t105 PRAMESA, JOHNNY
[] t184 RAMAZZOTTI, BOB
[] b22 RAMSDELL, WILLARD
[] t114 RAMSDELL, WILLARD
[] t153 RUSH, BOB
[] t173 SMALLEY, ROY
[] t157 USHER, BOB

1953

[] b94 ADDIS, BOB
[] t157 ADDIS, BOB
[] b112 ATWELL, TOBY
[] t23 ATWELL, TOBY
[] b42 BROWN, TOMMY
[] b7 CHITI, HARRY dnp
[] b138 CHURCH, BUBBA
[] t47 CHURCH, BUBBA
[] bw5 FONDY, DEE
[] b144 HACKER, WARREN
[] t179 HERMANSKI, GENE
[] bw12 JACKSON, RANDY
[] bw37 JEFFCOAT, HAL
[] t29 JEFFCOAT, HAL
[] t46 KLIPPSTEIN, JOHNNY
[] bw50 LEONARD, DUTCH

[] t155 LEONARD, DUTCH
[] b154 LOWN, TURK
[] t130 LOWN, TURK
[] t58 METKOVICH, GEORGE
[] t39 MIKSIS, EDDIE
[] b71 MINNER, PAUL
[] t92 MINNER, PAUL
[] t83 POLLET, HOWIE
[] bw41 RAMAZZOTTI, BOB
[] b110 RUSH, BOB
[] t111 SAUER, HANK
[] t202 SAWATSKI, CARL
[] t144 SCHULTZ, BOB
[] b122 SERENA, BILL
[] bw52 SMALLEY, ROY
[] t173 WARD, PRESTON

1954

[] b221 BAUMHOLTZ, FRANK
[] t60 BAUMHOLTZ, FRANK
[] b206 BILKO, STEVE
[] t116 BILKO, STEVE
[] t243 BLADES, RAY
[] b173 FONDY, DEE
[] b125 HACKER, WARREN
[] b189 JACKSON, RANDY
[] b205 JEFFCOAT, HAL
[] b29 KLIPPSTEIN, JOHNNY
[] t31 KLIPPSTEIN, JOHNNY

[] b157 LOWN, TURK
[] b61 MIKSIS, EDDIE
[] b13 MINNER, PAUL
[] t89 POLLET, HOWIE
[] b219 RICE, HAL
[] b211 ROBERTSON, AL
[] b77 RUSH, BOB
[] b93 SERENA, BILL
[] t229 TALBOT, BOB
[] t67 WILLIS, JIM

1955

[] b7 BAKER, GENE
[] b227 BAUMHOLTZ, FRANK
[] t172 BAUMHOLTZ, FRANK
[] b88 BILKO, STEVE
[] t93 BILKO, STEVE dnp
[] t179 BOLGER, JIM
[] b304 CHITI, HARRY
[] b273 CHURCH, BUBBA
[] t68 DAVIS, JIM
[] b224 FONDY, DEE
[] b256 FRIEND, OWEN
[] b8 HACKER, WARREN
[] b87 JACKSON, RANDY
[] b223 JEFFCOAT, HAL

[] b247 LEONARD, DUTCH dnp
[] b280 McCULLOUGH, CLYDE
[] b135 MERRIMAN, LLOYD
[] b181 MIKSIS, EDDIE
[] t184 PERKOWSKI, HARRY
[] t76 POLLET, HOWIE
[] b52 RICE, HAL dnp
[] b182 RUSH, BOB
[] b233 SERENA, BILL dnp
[] b137 TALBOT, BOB dnp
[] b51 TAPPE, ELVIN
[] t52 TREMEL, BILL
[] t196 WADE, GALE

1956
(all topps)

[] 142 BAKER, GENE
[] 102 DAVIS, JIM
[] 112 FONDY, DEE
[] 282 HACKER, WARREN
[] 124 KAISER, DON
[] 291 KELLERT, FRANK
[] 74 KING, JIM

[] 314 LANDRITH, HOBIE
[] 227 MEYER, RUSS
[] 285 MIKSIS, EDDIE
[] 182 MINNER, PAUL
[] 17 RUSH, BOB
[] 66 SPEAKE, BOB dnp
[] 96 TREMEL, BILL

1957
(all topps)

[] 289 BOLGER, JIM
[] 268 COLLUM, JACK
[] 94 DEL GRECO, BOBBY
[] 159 DRAKE, SOLLY dnp
[] 376 ELSTON, DON
[] 42 FONDY, DEE
[] 351 HILLMAN, DAVE
[] 134 KAISER, DON
[] 371 LENNON, BOB
[] 346 LITTLEFIELD, DICK

[] 247 LOWN, TURK
[] 16 MORYN, WALT
[] 353 NEEMAN, CAL
[] 235 POHOLSKY, TOM
[] 137 RUSH, BOB
[] 378 SINGLETON, BERT
[] 339 SPEAKE, BOB
[] 74 VALENTINETTI, VITO
[] 52 WALLS, LEE
[] 396 WISE, CASEY

1958
(all topps)

[] 99 ADAMS, BOBBY

[] 209 ANDERSON, BOB

[] 201 BOLGER, JIM
[] 80 DROTT, DICK
[] 363 ELSTON, DON
[] 449 FODGE, GENE
[] 27 FREEMAN, HERSHALL
[] 384 GORYL, JOHN
[] 41 HILLMAN, DAVE
[] 467 HOBBIE, GLEN
[] 221 KINDALL, JERRY
[] 261 LOWN, TURK

[] 461 MAYER, ED
[] 144 MORGAN, BOBBY
[] 122 MORYN, WALT
[] 33 NEEMAN, CAL
[] 159 PHILLIPS, TAYLOR
[] 269 SMITH, PAUL LESLIE
[] 184 TAPPE, ELVIN
[] 281 TAYLOR, SAMMY
[] 66 WALLS, LEE

1959
(all topps)

[] 249 ADAMS, BOBBY
[] 512 ALTMAN, GEORGE
[] 447 ANDERSON, BOB
[] 301 AVERILL, EARL
[] 118 BUZHARDT, JOHN
[] 226 CECCARELLI, ART
[] 15 DROTT, DICK
[] 520 ELSTON, DON
[] 77 GORYL, JOHN
[] 46 HENRY, BILL
[] 319 HILLMAN, DAVE
[] 334 HOBBIE, GLEN
[] 130 JACKSON, LOU
[] 394 JACKSON, RANDY
[] 538 KING, CHARLES

[] 153 MARSHALL, JIM
[] 38 MARTIN, MORRIE
[] 253 MOREHEAD, SETH
[] 488 MORYN, WALT
[] 367 NEEMAN, CAL
[] 362 NICHOLS, DOLAN dnp
[] 113 PHILLIPS, TAYLOR
[] 181 PORTERFIELD, BOB
[] 548 SINGLETON, BERT
[] 214 SOLIS, MARCELINO dnp
[] 193 TAYLOR, SAMMY
[] 62 TAYLOR, TONY
[] 474 THACKER, MOE dnp
[] 105 WALLS, LEE
[] 388 WILL, BOB dnp

Chicago White Sox

1949
(all bowman)

[] 119 BAKER, FLOYD
[] 87 GUMPERT, RANDY
[] 141 LUPIEN, TONY dnp
[] 12 MICHAELS, CASS
[] 159 MOULDER, GLEN dnp

[] 44 PHILLEY, DAVE
[] 217 PIERETTI, MARINO
[] 103 TIPTON, JOE

1950
(all bowman)

[] 146 BAKER, FLOYD
[] 236 CAIN, BOB
[] 183 HAEFNER, MICKEY
[] 15 KOZAR, AL
[] 92 MAJESKI, HANK
[] 128 MASI, PHIL

[] 154 NIARHOS, GUS
[] 127 PHILLEY, DAVE
[] 18 ROBINSON, EDDIE
[] 237 SALKELD, BILL
[] 108 SCARBOROUGH, RAY

1951
(all bowman)

[] 231 ALOMA, LUIS
[] 87 BAKER, FLOYD
[] 302 BUSBY, JIM
[] 197 CAIN, BOB
[] 136 COLEMAN, RAY
[] 63 DILLINGER, BOB
[] 36 DOBSON, JOE
[] 266 DORISH, HARRY
[] 59 GUMPERT, RANDY
[] 267 HOLCOMBE, KEN

[] 123 JUDSON, HOWIE
[] 8 LEHNER, PAUL
[] 12 MAJESKI, HANK
[] 160 MASI, PHIL
[] 124 NIARHOS, GUS
[] 297 PHILLEY, DAVE
[] 88 ROBINSON, EDDIE
[] 303 ROTBLATT, MARV
[] 159 STEWART, ED
[] 35 ZARRILLA, AL

1952

[] t308 ALOMA, LUIS
[] b68 BUSBY, JIM
[] t251 CARRASQUEL, CHICO
[] b201 COLEMAN, RAY
[] t211 COLEMAN, RAY
[] t304 DENTE, SAM
[] t254 DOBSON, JOE
[] t303 DORISH, HARRY
[] b141 EDWARDS, HANK
[] t176 EDWARDS, HANK
[] t95 HOLCOMBE, KEN
[] b149 JUDSON, HOWIE
[] t169 JUDSON, HOWIE
[] t102 KENNEDY, BILL
[] b221 KRETLOW, LOU
[] t42 KRETLOW, LOU

[] b237 LOLLAR, SHERM
[] t283 MASI, PHIL
[] b15 MELE, SAM
[] t94 MELE, SAM
[] t50 RICKERT, MARV dnp
[] b77 ROBINSON, EDDIE
[] t50 ROBINSON, EDDIE
[] b165 ROGOVIN, SAUL
[] t159 ROGOVIN, SAUL
[] b185 STEWART, ED
[] t279 STEWART, ED
[] t62 STOBBS, CHUCK
[] t133 WIDMAR, AL
[] b113 ZARRILLA, AL
[] t70 ZARRILLA, AL

1953

[] t257 BOYD, BOB
[] t123 BYRNE, TOMMY
[] b54 CARRASQUEL, CHICO
[] b155 CLARK, ALLIE
[] b89 CONSUEGRA, SANDY
[] b137 DENTE, SAM
[] b88 DOBSON, JOE
[] t5 DOBSON, JOE
[] t145 DORISH, HARRY
[] t65 HARRIST, EARL

[] t196 KEEGAN, BOB
[] b50 KRETLOW, LOU
[] t229 KRSNICH, ROCKY
[] t53 LOLLAR, SHERM
[] t240 MARSH, FRED
[] t156 RIVERA, JIM
[] b98 RODRIGUEZ, HECTOR dnp
[] b75 ROGOVIN, SAUL
[] t102 RYAN, CONNIE
[] t250 WILSON, BOB

1954

[] b134 ALOMA, LUIS dnp
[] t57 ALOMA, LUIS dnp
[] b183 BATTS, MATT
[] t88 BATTS, MATT
[] b118 BOYD, BOB
[] t113 BOYD, BOB
[] b195 CAIN, BOB
[] b54 CARRASQUEL, CHICO
[] b 166 CONSUEGRA, SANDY
[] b86 DORISH, HARRY
[] t110 DORISH, HARRY
[] t154 FORNIELES, MIKE
[] b165 GROTH, JOHNNY
[] t173 HARSHMAN, JACK

[] t208 HATTON, GRADY
[] t146 JOHNSON, DON
[] t100 KEEGAN, BOB
[] t218 MARSH, FRED
[] b70 MARSHALL, WILLARD
[] b179 MARTIN, MORRIE
[] b150 MICHAELS, CASS
[] t34 RIVERA, JIM
[] b140 ROGOVIN, SAUL dnp
[] t198 SAWATSKI, CARL
[] t216 SIMA, AL
[] b198 TRUCKS, VIRGIL
[] t222 WILSON, BILL
[] t58 WILSON, BOB

1955

[] t178 ADAMS, BOBBY
[] b151 BRIDEWESER, JIM
[] b166 BUSBY, JIM
[] b159 BYRD, HARRY
[] b173 CARRASQUEL, CHICO
[] b148 CHAKALES, BOB
[] b78 COAN, GIL
[] b116 CONSUEGRA, SANDY
[] t146 DONOVAN, DICK
[] b266 FORNIELES, MIKE
[] b86 GRAY, TED

[] t104 HARSHMAN, JACK
[] t66 JACKSON, RON
[] b251 JOK, STAN
[] t10 KEEGAN, BOB
[] b131 MARSHALL, WILLARD
[] t32 McGHEE, ED
[] b135 MERRIMAN, LLOYD
[] b85 MICHAELS, CASS dnp
[] b145 NIEMAN, BOB
[] t58 RIVERA, JIM
[] t122 SAWATSKI, CARL dnp

1956
(all topps)

[] 265 CONSUEGRA, SANDY
[] 338 DELSING, JIM
[] 18 DONOVAN, DICK
[] 29 HARSHMAN, JACK
[] 318 HATFIELD, FRED
[] 149 HOWELL, DIXIE M
[] 186 JACKSON, RON
[] 326 JOHNSON, CONNIE

[] 54 KEEGAN, BOB
[] 336 KINDER, ELLIS
[] 267 NIEMAN, BOB
[] 222 PHILLEY, DAVE
[] 262 POLLET, HOWIE
[] 144 POWELL, LEROY dnp
[] 70 RIVERA, JIM
[] 171 WILSON, JIM

1957
(all topps)

[] 181 DONOVAN, DICK
[] 257 DROPO, WALT

[] 301 ESPOSITO, SAMMY
[] 152 HARSHMAN, JACK

[] 278 HATFIELD, FRED
[] 221 HOWELL, DIXIE M
[] 99 KEEGAN, BOB
[] 352 KINDER, ELLIS
[] 344 LaPALME, PAUL
[] 213 MOSS, LES

[] 31 NORTHY, RON
[] 124 PHILLEY, DAVE
[] 395 PHILLIPS, BUBBA
[] 107 RIVERA, JIM
[] 227 STALEY, GERRY
[] 330 WILSON, JIM

1958
(all topps)

[] 364 BATTEY, EARL
[] 129 DERRINGTON, JIM dnp
[] 290 DONOVAN, DICK
[] 425 ESPOSITO, SAMMY
[] 66 FISCHER, BILL
[] 421 HOWELL, DIXIE M
[] 26 JACKSON, RON
[] 200 KEEGAN, BOB
[] 108 LANDIS, JIM
[] 261 LOWN, TURK
[] 249 MOORE, RAY

[] 153 MOSS, LES
[] 212 PHILLIPS, BUBBA
[] 453 QUALTERS, TOM
[] 11 RIVERA, JIM
[] 347 RUDOLPH, DON
[] 206 SHAW, BOB
[] 177 SMITH, AL
[] 412 STALEY, GERRY
[] 138 TORGESON, EARL
[] 163 WILSON, JIM

1959
(all topps)

[] 537 ARIAS, RUDOLPH
[] 438 ESPOSITO, SAMMY
[] 477 LATMAN, BARRY
[] 293 MOORE, RAY
[] 453 MOSS, LES dnp
[] 341 QUALTERS, TOM dnp

[] 138 ROMANO, JOHN
[] 179 RUDOLPH, DON
[] 333 SIMPSON, HARRY
[] 328 SKIZAS, LOU
[] 351 TORGESON, EARL

Cincinnati Reds / Redlegs

1948
(all bowman)

[] 39 GALAN, AUGIE
[] 46 WEHMEIER, HERM

[] 44 WYROSTEK, JOHNNY

1949
(all bowman)

[] 160 BLACKBURN, JIM dnp
[] 117 COOPER, WALKER

[] 200 DOBERNIC, JESS
[] 192 GUMBERT, HARRY

[] 62 HATTON, GRADY
[] 113 LaMANNO, RAY dnp
[] 97 LITWHILER, DANNY
[] 22 LOWREY, PEANUTS
[] 176 RAFFENSBERGER, KEN

[] 81 STALLCUP, VIRGIL
[] 130 WALKER, HARRY
[] 51 WEHMEIER, HERM
[] 37 WYROSTEK, JOHNNY

1950
(all bowman)

[] 80 FOX, HOWIE
[] 26 HATTON, GRADY
[] 198 LITWHILER, DANNY
[] 172 LOWREY, PEANUTS
[] 173 MERRIMAN, LLOYD

[] 168 SCHEFFING, BOB
[] 116 STALLCUP, VIRGIL
[] 27 WEHMEIER, HERM
[] 197 WYROSTEK, JOHNNY

1951
(all bowman)

[] 288 ADAMS, BOBBY
[] 287 BLACKBURN, JIM
[] 180 FOX, HOWIE
[] 47 HATTON, GRADY
[] 252 HOWELL, DIXIE H
[] 179 LITWHILER, DANNY
[] 84 McCOSKY, BARNEY
[] 72 MERRIMAN, LLOYD

[] 215 PETERSON, KENT
[] 48 RAFFENSBERGER, KEN
[] 251 RAMSDELL, WILLARD
[] 216 RYAN, CONNIE
[] 108 STALLCUP, VIRGIL
[] 286 USHER, BOB
[] 144 WEHMEIER, HERM
[] 107 WYROSTEK, JOHNNY

1952

[] b86 ABRAMS, CAL
[] b166 ADAMS, BOBBY
[] t249 ADAMS, BOBBY
[] t144 BLAKE, ED
[] t161 BYERLY, BUD
[] t391 CHAPMAN, BEN
[] b40 CHURCH, BUBBA
[] t323 CHURCH, BUBBA
[] b141 EDWARDS, HANK
[] t176 EDWARDS, HANK
[] t171 ERAUTT, ED dnp
[] t198 HAUGSTAD, PHIL
[] b114 HILLER, FRANK
[] t156 HILLER, FRANK
[] b222 HOWELL, DIXIE H
[] t135 HOWELL, DIXIE H
[] t165 KAZAK, EDDIE
[] b92 MARSHALL, WILLARD
[] t96 MARSHALL, WILLARD

[] b238 McMILLAN, ROY
[] b78 MERRIMAN, LLOYD dnp
[] b202 PERKOWSKI, HARRY
[] t142 PERKOWSKI, HARRY
[] t188 PODBIELAN, BUD
[] b55 RAFFENSBERGER, KEN
[] t118 RAFFENSBERGER, KEN
[] t379 ROSSI, JOE
[] t297 SEMINICK, ANDY
[] b127 SISLER, DICK
[] b186 SMITH, FRANK
[] t179 SMITH, FRANK
[] b6 STALLCUP, VIRGIL
[] t69 STALLCUP, VIRGIL
[] b150 WEHMEIER, HERM
[] t38 WESTLAKE, WALLY
[] b42 WYROSTEK, JOHNNY
[] t13 WYROSTEK, JOHNNY

1953

[] b108 ADAMS, BOBBY
[] t152 ADAMS, BOBBY
[] tdp118 BELL, GUS
[] t7 BORKOWSKI, BOB
[] bw32 BRIDGES, ROCKY
[] t47 CHURCH, BUBBA
[] t226 ERAUTT, ED
[] t252 FOILES, HANK
[] t209 GREENGRASS, JIM
[] t45 HATTON, GRADY
[] bw42 JUDSON, HOWIE
[] t12 JUDSON, HOWIE
[] b58 MARSHALL, WILLARD
[] t95 MARSHALL, WILLARD

[] t259 McMILLAN, ROY
[] tdp105 NUXHALL, JOE
[] b87 PERKOWSKI, HARRY
[] t236 PERKOWSKI, HARRY
[] bw21 PODBIELAN, BUD
[] t237 PODBIELAN, BUD
[] b106 RAFFENSBERGER, KEN
[] t276 RAFFENSBERGER, KEN
[] bw7 SEMINICK, ANDY
[] t153 SEMINICK, ANDY
[] t116 SMITH, FRANK
[] b23 WEHMEIER, HERM
[] t110 WEHMEIER, HERM

1954

[] t123 ADAMS, BOBBY
[] b60 BACZEWSKI, FRED
[] t184 BAILEY, ED
[] t138 BORKOWSKI, BOB
[] b14 BRIDGES, ROCKY
[] b204 COLLUM, JACK
[] b191 DREWS, KARL
[] b28 GREENGRASS, JIM
[] t22 GREENGRASS, JIM
[] t146 HARMON, CHUCK
[] t208 HATTON, GRADY
[] b220 LANDRITH, HOBIE

[] t97 LANE, JERALD HAL
[] t19 LIPON, JOHNNY
[] b44 PERKOWSKI, HARRY
[] t125 PERKOWSKI, HARRY
[] t69 PODBIELAN, BUD
[] b92 RAFFENSBERGER, KEN
[] t46 RAFFENSBERGER, KEN
[] t136 RYAN, CONNIE
[] b172 SEMINICK, ANDY
[] b188 SMITH, FRANK
[] t71 SMITH, FRANK
[] t162 WEHMEIER, HERM

1955

[] b118 ADAMS, BOBBY
[] t178 ADAMS, BOBBY
[] b190 BACZEWSKI, FRED
[] b161 BATTS, MATT
[] t74 BORKOWSKI, BOB
[] b136 BRIDGES, ROCKY
[] b189 COLLUM, JACK
[] b290 FREEMAN, HERSHALL
[] t82 HARMON, CHUCK
[] b271 HOOPER, BOB

[] t56 JABLONSKI, RAY
[] b193 JUDSON, HOWIE dnp
[] b152 KLIPPSTEIN, JOHNNY
[] b50 LANDRITH, HOBIE
[] b147 MELE, SAM
[] t174 MINARCIN, RUDY
[] t170 PEARCE, JIM
[] b111 RIDZIK, STEVE
[] b155 STALEY, GERRY
[] t44 VALENTINE, CORKY

1956
(all topps)

[] 254 CROWE, GEORGE
[] 303 DYCK, JIM
[] 47 FOWLER, ART
[] 141 FRAZIER, JOE
[] 242 FREEMAN, HERSHALL
[] 37 GRAMMAS, ALEX
[] 308 HARMON, CHUCK
[] 86 JABLONSKI, RAY

[] 289 JEFFCOAT, HAL
[] 249 KLIPPSTEIN, JOHNNY
[] 305 LAWRENCE, BROOKS
[] 227 MEYER, RUSS
[] 224 PODBIELAN, BUD dnp
[] 137 SILVERA, AL
[] 212 TEMPLE, JOHNNY

1957
(all topps)

[] 219 ACKER, TOM
[] 294 BRIDGES, ROCKY
[] 73 CROWE, GEORGE
[] 233 FOWLER, ART
[] 32 FREEMAN, HERSHALL
[] 222 GRAMMAS, ALEX
[] 341 GROSS, DON
[] 370 HACKER, WARREN

[] 274 HOAK, DON
[] 93 JEFFCOAT, HAL
[] 296 KLIPPSTEIN, JOHNNY
[] 66 LAWRENCE, BROOKS
[] 393 SANCHEZ, RAUL
[] 279 THURMAN, BOB
[] 373 WHISENANT, PETE

1958
(all topps)

[] 149 ACKER, TOM
[] 346 BILKO, STEVE
[] 12 CROWE, GEORGE
[] 396 DOTTERER, DUTCH
[] 157 FONDY, DEE
[] 27 FREEMAN, HERSHALL
[] 254 GRAMMAS, ALEX
[] 339 HATFIELD, FRED
[] 131 HENRICH, BOB
[] 294 JEFFCOAT, HAL
[] 3 KELLNER, ALEX

[] 242 KLIPPSTEIN, JOHNNY
[] 374 LAWRENCE, BROOKS
[] 261 LOWN, TURK
[] 121 MIKSIS, EDDIE
[] 126 PALYS, STAN dnp
[] 311 PURKEY, BOB
[] 376 RABE, CHARLEY
[] 214 SCHMIDT, WILLARD
[] 34 THURMAN, BOB
[] 466 WHISENANT, PETE
[] 237 WIGHT, BILL

1959
(all topps)

[] 201 ACKER, TOM
[] 210 BAILEY, ED
[] 120 COLES, CHUCK dnp
[] 288 DOTTERER, DUTCH
[] 431 DOUGLAS, WHAMMY dnp

[] 158 DROPO, WALT
[] 81 JEFFCOAT, HAL
[] 208 JONES, WILLIE
[] 232 KASKO, EDDIE
[] 67 LAWRENCE, BROOKS

[] 356 MABE, BOB
[] 58 MIKSIS, EDDIE dnp
[] 136 O'TOOLE, JIM
[] 494 PAVLETICH, DON
[] 271 PENA, ORLANDO
[] 174 PENDLETON, JIM

[] 489 POWERS, JOHN
[] 506 PURKEY, BOB
[] 179 RUDOLPH, DON
[] 171 SCHMIDT, WILLARD
[] 541 THURMAN, BOB
[] 14 WHISENANT, PETE

Cleveland Indians

1949
(all bowman)

[] 150 CLARK, ALLIE
[] 198 GROMEK, STEVE
[] 182 PECK, HAL

[] 166 TRESH, MIKE
[] 78 ZOLDAK, SAM

1950
(all bowman)

[] 233 CLARK, ALLIE
[] 131 GROMEK, STEVE

[] 181 PIERETTI, MARINO
[] 182 ZOLDAK, SAM

1951
(all bowman)

[] 155 BRISSIE, LOU
[] 9 CHAPMAN, SAM
[] 29 CLARK, ALLIE
[] 115 GROMEK, STEVE

[] 8 LEHNER, PAUL
[] 84 McCOSKY, BARNEY
[] 222 TUCKER, THURMAN

1952

[] b214 BOONE, RAY
[] b79 BRISSIE, LOU
[] t270 BRISSIE, LOU
[] t170 CHAKALES, BOB
[] t18 COMBS, MERRILL
[] t399 FRIDLEY, JIM
[] b203 GROMEK, STEVE
[] b135 HARRIS, MICKEY
[] t207 HARRIS, MICKEY
[] b58 MAJESKI, HANK
[] t112 MAJESKI, HANK

[] b239 MITCHELL, DALE
[] b223 SIMPSON, HARRY
[] b207 STRICKLAND, GEORGE
[] t197 STRICKLAND, GEORGE
[] b124 TEBBETTS, BIRDIE
[] t134 TIPTON, JOE
[] t38 WESTLAKE, WALLY
[] b138 WILKS, TED
[] t109 WILKS, TED
[] t199 ZUVERINK, GEORGE

1953

[] t233 ABER, AL
[] t2 EASTER, LUKE
[] t252 FOILES, HANK
[] t187 FRIDLEY, JIM dnp
[] b6 GINSBERG, JOE
[] t171 GLYNN, BILL
[] t84 HOOPER, BOB
[] b4 HOUTTEMAN, ART
[] tdp33 KENNEDY, BOB

[] t26 MITCHELL, DALE
[] tdp135 ROSEN, AL
[] b86 SIMPSON, HARRY
[] t150 SIMPSON, HARRY
[] bw13 TIPTON, JOE
[] t192 WESTLAKE, WALLY
[] b100 WIGHT, BILL
[] t101 WILKS, TED

1954

[] b85 DYCK, JIM
[] b212 FRIEND, OWEN dnp
[] b52 GINSBERG, JOE
[] t178 GLYNN, BILL
[] b184 GRASSO, MICKEY
[] b4 HOOPER, BOB
[] t81 HOSKINS, DAVE

[] b20 HOUTTEMAN, ART
[] t160 KRESS, RALPH
[] t199 NELSON, ROCKY
[] t159 PHILLEY, DAVE
[] b36 STRICKLAND, GEORGE
[] t92 WESTLAKE, WALLY

1955

[] t39 GLYNN, BILL dnp
[] b86 GRAY, TED
[] t133 HOSKINS, DAVE dnp
[] b144 HOUTTEMAN, ART
[] t151 KRESS, RALPH
[] b127 MAJESKI, HANK
[] b129 NARAGON, HAL

[] b96 NARLESKI, RAY
[] t160 NARLESKI, RAY
[] b198 POPE, DAVE
[] b142 REGALADO, RUDY
[] b192 STRICKLAND, GEORGE
[] t102 WESTLAKE, WALLY

1956
(all topps)

[] 132 AVILA, BOBBY
[] 230 CARRASQUEL, CHICO
[] 281 HOUTTEMAN, ART
[] 266 KUHN, KEN

[] 144 NARLESKI, RAY
[] 154 POPE, DAVE
[] 105 SMITH, AL

1957
(all topps)

[] 96 AGUIRRE, HANK
[] 195 AVILA, BOBBY

[] 230 CARRASQUEL, CHICO
[] 385 HOUTTEMAN, ART

[] 266 KUHN, KEN
[] 144 NARLESKI, RAY
[] 249 POPE, DAVE dnp
[] 238 ROBINSON, EDDIE

[] 145 SMITH, AL
[] 263 STRICKLAND, GEORGE
[] 74 VALENTINETTI, VITO
[] 226 WARD, PRESTON

1958
(all topps)

[] 276 AVILA, BOBBY
[] 456 BROWN, DICK
[] 182 CAFFIE, JOE dnp
[] 55 CARRASQUEL, CHICO
[] 469 FERRARESE, DON
[] 394 GRANT, JIM
[] 339 HATFIELD, FRED
[] 202 HELD, WOODY
[] 98 HUNTER, BILLY
[] 301 JACKSON, RANDY

[] 53 MARTIN, MORRIE
[] 208 McLISH, CAL
[] 388 MORAN, BILLY
[] 22 NARAGON, HAL
[] 439 NARLESKI, RAY
[] 133 NIXON, RUSS
[] 32 PORTER, J W
[] 243 RAINES, LARRY
[] 102 STRICKLAND, GEORGE dnp
[] 123 TOMANEK, DICK

1959
(all topps)

[] 547 BAXES, JIM
[] 327 BELL, GARY
[] 29 BOLGER, JIM
[] 177 BRIGGS, JOHN
[] 371 BRODOWSKI, DICK
[] 61 BROWN, DICK
[] 57 CICOTTE, AL
[] 123 DILLARD, DON
[] 247 FERRARESE, DON
[] 33 FITZGERALD, ED
[] 268 FRANCONA, TITO
[] 436 HAMNER, GRANNY
[] 168 HARDY, CARROLL
[] 475 HARSHMAN, JACK

[] 266 HELD, WOODY
[] 283 HEMAN, RUSS dnp
[] 394 JACKSON, RANDY
[] 208 JONES, WILLIE
[] 445 McLISH, CAL
[] 196 MORAN, BILLY
[] 376 NARAGON, HAL
[] 344 NIXON, RUSS
[] 366 ROBINSON, HUMBERTO
[] 142 STIGMAN, DICK dnp
[] 207 STRICKLAND, GEORGE
[] 501 TIEFENAUER, BOB dnp
[] 531 WEBSTER, RAY

Detroit Tigers

1949
(all bowman)

[] 180 BERRY, NEIL
[] 42 EVERS, HOOT
[] 10 GRAY, TED
[] 28 KOLLOWAY, DON
[] 107 LAKE, EDDIE

[] 56 MULLIN, PAT
[] 133 ROBINSON, AARON
[] 148 SWIFT, BOB
[] 122 VICO, GEORGE
[] 91 WAKEFIELD, DICK

1950

(all bowman)

[] 241 BERRY, NEIL
[] 177 BOROWY, HANK
[] 41 EVERS, HOOT
[] 210 GRAY, TED
[] 243 GROTH, JOHNNY
[] 42 HOUTTEMAN, ART
[] 133 KOLLOWAY, DON
[] 242 KRYHOSKI, DICK

[] 240 LAKE, EDDIE
[] 135 MULLIN, PAT
[] 212 PRIDDY, JERRY
[] 95 ROBINSON, AARON
[] 149 SWIFT, BOB
[] 134 TROUT, DIZZY
[] 150 VICO, GEORGE dnp

1951

(all bowman)

[] 213 BERRY, NEIL
[] 250 BOROWY, HANK
[] 197 CAIN, BOB
[] 23 EVERS, HOOT
[] 178 GRAY, TED
[] 249 GROTH, JOHNNY
[] 45 HOUTTEMAN, ART dnp
[] 321 JOHNSON, EARL

[] 105 KOLLOWAY, DON
[] 140 LAKE, EDDIE dnp
[] 285 LIPON, JOHNNY
[] 106 MULLIN, PAT
[] 71 PRIDDY, JERRY
[] 142 ROBINSON, AARON
[] 214 SWIFT, BOB
[] 320 WHITE, HAL

1952

[] b216 BATTS, MATT
[] t230 BATTS, MATT
[] b219 BERRY, NEIL
[] b157 DELSING, JIM
[] t235 DROPO, WALT
[] b111 EVERS, HOOT
[] t222 EVERS, HOOT
[] b29 GARVER, NED
[] t212 GARVER, NED
[] t192 GINSBERG, JOE
[] b199 GRAY, TED
[] t86 GRAY, TED
[] b67 GROTH, JOHNNY
[] t25 GROTH, JOHNNY
[] b153 HATFIELD, FRED
[] t146 HOUSE, FRANK dnp
[] t238 HOUTTEMAN, ART
[] b91 KOLLOWAY, DON
[] t104 KOLLOWAY, DON
[] t4 LENHARDT, DON

[] b163 LIPON, JOHNNY
[] t89 LIPON, JOHNNY
[] b209 LITTLEFIELD, DICK
[] t366 MADISON, DAVE
[] b13 MAPES, CLIFF
[] t103 MAPES, CLIFF
[] b183 MULLIN, PAT
[] t275 MULLIN, PAT
[] b139 PRIDDY, JERRY
[] t28 PRIDDY, JERRY
[] t296 ROLFE, RED
[] b235 SOUCHOCK, STEVE
[] t234 SOUCHOCK, STEVE
[] b147 STUART, MARLIN
[] t208 STUART, MARLIN
[] b131 SWIFT, BOB
[] t181 SWIFT, BOB
[] t244 WERTZ, VIC
[] b117 WIGHT, BILL
[] t177 WIGHT, BILL

1953

[] t233 ABER, AL
[] bw44 DELSING, JIM
[] t239 DELSING, JIM
[] b47 GARVER, NED
[] t112 GARVER, NED
[] b6 GINSBERG, JOE
[] b72 GRAY, TED
[] t52 GRAY, TED
[] bw63 GROMEK, STEVE
[] t65 HARRIST, EARL
[] b125 HATFIELD, FRED
[] t163 HATFIELD, FRED

[] t17 HITCHCOCK, BILLY
[] t165 HOEFT, BILLY
[] t194 KAZAK, EDDIE dnp
[] t277 LUND, DON
[] t99 MADISON, DAVE
[] bw4 MULLIN, PAT
[] t245 NORMAN, BILL
[] t211 PORTER, J W dnp
[] t113 PRIDDY, JERRY
[] t213 SCARBOROUGH, RAY
[] b91 SOUCHOCK, STEVE
[] b100 WIGHT, BILL

1954

[] t238 ABER, AL
[] t88 BATTS, MATT
[] b215 BUCHA, JOHNNY dnp
[] b55 DELSING, JIM
[] t111 DELSING, JIM
[] b18 EVERS, HOOT
[] b39 GARVER, NED
[] t44 GARVER, NED
[] b71 GRAY, TED
[] b199 GROMEK, STEVE
[] b119 HATFIELD, FRED

[] t190 HERBERT, RAY
[] b167 HOEFT, BILLY
[] t163 HOUSE, FRANK
[] t219 KRESS, CHUCK
[] b87 LUND, DON
[] t167 LUND, DON
[] t241 MILLER, BOB
[] b151 MULLIN, PAT dnp
[] b103 SOUCHOCK, STEVE
[] t65 SWIFT, BOB
[] t224 WEIK, DICK

1955

[] b24 ABER, AL
[] b36 BELARDI, WAYNE
[] t94 BERTOIA, RENO
[] t162 COLEMAN, JOE
[] b274 DELSING, JIM
[] b254 FLOWERS, BENNET
[] b188 GARVER, NED
[] b203 GROMEK, STEVE
[] b187 HATFIELD, FRED

[] t87 HOUSE, FRANK
[] b133 KING, CHARLES
[] b91 MARLOWE, DICK
[] b162 MAXWELL, CHARLIE
[] t9 MILLER, BOB G
[] b228 PHILLIPS, BUBBA
[] t49 PORTER, J W
[] b210 TORGESON, EARL
[] b35 TUTTLE, BILL

1956
(all topps)

[] 317 ABER, AL
[] 126 BRADY, JIM
[] 189 GARVER, NED

[] 310 GROMEK, STEVE
[] 318 HATFIELD, FRED
[] 32 HOUSE, FRANK

[] 57 MAAS, DUKE
[] 263 MILLER, BOB G
[] 207 SMALL, JIM

[] 147 TORGESON, EARL
[] 203 TUTTLE, BILL
[] 92 WILSON, BOB

1957
(all topps)

[] 141 ABER, AL
[] 390 BERTOIA, RENO
[] 325 BOLLING, FRANK
[] 297 CRIMIAN, JACK
[] 282 DITTMER, JACK
[] 248 FINIGAN, JIM
[] 77 FOYTACK, PAUL
[] 258 GROMEK, STEVE
[] 360 GROTH, JOHNNY
[] 223 HOUSE, FRANK

[] 379 LEE, DON
[] 405 MAAS, DUKE
[] 153 OLSON, KARL
[] 124 PHILLEY, DAVE
[] 307 PHILLIPS, JACK
[] 238 ROBINSON, EDDIE
[] 33 SMALL, JIM
[] 357 TORGESON, EARL
[] 72 TUTTLE, BILL
[] 19 WILSON, BOB

1958
(all topps)

[] 337 AGUIRRE, HANK
[] 232 BERTOIA, RENO
[] 95 BOLLING, FRANK
[] 188 BOLLING, MILT
[] 81 BOROS, STEVE
[] 154 BYRD, HARRY dnp
[] 382 CICOTTE, AL
[] 56 FISCHER, BILL
[] 282 FOYTACK, PAUL
[] 262 GROTH, JOHNNY
[] 309 HARRIS, GAIL
[] 83 HAZLE, BOB

[] 13 HOEFT, BILLY
[] 365 MORGAN, TOM
[] 206 SHAW, BOB
[] 319 SKIZAS, LOU
[] 46 SLEATER, LOU
[] 189 SUSCE, GEORGE
[] 389 TAYLOR, BILL
[] 57 THOMPSON, CHUCK
[] 463 VALENTINETTI, VITO
[] 107 VIRGIL, OZZIE
[] 248 WEHMEIER, HERM
[] 213 WILSON, BOB

1959
(all topps)

[] 36 AGUIRRE, HANK
[] 504 ALVAREZ, OSSIE
[] 96 BERBERET, LOU
[] 280 BOLLING, FRANK
[] 331 BOROS, STEVE dnp
[] 318 BRIDGES, ROCKY
[] 354 BURNSIDE, PETE
[] 189 CHRISLEY, NEIL
[] 256 DAVIE, JERRY
[] 233 FOYTACK, PAUL
[] 164 GROTH, JOHNNY

[] 378 HARRIS, GAIL
[] 343 HOEFT, BILLY
[] 132 LEE, DONdnp
[] 348 LEPCIO, TED
[] 545 MORGAN, TOM
[] 442 NARLESKI, RAY
[] 524 OSBORNE, LARRY
[] 384 SISLER, DAVE
[] 83 SMITH, BOB G
[] 511 SUSCE, GEORGE
[] 52 VEAL, COOT

[] 203 VIRGIL, OZZIE
[] 421 WEHMEIER, HERM

[] 24 WILSON, BOB

New York / San Francisco Giants

1948
(all bowman)

[] 9 COOPER, WALKER
[] 37 HARTUNG, CLINT

[] 42 POAT, RAY
[] 32 RIGNEY, BILL

1949
(all bowman)

[] 117 COOPER, WALKER
[] 101 GORDON, SID
[] 215 HIGBE, KIRBY
[] 223 HOFMAN, BOBBY
[] 68 JONES, SHELDON
[] 237 KENNEDY, MONTE

[] 186 KERR, BUDDY
[] 34 KOSLO, DAVE
[] 59 LOHRKE, JACK
[] 48 MARSHALL, WILLARD
[] 220 McCARTHY, JOHN dnp

1950
(all bowman)

[] 235 GILBERT, TOOKIE
[] 118 HARTUNG, CLINT
[] 208 HEARN, JIM
[] 83 JONES, SHELDON

[] 175 KENNEDY, MONTE
[] 65 KOSLO, DAVE
[] 199 KRAMER, JACK
[] 117 RIGNEY, BILL

1951
(all bowman)

[] 304 GETTELL, AL
[] 199 JONES, SHELDON
[] 163 KENNEDY, MONTE
[] 90 KOSLO, DAVE

[] 200 KRAMER, JACK
[] 235 LOHRKE, JACK
[] 269 NOBLE, RAY
[] 161 WESTRUM, WES

1952

[] b121 CORWIN, AL
[] b198 DIERING, CHUCK
[] t265 DIERING, CHUCK

[] t385 FRANKS, HERMAN
[] t61 GILBERT, TOOKIE dnp
[] t141 HARTUNG, CLINT

124

[] b49 HEARN, JIM
[] t371 HOFMAN, BOBBY
[] b119 HOWERTON, BILL
[] t167 HOWERTON, BILL
[] b215 JONES, SHELDON dnp
[] t130 JONES, SHELDON dnp
[] b213 KENNEDY, MONTE
[] t124 KENNEDY, MONTE

[] b182 KOSLO, DAVE
[] t336 KOSLO, DAVE
[] b110 LANIER, MAX
[] t101 LANIER, MAX
[] t123 RIGNEY, BILL
[] t346 SPENCER, GEORGE
[] b249 THOMPSON, HANK

1953

[] t260 CALDERONE, SAM
[] t126 CONNELLY, BILL
[] b126/149 CORWIN, AL
[] b76 HEARN, JIM
[] t38 HEARN, JIM
[] t182 HOFMAN, BOBBY

[] bw40 JANSEN, LARRY
[] t132 MORGAN, TOM dnp
[] bw3 RIGNEY, BILL
[] t115 SPENCER, GEORGE
[] t11 YVARS, SAL

1954

[] b137 CORWIN, AL
[] b18 EVERS, HOOT
[] t99 HOFMAN, BOBBY
[] b121 KATT, RAY
[] t225 LIDDLE, DON

[] b185 SPENCER, DARYL dnp
[] b128 ST CLAIRE, EBBA
[] t74 TAYLOR, BILL
[] t64 THOMPSON, HANK
[] b9 WILLIAMS, DAVE

1955

[] t144 AMALFITANO, JOE
[] b78 COAN, GIL
[] b122 CORWIN, AL
[] t71 GOMEZ, RUBEN
[] b123 GRISSOM, MARV
[] b220 HEARN, JIM
[] t17 HOFMAN, BOBBY

[] b183 KATT, RAY
[] t119 LENNON, BOB dnp
[] b146 LIDDLE, DON
[] t42 McCALL, WINDY
[] t53 TAYLOR, BILL
[] t34 TERWILLIGER, WAYNE

1956
(all topps)

[] 271 CASTLEMAN, FOSTER
[] 9 GOMEZ, RUBEN
[] 301 GRISSOM, MARV
[] 91 HARRIS, GAIL
[] 202 HEARN, JIM
[] 28 HOFMAN, BOBBY
[] 104 LENNON, BOB

[] 325 LIDDLE, DON
[] 44 McCALL, WINDY
[] 264 MONZANT, RAY
[] 247 SARNI, BILL
[] 277 SPENCER, DARYL
[] 209 SURKONT, MAX
[] 73 TERWILLIGER, WAYNE

1957

(all topps)

[] 361 BARCLAY, CURT
[] 237 CASTLEMAN, FOSTER
[] 68 CRONE, RAY
[] 273 DAVIS, JIM
[] 58 GOMEZ, RUBEN
[] 216 GRISSOM, MARV
[] 281 HARRIS, GAIL
[] 218 JABLONSKI, RAY
[] 331 KATT, RAY
[] 191 MARGONERI, JOE

[] 291 McCALL, WINDY
[] 271 O'CONNELL, DANNY
[] 123 RIDZIK, STEVE
[] 377 RODGERS, ANDRE
[] 86 SARNI, BILL dnp
[] 49 SPENCER, DARYL
[] 310 SURKONT, MAX
[] 109 THOMPSON, HANK dnp
[] 365 VIRGIL, OZZIE
[] 39 WORTHINGTON, AL

1958

(all topps)

[] 21 BARCLAY, CURT
[] 211 BURNSIDE, PETE
[] 272 CRONE, RAY
[] 413 DAVENPORT, JIM
[] 136 FINIGAN, JIM
[] 335 GOMEZ, RUBEN
[] 399 GRISSOM, MARV
[] 362 JABLONSKI, RAY
[] 183 JOLLY, DAVE dnp

[] 332 KING, JIM
[] 128 KIRKLAND, WILLIE
[] 447 MONZANT, RAY
[] 166 O'CONNELL, DANNY
[] 468 SCHMIDT, BOB
[] 437 SPEAKE, BOB
[] 68 SPENCER, DARYL
[] 86 THOMAS, VALMY
[] 427 WORTHINGTON, AL

1959

(all topps)

[] 307 BARCLAY, CURT
[] 297 BRANDT, JACKIE
[] 19 BRESSOUD, EDDIE
[] 458 JONES, GORDON
[] 484 KIRKLAND, WILLIE
[] 422 LANDRITH, HOBIE
[] 332 MONZANT, RAY dnp
[] 241 MUFFETT, BILLY

[] 87 O'CONNELL, DANNY
[] 216 RODGERS, ANDRE
[] 109 SCHMIDT, BOB
[] 141 SHIPLEY, JOE
[] 526 SPEAKE, BOB
[] 443 SPENCER, DARYL
[] 28 WORTHINGTON, AL
[] 145 ZANNI, DOM

New York Yankees

1949

(all bowman)

[] 218 KRYHOSKI, DICK
[] 181 NIARHOS, GUS

[] 3 PORTERFIELD, BOB
[] 236 SANFORD, FRED

1950
(all bowman)

[] 209 LINDELL, JOHNNY
[] 154 NIARHOS, GUS

[] 219 PORTERFIELD, BOB

1951
(all bowman)

[] 73 BYRNE, TOMMY
[] 182 FERRICK, TOM
[] 200 KRAMER, JACK

[] 97 KUZAVA, BOB
[] 280 OVERMIRE, FRANK

1952

[] t128 BOLLWEG, DON dnp
[] t9 HOGUE, BOB
[] b233 KUZAVA, BOB
[] t206 OSTROWSKI, JOE
[] t155 OVERMIRE, FRANK dnp
[] b140 SCARBOROUGH, RAY
[] t43 SCARBOROUGH, RAY

[] b224 SCHMITZ, JOHNNY
[] b230 SHEA, FRANK dnp
[] t248 SHEA, FRANK dnp
[] b197 SILVERA, CHARLIE
[] b210 WILSON, AL
[] t327 WILSON, AL

1953

[] b136 BRIDEWESER, JIM
[] bw61 GORMAN, TOM
[] bw33 KUZAVA, BOB
[] bw54 MILLER, BILL
[] t100 MILLER, BILL
[] t278 MIRANDA, WILLIE

[] bw45 NOREN, IRV
[] t35 NOREN, IRV
[] tdp141 REYNOLDS, ALLIE
[] t213 SCARBOROUGH, RAY
[] t167 SCHULT, ART
[] t264 WOODLING, GENE

1954

[] b49 BYRD, HARRY
[] b17 GORMAN, TOM
[] t56 MIRANDA, WILLIE

[] b193 ROBINSON, EDDIE
[] t62 ROBINSON, EDDIE
[] b209 WOODLING, GENE

1955

[] b86 GRAY, TED
[] t139 KRALY, STEVE dnp
[] t99 LEJA, FRANK

[] b100 MORGAN, TOM
[] b153 ROBINSON, EDDIE
[] t188 SILVERA, CHARLIE

1956

[] t302 ROBINSON, EDDIE

1957
(all topps)

[] 164 CARROLL, TOMMY dnp
[] 94 DEL GRECO, BOBBY
[] 36 GRIM, BOB

[] 306 JOHNSON, DARRELL
[] 225 SIMPSON, HARRY

1958
(all topps)

[] 349 DICKSON, MURRY
[] 61 JOHNSON, DARRELL
[] 87 KUCKS, JOHNNY

[] 193 LUMPE, JERRY
[] 228 MAAS, DUKE
[] 299 SIMPSON, HARRY

1959
(all topps)

[] 539 BLAYLOCK, GARY
[] 532 FREEMAN, MARK
[] 272 LUMPE, JERRY
[] 167 MAAS, DUKE

[] 259 PISONI, JIM
[] 308 SIEBERN, NORM
[] 471 STURDIVANT, TOM

Philadelphia / Kansas City Athletics

1948
(all bowman)

[] 15 JOOST, EDDIE
[] 31 McCAHAN, BILL

[] 25 McCOSKY, BARNEY
[] 10 ROSAR, BUDDY

1949
(all bowman)

[] 41 BRISSIE, LOU
[] 171 FOWLER, DICK
[] 155 GUERRA, MIKE

[] 55 JOOST, EDDIE
[] 222 KELLNER, ALEX
[] 127 MAJESKI, HANK

[] 187 MARCHILDON, PHIL
[] 80 McCAHAN, BILL
[] 203 McCOSKY, BARNEY dnp
[] 138 ROSAR, BUDDY

[] 25 SCHEIB, CARL
[] 66 VALO, ELMER
[] 96 WRIGHT, TAFT

1950
(all bowman)

[] 48 BRISSIE, LOU
[] 104 CHAPMAN, SAM
[] 105 DILLINGER, BOB
[] 214 FOWLER, DICK
[] 157 GUERRA, MIKE
[] 103 JOOST, EDDIE

[] 14 KELLNER, ALEX
[] 158 LEHNER, PAUL
[] 213 SCHEIB, CARL
[] 140 SUDER, PETE
[] 159 TIPTON, JOE
[] 49 VALO, ELMER

1951
(all bowman)

[] 298 ASTROTH, JOE
[] 155 BRISSIE, LOU
[] 9 CHAPMAN, SAM
[] 29 CLARK, ALLIE
[] 226 DYKES, JIMMY
[] 191 HITCHCOCK, BILLY
[] 33 HOOPER, BOB
[] 119 JOOST, EDDIE
[] 57 KELLNER, ALEX

[] 8 LEHNER, PAUL
[] 12 MAJESKI, HANK
[] 84 McCOSKY, BARNEY
[] 297 PHILLEY, DAVE
[] 83 SCHEIB, CARL
[] 82 TIPTON, JOE
[] 192 WYSE, HANK
[] 114 ZOLDAK, SAM

1952

[] b170 ASTROTH, JOE
[] t290 ASTROTH, JOE
[] b130 CLARK, ALLIE
[] t278 CLARK, ALLIE
[] b190 FOWLER, DICK
[] t210 FOWLER, DICK
[] b89 HITCHCOCK, BILLY
[] t182 HITCHCOCK, BILLY
[] b10 HOOPER, BOB
[] b26 JOOST, EDDIE
[] t45 JOOST, EDDIE
[] b242 KELL, EVERETT
[] b226 KELLNER, ALEX
[] t201 KELLNER, ALEX
[] b58 MAJESKI, HANK

[] t112 MAJESKI, HANK
[] t131 MARTIN, MORRIE
[] b36 MICHAELS, CASS
[] t178 MICHAELS, CASS
[] b118 MURRAY, RAY
[] t226 PHILLEY, DAVE
[] t245 ROBERTSON, SHERRY
[] b46 SCHEIB, CARL
[] b179 SUDER, PETE
[] t256 SUDER, PETE
[] t134 TIPTON, JOE
[] b206 VALO, ELMER
[] t34 VALO, ELMER
[] t41 WELLMAN, BOB dnp
[] t231 ZOLDAK, SAM

1953

[] b82 ASTROTH, JOE
[] t103 ASTROTH, JOE
[] bw43 BEVAN, HAL dnp
[] t186 BISHOP, CHARLIE
[] b38 BYRD, HARRY
[] t131 BYRD, HARRY
[] b155 CLARK, ALLIE
[] t279 COLEMAN, JOE
[] t199 FRICANO, MARION
[] b105 JOOST, EDDIE
[] b107 KELLNER, ALEX
[] t97 KOLLOWAY, DON
[] bw53 MARTIN, MORRIE
[] t227 MARTIN, MORRIE
[] t195 McGHEE, ED

[] b130 MICHAELS, CASS
[] bw6 MURRAY, RAY
[] t234 MURRAY, RAY
[] tdp15 NEWSOM, BOBO
[] t64 PHILLEY, DAVE
[] bw20 ROBINSON, EDDIE
[] t73 ROBINSON, EDDIE
[] b150 SCHEIB, CARL
[] t57 SCHEIB, CARL
[] bw8 SUDER, PETE
[] bw62 THOMAS, KEITH
[] t129 THOMAS, KEITH
[] t122 VALO, ELMER
[] t42 ZERNIAL, GUS

1954

[] b131 ASTROTH, JOE
[] b115 BOLLWEG, DON
[] t61 CAIN, BOB dnp
[] b147 DeMAESTRI, JOE
[] b3 FRICANO, MARION
[] t124 FRICANO, MARION
[] t233 GALAN, AUGIE
[] t143 HEMSLEY, ROLLIE
[] t129 JACOBS, FORREST
[] b35 JOOST, EDDIE
[] b51 KELLNER, ALEX

[] t232 LIMMER, LOU
[] t214 PORTOCARRERO, ARNIE
[] t112 RENNA, BILL
[] t149 ROBERTSON, AL
[] b67 SCHEIB, CARL
[] t118 SCHEIB, CARL
[] b99 SUDER, PETE
[] t148 TRICE, BOB
[] t145 VALO, ELMER
[] t244 WHEAT, LEROY
[] t222 WILSON, BILL

1955

[] b119 ASTROTH, JOE
[] t96 BISHOP, CHARLIE
[] b54 BOLLWEG, DON
[] b149 BOYER, CLOYD
[] b120 BURTSCHY, ED
[] b176 DeMAESTRI, JOE
[] b90 DITMAR, ART
[] b211 DIXON, SONNY
[] t14 FINIGAN, JIM
[] b316 FRICANO, MARION
[] t101 GRAY, JOHNNY
[] t138 HERBERT, RAY
[] t61 JACOBS, FORREST
[] b55 KELLNER, ALEX

[] b14 KERIAZAKOS, GUS
[] b80 LIMMER, LOU dnp
[] t54 LIMMER, LOU dnp
[] b294 MOSES, WALLY dnp
[] t77 PORTOCARRERO, ARNIE
[] b185 RASCHI, VIC
[] t121 RENNA, BILL
[] t177 ROBERTSON, AL
[] b175 SHANTZ, WILMER
[] b6 SUDER, PETE
[] t132 TRICE, BOB
[] t145 VALO, ELMER
[] t86 WILSON, BILL

1956
(all topps)

[] 106 ASTROTH, JOE
[] 319 CRIMIAN, JACK
[] 161 DeMAESTRI, JOE
[] 22 FINIGAN, JIM
[] 246 GORMAN, TOM
[] 279 GROTH, JOHNNY
[] 176 KELLNER, ALEX

[] 339 PLESS, RANCE
[] 53 PORTOCARRERO, ARNIE
[] 82 RENNA, BILL
[] 302 ROBINSON, EDDIE
[] 59 SANTIAGO, JOSE
[] 239 SIMPSON, HARRY

1957
(all topps)

[] 141 ABER, AL
[] 13 BURNETTE, WALLY
[] 354 COLEMAN, RIP
[] 44 DeMAESTRI, JOE
[] 285 GARVER, NED
[] 87 GORMAN, TOM
[] 369 GRAFF, MILT
[] 360 GROTH, JOHNNY
[] 207 HUNTER, BILLY
[] 280 KELLNER, ALEX

[] 139 KRETLOW, LOU dnp
[] 318 McDERMONT, MICKEY
[] 239 MORGAN, TOM
[] 298 NOREN, IRV
[] 402 PISONI, JIM
[] 225 SIMPSON, HARRY
[] 83 SKIZAS, LOU
[] 41 SMITH, HAL W
[] 142 THOMPSON, CHUCK

1958
(all topps)

[] 302 BAXES, MIKE
[] 139 BRUNET, GEORGE dnp
[] 69 BURNETTE, WALLY
[] 55 CARRASQUEL, CHICO
[] 119 CHITI, HARRY
[] 222 DALEY, BUD
[] 62 DeMAESTRI, JOE
[] 349 DICKSON, MURRY
[] 292 GARVER, NED
[] 235 GORMAN, TOM
[] 192 GRAFF, MILT
[] 202 HELD, WOODY

[] 379 HERBERT, RAY
[] 318 HOUSE, FRANK
[] 98 HUNTER, BILLY
[] 3 KELLNER, ALEX
[] 228 MAAS, DUKE
[] 39 MARTYN, BOB
[] 391 MELTON, DAVE
[] 299 SIMPSON, HARRY
[] 257 SMITH, HAL W
[] 123 TOMANEK, DICK
[] 23 TUTTLE, BILL
[] 367 URBAN, JACK

1959
(all topps)

[] 381 BAXES, MIKE dnp
[] 254 BELLA, ZEKE
[] 513 CARROLL, TOMMY
[] 79 CHITI, HARRY

[] 51 COLEMAN, RIP
[] 281 CRADDOCK, WALT dnp
[] 263 DALEY, BUD
[] 532 FREEMAN, MARK

131

[] 245 GARVER, NED
[] 449 GORMAN, TOM
[] 182 GRAFF, MILT dnp
[] 127 HADLEY, KENT
[] 154 HERBERT, RAY
[] 313 HOUSE, FRANK
[] 342 JABLONSKI, RAY
[] 272 LUMPE, JERRY
[] 41 MARTYN, BOB

[] 482 MEYER, RUSS
[] 140 SECREST, CHARLIE dnp
[] 333 SIMPSON, HARRY
[] 227 SMITH, HAL W
[] 471 STURDIVANT, TOM
[] 496 TERWILLIGER, WAYNE
[] 369 TOMANEK, DICK
[] 459 TUTTLE, BILL
[] 176 WARD, PRESTON

Philadelphia Phillies

1949
(all bowman)

[] 123 BLATNICK, JOHNNY
[] 134 BOROWY, HANK
[] 145 DONNELLY, BLIX
[] 108 HEINTZELMAN, KEN

[] 228 MAYO, JACKIE
[] 161 THOMPSON, JOHN
[] 193 TRINKLE, KEN

1950
(all bowman)

[] 177 BOROWY, HANK
[] 176 DONNELLY, BLIX
[] 205 GOLIAT, MIKE

[] 85 HEINTZELMAN, KEN
[] 120 THOMPSON, JOHN

1951
(all bowman)

[] 185 BLOODWORTH, JIMMY
[] 255 CANDINI, MILO
[] 149 CHURCH, BUBBA
[] 77 GOLIAT, MIKE
[] 148 HAMNER, GRANNY
[] 147 HEINTZELMAN, KEN
[] 293 JOHNSON, KEN
[] 112 JONES, WILLIE

[] 220 MILLER, BOB
[] 113 NICHOLSON, BILL
[] 292 PELLAGRINI, EDDIE
[] 51 SEMINICK, ANDY
[] 294 THOMPSON, JOHN
[] 28 WAITKUS, EDDIE
[] 221 WHITMAN, DICK

1952

[] b40 CHURCH, BUBBA
[] t323 CHURCH, BUBBA
[] t44 DEMPSEY, CON dnp
[] b125 FOX, HOWIE

[] t209 FOX, HOWIE
[] b35 HAMNER, GRANNY
[] t221 HAMNER, GRANNY
[] t74 HANSEN, ANDY

[] b148 HEINTZELMAN, KEN
[] t213 JONES, NIPPY
[] b20 JONES, WILLIE
[] b251 LOHRKE, JACK
[] b220 MEYER, RUSS
[] t187 MILLER, BOB
[] b164 RYAN, CONNIE

[] t107 RYAN, CONNIE
[] b200 SILVESTRI, KEN dnp
[] t158 WAITKUS, EDDIE
[] b225 WILBER, DEL
[] t383 WILBER, DEL
[] b42 WYROSTEK, JOHNNY
[] t 13 WYROSTEK, JOHNNY

1953

[] b67 CLARK, MEL
[] b113 DREWS, KARL
[] t59 DREWS, KARL
[] b158 FOX, HOWIE
[] t22 FOX, HOWIE
[] t140 GLAVIANO, TOMMY
[] b60 HAMNER, GRANNY
[] t146 HAMNER, GRANNY
[] t136 HEINTZELMAN, KEN dnp
[] b133 JONES, WILLIE

[] t88 JONES, WILLIE
[] t230 LINDELL, JOHNNY
[] bw47 LOHRKE, JACK
[] bw14 NICHOLSON, BILL
[] bw48 RIDZIK, STEVE
[] b131 RYAN, CONNIE
[] t102 RYAN, CONNIE
[] bw35 WYROSTEK, JOHNNY
[] t79 WYROSTEK, JOHNNY

1954

[] b175 CLARK, MEL
[] b111 DICKSON, MURRY
[] b191 DREWS, KARL
[] b47 HAMNER, GRANNY
[] t24 HAMNER, GRANNY
[] t196 JOK, STAN
[] b143 JONES, WILLIE
[] t41 JONES, WILLIE
[] t78 KAZANSKI, TED
[] t108 KIPPER, THORNTON
[] b159 LINDELL, JOHNNY

[] t51 LINDELL, JOHNNY
[] b207 LOPATA, STAN
[] t247 MAYO, ED
[] t212 MICELOTTA, BOB
[] t127 O'NEILL, STEVE
[] t236 PENSON, PAUL
[] t174 QUALTERS, TOM
[] b223 RIDZIK, STEVE
[] t104 SANDLOCK, MIKE
[] b63 TORGESON, EARL

1955

[] b292 BLAYLOCK, MARV
[] t167 CASAGRANDE, TOM dnp
[] b41 CLARK, MEL
[] b236 DICKSON, MURRY
[] b49 GREENGRASS, JIM
[] b42 GREENWOOD, BOB
[] b172 JONES, WILLIE
[] t46 KAZANSKI, TED
[] t62 KIPPER, THORNTON
[] b215 KUZAVA, BOB
[] b18 LOPATA, STAN
[] b110 MILLER, BOB
[] t157 MILLER, BOB

[] b81 MORGAN, BOBBY
[] b287 MROZINSKI, RON
[] t114 ORTIZ, LOUIS dnp
[] t202 OWENS, JIM
[] t33 QUALTERS, TOM
[] b111 RIDZIK, STEVE
[] t79 SCHELL, DANNY
[] b93 SEMINICK, ANDY
[] b252 SMALLEY, ROY
[] t130 SMITH, MAYO
[] t29 WEHMEIER, HERM
[] b237 WYROSTEK, JOHNNY dnp

1956
(all topps)

[] 274 BAUMHOLTZ, FRANK
[] 211 DICKSON, MURRY
[] 174 GORBOUS, GLEN
[] 275 GREENGRASS, JIM
[] 197 HAMNER, GRANNY
[] 269 MEYER, JACK

[] 337 MORGAN, BOBBY
[] 7 NEGRAY, RON
[] 296 SEMINICK, ANDY
[] 60 SMITH, MAYO
[] 78 WEHMEIER, HERM
[] 81 WESTLAKE, WALLY

1957
(all topps)

[] 404 ANDERSON, HARRY
[] 224 BLAYLOCK, MARV
[] 314 BOUCHEE, ED
[] 332 BOWMAN, BOB
[] 91 BURK, MACK
[] 374 CARDWELL, DON
[] 305 FERNANDEZ, CHICO
[] 370 HACKER, WARREN
[] 265 HADDIX, HARVEY
[] 335 HAMNER, GRANNY
[] 299 HARMON, CHUCK
[] 348 HEARN, JIM

[] 231 HEMUS, SOLLY
[] 174 JONES, WILLIE
[] 27 KAZANSKI, TED
[] 241 LONNETT, JOE
[] 119 LOPATA, STAN
[] 162 MEYER, JACK
[] 46 MILLER, BOB
[] 254 NEGRAY, RON dnp
[] 31 NORTHY, RON
[] 245 REPULSKI, RIP
[] 129 ROGOVIN, SAUL
[] 397 SMALLEY, ROY

1958
(all topps)

[] 404 ANDERSON, HARRY
[] 415 BOWMAN, BOB
[] 278 BURK, MACK
[] 372 CARDWELL, DON
[] 460 ESSEGIAN, CHUCK
[] 76 FARRELL, DICK
[] 348 FERNANDEZ, CHICO
[] 251 HACKER, WARREN
[] 268 HAMNER, GRANNY
[] 48 HARMON, CHUCK dnp
[] 298 HEARN, JIM
[] 207 HEMUS, SOLLY

[] 181 JONES, WILLIE
[] 36 KAZANSKI, TED
[] 291 LANDRUM, DON dnp
[] 64 LONNETT, JOE
[] 353 LOPATA, STAN
[] 186 MEYER, JACK
[] 326 MILLER, BOB
[] 116 PHILLEY, DAVE
[] 453 QUALTERS, TOM
[] 14 REPULSKI, RIP
[] 234 SAWATSKI, CARL
[] 474 SEMPROCH, ROMAN

1959
(all topps)

[] 85 ANDERSON, HARRY

[] 29 BOLGER, JIM

[] 39 BOUCHEE, ED
[] 221 BOWMAN, BOB
[] 314 CARDWELL, DON
[] 121 CONLEY, BOB dnp
[] 406 DRAKE, SOLLY
[] 452 FERNANDEZ, CHICO
[] 472 FREESE, GENE
[] 535 GOMEZ, RUBEN
[] 436 HAMNER, GRANNY
[] 63 HEARN, JIM
[] 129 HERRERA, FRANK dnp
[] 208 JONES, WILLIE
[] 99 KAZANSKI, TED dnp

[] 517 KOPPE, JOE
[] 31 LEHMAN, KEN dnp
[] 269 MEYER, JACK
[] 253 MOREHEAD, SETH
[] 503 OWENS, JIM
[] 92 PHILLEY, DAVE
[] 113 PHILLIPS, TAYLOR
[] 366 ROBINSON, HUMBERTO
[] 56 SAWATSKI, CARL
[] 546 SCHROLL, AL
[] 197 SEMPROCH, ROMAN
[] 235 THOMAS, VALMY

Pittsburgh Pirates

1949
(all bowman)

[] 195 BOCKMAN, EDDIE
[] 77 BONHAM, ERNIE
[] 13 CHESNES, BOB
[] 8 DICKSON, MURRY
[] 109 FITZGERALD, ED
[] 192 GUMBERT, HARRY
[] 215 HIGBE, KIRBY
[] 207 HOPP, JOHNNY

[] 153 MASI, PHIL
[] 163 McCULLOUGH, CLYDE
[] 227 OSTERMUELLER, FRITZ dnp
[] 135 ROJEK, STAN
[] 234 SEWELL, RIP
[] 147 SINGLETON, BERT dnp
[] 45 WESTLAKE, WALLY

1950
(all bowman)

[] 177 BOROWY, HANK
[] 201 CASTIGLIONE, PETE
[] 202 CHAMBERS, CLIFF
[] 70 CHESNES, BOB
[] 244 COOGAN, DALE
[] 34 DICKSON, MURRY
[] 105 DILLINGER, BOB
[] 178 FITZGERALD, ED

[] 171 GUMBERT, HARRY
[] 122 HOPP, JOHNNY
[] 124 McCULLOUGH, CLYDE
[] 123 RESTELLI, DINO dnp
[] 86 ROJEK, STAN
[] 87 WERLE, BILL
[] 69 WESTLAKE, WALLY

1951
(all bowman)

[] 308 BEARD, TED
[] 17 CASTIGLIONE, PETE
[] 131 CHAMBERS, CLIFF
[] 167 DICKSON, MURRY
[] 63 DILLINGER, BOB

[] 310 DUSAK, ERV
[] 229 HOWERTON, BILL
[] 204 LOMBARDI, VIC dnp
[] 239 MacDONALD, BILL dnp
[] 94 McCULLOUGH, CLYDE

[] 272 MEYER, BILLY
[] 93 O'CONNELL, DANNY dnp
[] 309 QUEEN, MEL
[] 166 ROJEK, STAN

[] 130 SAFFELL, TOM
[] 64 WERLE, BILL
[] 193 WILKS, TED

1952

[] t12 BASGALL, MONTE dnp
[] t150 BEARD, TED
[] b47 CASTIGLIONE, PETE
[] t260 CASTIGLIONE, PETE
[] t87 COOGAN, DALE
[] b59 DICKSON, MURRY
[] t266 DICKSON, MURRY
[] t183 DUSAK, ERV
[] b180 FITZGERALD, ED
[] t236 FITZGERALD, ED
[] b119 HOWERTON, BILL
[] t167 HOWERTON, BILL
[] t380 KOSHOREK, CLEM
[] t166 LaPALME, PAUL
[] t138 MacDONALD, BILL dnp
[] t379 MAIN, FORREST
[] b99 McCULLOUGH, CLYDE
[] t218 McCULLOUGH, CLYDE

[] t375 MERSON, JOHN
[] b108 METKOVICH, GEORGE
[] b155 MEYER, BILLY
[] t387 MEYER, BILLY
[] t154 MUIR, JOE
[] b243 MUNGER, GEORGE
[] t115 MUNGER, GEORGE
[] t240 PHILLIPS, JACK
[] b83 POLLET, HOWIE
[] t63 POLLET, HOWIE
[] t361 POSEDEL, BILL
[] b171 QUEEN, MEL
[] b207 STRICKLAND, GEORGE
[] t197 STRICKLAND, GEORGE
[] b248 WERLE, BILL
[] t73 WERLE, BILL
[] b138 WILKS, TED
[] t109 WILKS, TED

1953

[] t98 ABRAMS, CAL
[] b94 ADDIS, BOB
[] t157 ADDIS, BOB
[] b112 ATWELL, TOBY
[] t23 ATWELL, TOBY
[] t71 BARTIROME, TONY dnp
[] t243 BERNIER, CARLOS
[] t48 DEL GRECO, BOBBY dnp
[] tdp246 FACE, ROY
[] t235 HETKI, JOHN
[] t238 HOGUE, CAL
[] t222 JANOWICZ, VIC
[] t175 KLINE, RON
[] b147 KOSHOREK, CLEM
[] t8 KOSHOREK, CLEM

[] bw19 LaPALME, PAUL
[] t201 LaPALME, PAUL
[] t230 LINDELL, JOHNNY
[] t198 MAIN, FORREST
[] t58 METKOVICH, GEORGE
[] t249 O'BRIEN, EDDIE
[] t223 O'BRIEN, JOHNNY
[] t28 PELLAGRINI, EDDIE
[] t83 POLLET, HOWIE
[] t93 RICE, HAL
[] t74 ROSSI, JOE dnp
[] t247 SANDLOCK, MIKE
[] t144 SCHULTZ, BOB
[] t173 WARD, PRESTON
[] t178 WAUGH, JIM

1954

[] t179 ALLIE, GAIR
[] b123 ATWELL, TOBY
[] b171 BERNIER, CARLOS dnp
[] b27 COLE, DICK
[] t84 COLE, DICK
[] t213 FITZPATRICK, JOHN
[] b11 GORDON, SID
[] t75 HANEY, FRED
[] t228 HERMANSKI, GENE dnp
[] t161 HETKI, JOHN
[] t134 HOGUE, CAL

[] b107 LaPALME, PAUL
[] b213 LITTLEFIELD, DICK
[] t234 LYNCH, JERRY
[] b219 RICE, HAL
[] t95 RICE, HAL
[] t242 ROBERTS, CURT
[] b59 SCHULTZ, BOB dnp
[] t11 SMITH, PAUL LESLIE dnp
[] b75 SURKONT, MAX
[] b139 WARD, PRESTON
[] t72 WARD, PRESTON

1955

[] t55 ALLIE, GAIR dnp
[] b164 ATWELL, TOBY
[] b115 BOWMAN, ROGER
[] b28 COLE, DICK
[] b84 FREESE, GEORGE
[] b113 HALL, BOB
[] t126 HALL, DICK
[] t112 KING, NELSON
[] b200 LITTLEFIELD, DICK
[] t147 PEPPER, HUGH

[] t118 PURKEY, BOB
[] t107 ROBERTS, CURT
[] t73 SHEPARD, JACK
[] b288 SMITH, DICK
[] b83 SURKONT, MAX
[] t12 THIES, JAKE
[] b82 WALLS, LEE dnp
[] b27 WARD, PRESTON
[] t95 WARD, PRESTON

1956
(all topps)

[] 64 ARROYO, LUIS
[] 232 ATWELL, TOBY
[] 46 FREESE, GENE
[] 331 HALL, DICK
[] 94 KLINE, RON
[] 129 MARTIN, JAKE dnp
[] 116 O'BRIEN, EDDIE

[] 108 PEPPER, HUGH
[] 262 POLLET, HOWIE
[] 306 ROBERTS, CURT
[] 209 SURKONT, MAX
[] 204 SWANSON, ART
[] 328 WARD, PRESTON

1957
(all topps)

[] 104 FOILES, HANK
[] 42 FONDY, DEE
[] 308 HALL, DICK
[] 349 KING, NELSON
[] 256 KLINE, RON
[] 267 KRAVITZ, DANNY

[] 362 MEJIAS, ROMAN
[] 259 O'BRIEN, EDDIE
[] 327 PENDLETON, JIM
[] 368 PURKEY, BOB
[] 345 SMITH, PAUL LESLIE
[] 52 WALLS, LEE

1958

(all topps)

[] 358 BAKER, GENE
[] 459 BLACKBURN, RON
[] 392 DANIELS, BENNIE
[] 306 DOUGLAS, WHAMMY dnp
[] 4 FOILES, HANK
[] 293 FREESE, GENE
[] 172 GROSS, DON
[] 82 KLINE, RON
[] 444 KRAVITZ, DANNY

[] 452 MEJIAS, ROMAN
[] 104 PENDLETON, JIM
[] 344 PORTERFIELD, BOB
[] 432 POWERS, JOHN
[] 151 PRITCHARD, BUDDY dnp
[] 218 RAND, DICK dnp
[] 226 SMITH, BOB G
[] 269 SMITH, PAUL LESLIE
[] 470 STEVENS, R C

1959

(all topps)

[] 238 BAKER, GENE dnp
[] 401 BLACKBURN, RON
[] 523 BRIGHT, HARRY
[] 428 BUC HILL ACES
[] 122 DANIELS, BENNIE
[] 294 FOILES, HANK
[] 228 GROSS, DON
[] 49 HALL, BILL dnp
[] 265 KLINE, RON

[]536 KRAVITZ, DANNY
[] 134 McDANIEL, JIM dnp
[] 218 MEJIAS, ROMAN
[] 446 NELSON, ROCKY
[] 181 PORTERFIELD, BOB
[] 305 RAYDON, CURT dnp
[] 333 SIMPSON, HARRY
[] 83 SMITH, BOB G
[] 282 STEVENS, R C

St Louis Browns / Baltimore Orioles

1949

(all bowman)

[] 139 ARFT, HANK
[] 188 DREWS, KARL
[] 120 FANNIN, CLIFF
[] 15 GARVER, NED
[] 105 KENNEDY, BILL
[] 31 KOKOS, DICK
[] 131 LEHNER, PAUL

[] 149 PARTEE, ROY dnp
[] 172 PELLAGRINI, EDDIE
[] 89 PLATT, MIZELL
[] 4 PRIDDY, JERRY
[] 204 SAVAGE, BOB
[] 102 SPENCE, STAN

1950

(all bowman)

[] 250 COLEMAN, RAY
[] 106 FANNIN, CLIFF
[] 189 FRIEND, OWEN
[] 51 GARVER, NED
[] 145 GRAHAM, JACK dnp

[] 50 KOKOS, DICK
[] 251 MOSS, LES
[] 191 STARR, DICK
[] 190 WOOD, KEN

1951

(all bowman)

[] 173 ARFT, HANK
[] 129 BATTS, MATT
[] 73 BYRNE, TOMMY
[] 136 COLEMAN, RAY
[] 279 DELSING, JIM
[] 43 DeMARS, BILLY
[] 244 FANNIN, CLIFF
[] 101 FRIEND, OWEN dnp
[] 172 GARVER, NED

[] 77 GOLIAT, MIKE
[] 68 KOKOS, DICK dnp
[] 8 LEHNER, PAUL
[] 210 MOSS, LES
[] 280 OVERMIRE, FRANK
[] 316 PILLETTE, DUANE
[] 315 TAYLOR, ZACK dnp
[] 281 WIDMAR, AL
[] 209 WOOD, KEN

1952

[] b229 ARFT, HANK
[] t284 ARFT, HANK
[] b173 BEARDEN, GENE
[] t229 BEARDEN, GENE
[] b61 BYRNE, TOMMY
[] t241 BYRNE, TOMMY
[] b19 CAIN, BOB
[] b201 COLEMAN, RAY
[] t211 COLEMAN, RAY
[] t286 DeMAESTRI, JOE
[] t285 FANNIN, CLIFF
[] t160 FRIEND, OWEN dnp
[] b29 GARVER, NED
[] t212 GARVER, NED
[] t46 GOLDSBERRY, GORDON
[] t9 HOGUE, BOB
[] t95 HOLCOMBE, KEN
[] b133 KRYHOSKI, DICK
[] t149 KRYHOSKI, DICK
[] t4 LENHARDT, DON

[] b209 LITTLEFIELD, DICK
[] t366 MADISON, DAVE
[] t58 MAHONEY, BOB
[] t8 MARSH, FRED
[] b36 MICHAELS, CASS
[] t178 MICHAELS, CASS
[] t143 MOSS, LES
[] t155 OVERMIRE, FRANK
[] t82 PILLETTE, DUANE
[] b137 ROJEK, STAN
[] t163 ROJEK, STAN
[] b245 SCHMEES, GEORGE
[] t306 SLEATER, LOU
[] b147 STUART, MARLIN
[] t208 STUART, MARLIN
[] t244 WERTZ, VIC
[] b193 YOUNG, BOBBY
[] t147 YOUNG, BOBBY
[] b113 ZARRILLA, AL
[] t70 ZARRILLA, AL

1953

[] b56 CAIN, BOB
[] t266 CAIN, BOB
[] b70 COURTNEY, CLINT
[] t127 COURTNEY, CLINT
[] b111 DYCK, JIM
[] t177 DYCK, JIM
[] t90 EDWARDS, HANK
[] t203 FANNIN, CLIFF dnp
[] t200 GOLDSBERRY, GORDON dnp
[] t36 GROTH, JOHNNY
[] t166 HUNTER, BILLY
[] t232 KOKOS, DICK

[] b50 KRETLOW, LOU
[] b127 KRYHOSKI, DICK
[] b20 LENHARDT, DON
[] b123 LIPON, JOHNNY
[] t40 LIPON, JOHNNY
[] t278 MIRANDA, WILLIE
[] t245 NORMAN, BILL
[] b59 PILLETTE, DUANE
[] t269 PILLETTE, DUANE
[] t dp67 SIEVERS, ROY
[] b120 STUART, MARLIN
[] t160 YOUNG, BOBBY

1954

[] b91 ABRAMS, CAL
[] b40 COAN, GIL
[] b69 COURTNEY, CLINT
[] t246 FOX, HOWIE
[] b5 HUNTER, BILLY
[] b37 KOKOS, DICK
[] t106 KOKOS, DICK
[] b197 KRETLOW, LOU
[] b117 KRYHOSKI, DICK
[] t150 KRYHOSKI, DICK

[] b53 LENHARDT, DON
[] b22 MELE, SAM
[] b181 MOSS, LES
[] b83 MURRAY, RAY
[] t49 MURRAY, RAY
[] t207 OLIVER, TOM
[] b133 PILLETTE, DUANE
[] t107 PILLETTE, DUANE
[] b149 YOUNG, BOBBY
[] t8 YOUNG, BOBBY

1955

[] b55 ABRAMS, CAL
[] b221 BROWN, HECTOR
[] t148 BROWN, HECTOR
[] b78 COAN, GIL
[] t162 COLEMAN, JOE
[] b121 CRAWFORD, RUFUS dnp
[] t105 DIERING, CHUCK
[] b248 DORISH, HARRY
[] t185 FERRARESE, DON
[] b86 GRAY, TED
[] t165 JOHNSON, DON
[] b108 KRETLOW, LOU
[] b215 KUZAVA, BOB
[] b127 MAJESKI, HANK
[] t13 MARSH, FRED

[] b162 MAXWELL, CHARLIE
[] b77 McDONALD, JIM
[] b245 MILLER, BILL
[] b79 MIRANDA, WILLIE
[] t154 MIRANDA, WILLIE
[] t57 O'DELL, BILLY dnp
[] b244 PILLETTE, DUANE
[] t168 PILLETTE, DUANE
[] b198 POPE, DAVE
[] b225 RICHARDS, PAUL
[] t8 SMITH, HAL W
[] t102 WESTLAKE, WALLY
[] b312 WIGHT, BILL
[] b253 WILSON, JIM
[] b92 ZUVERINK, GEORGE

1956
(all topps)

[] 287 ADAMS, BOBBY
[] 84 BIRRER, BABE
[] 265 CONSUEGRA, SANDY
[] 19 DIERING, CHUCK
[] 167 DORISH, HARRY
[] 303 DYCK, JIM
[] 266 FERRARESE, DON
[] 141 FRAZIER, JOE
[] 231 HALE, BOB
[] 26 HATTON, GRADY
[] 326 JOHNSON, CONNIE
[] 23 MARSH, FRED
[] 129 MARTIN, MORRIE

[] 103 MIRANDA, WILLIE
[] 43 MOORE, RAY
[] 169 NELSON, BOB
[] 267 NIEMAN, BOB
[] 206 PALICA, ERV
[] 222 PHILLEY, DAVE
[] 154 POPE, DAVE
[] 298 SCHMITZ, JOHNNY
[] 80 TRIANDOS, GUS
[] 286 WIGHT, BILL
[] 171 WILSON, JIM
[] 276 ZUVERINK, GEORGE

1957
(all topps)

[] 26 BOYD, BOB
[] 382 BRIDEWESER, JIM
[] 194 BROWN, HECTOR
[] 309 BUSBY, JIM
[] 146 FERRARESE, DON
[] 116 FORNIELES, MIKE
[] 184 FRANCONA, TITO
[] 17 GARDNER, BILLY
[] 236 GINSBERG, JOE
[] 406 HALE, BOB
[] 385 HOUTTEMAN, ART
[] 43 JOHNSON, CONNIE

[] 366 LEHMAN, KEN
[] 350 MIKSIS, EDDIE
[] 151 MIRANDA, WILLIE
[] 106 MOORE, RAY
[] 14 NIEMAN, BOB
[] 316 O'DELL, BILLY
[] 311 PILARCIK, AL
[] 276 PYBURN, JIM
[] 238 ROBINSON, EDDIE
[] 340 WIGHT, BILL
[] 11 ZUVERINK, GEORGE

1958
(all topps)

[] 279 BOYD, BOB
[] 381 BROWN, HECTOR
[] 28 BUSBY, JIM
[] 416 CASTLEMAN, FOSTER
[] 191 CECCARELLI, ART dnp
[] 96 DURHAM, JOE dnp
[] 105 GARDNER, BILLY
[] 67 GINSBERG, JOE
[] 471 GREEN, LENNY
[] 336 HAMRIC, BERT
[] 217 HARSHMAN, JACK
[] 266 JOHNSON, CONNIE

[] 141 LEHMAN, KEN
[] 121 MIKSIS, EDDIE
[] 179 MIRANDA, WILLIE
[] 165 NIEMAN, BOB
[] 84 O'DELL, BILLY
[] 259 PILARCIK, AL
[] 465 PORTOCARRERO, ARNIE
[] 46 SLEATER, LOU
[] 451 TAYLOR, JOE
[] 113 WALKER, JERRY
[] 229 ZUPO, FRANK
[] 6 ZUVERINK, GEORGE

1959
(all topps)

[] 363 AVILA, BOBBY
[] 192 BEAMON, CHARLIE dnp
[] 82 BOYD, BOB
[] 487 BROWN, HECTOR
[] 264 CARRASQUEL, CHICO
[] 51 COLEMAN, RIP
[] 158 DROPO, WALT
[] 47 FINIGAN, JIM
[] 89 GARDNER, BILLY
[] 66 GINSBERG, JOE
[] 209 GREEN, LENNY
[] 507 HALE, BOB
[] 475 HARSHMAN, JACK

[] 343 HOEFT, BILLY
[] 21 JOHNSON, CONNIE
[] 279 JOHNSON, ERNIE
[] 299 KLAUS, BILLY
[] 540 MIRANDA, WILLIE
[] 375 NIEMAN, BOB
[] 250 O'DELL, BILLY
[] 7 PILARCIK, AL
[] 98 PORTOCARRERO, ARNIE
[] 143 TASBY, WILLIE
[] 144 WALKER, JERRY
[] 219 ZUVERINK, GEORGE

St Louis Cardinals

1949
(all bowman)

[] 126 BRAZLE, AL
[] 190 HEARN, JIM
[] 40 MUNGER, GEORGE

[] 79 NORTHY, RON
[] 95 POLLET, HOWIE
[] 137 WILKS, TED

1950
(all bowman)

[] 126 BRAZLE, AL
[] 179 DIERING, CHUCK
[] 239 HOWERTON, BILL
[] 238 JONES, NIPPY
[] 207 LANIER, MAX

[] 209 LINDELL, JOHNNY
[] 89 MUNGER, GEORGE
[] 245 PAPAI, AL
[] 72 POLLET, HOWIE
[] 125 RICE, DEL

1951
(all bowman)

[] 265 BILKO, STEVE
[] 157 BRAZLE, AL
[] 131 CHAMBERS, CLIFF
[] 158 DIERING, CHUCK
[] 310 DUSAK, ERV
[] 301 GLAVIANO, TOMMY
[] 229 HOWERTON, BILL
[] 85 KAZAK, EDDIE
[] 230 LANIER, MAX

[] 194 LOWREY, PEANUTS
[] 11 MUNGER, GEORGE
[] 300 RICE, HAL
[] 264 RICHMOND, DON
[] 166 ROJEK, STAN
[] 121 STALEY, GERRY
[] 137 STARR, DICK
[] 193 WILKS, TED

1952

[] t287 BILKO, STEVE
[] b134 BRAZLE, AL
[] t228 BRAZLE, AL
[] t19 BUCHA, JOHNNY dnp
[] b14 CHAMBERS, CLIFF
[] t68 CHAMBERS, CLIFF
[] t56 GLAVIANO, TOMMY
[] b212 HEMUS, SOLLY
[] b122 JOHNSON, BILLY
[] t83 JOHNSON, BILLY
[] t165 KAZAK, EDDIE
[] t102 KENNEDY, BILL dnp
[] b102 LOWREY, PEANUTS
[] b243 MUNGER, GEORGE

[] t115 MUNGER, GEORGE
[] b62 PRESKO, JOE
[] t220 PRESKO, JOE
[] b107 RICE, DEL
[] t100 RICE, DEL
[] t398 RICE, HAL
[] b127 SISLER, DICK
[] b50 STALEY, GERRY
[] t79 STALEY, GERRY
[] b6 STALLCUP, VIRGIL
[] t69 STALLCUP, VIRGIL
[] b248 WERLE, BILL
[] t73 WERLE, BILL
[] t38 WESTLAKE, WALLY

1953

[] t205 BENSON, VERN
[] t204 BOKELMAN, DICK
[] b115 BOYER, CLOYD dnp
[] t60 BOYER, CLOYD dnp
[] b140 BRAZLE, AL
[] t193 CLARK, MIKE
[] t226 ERAUTT, ED
[] t218 FUSSELMAN, LES
[] b85 HEMUS, SOLLY
[] t231 HEMUS, SOLLY
[] t189 JABLONSKI, RAY
[] t21 JOHNSON, BILLY
[] t16 LOWREY, PEANUTS
[] b142 MIGGINS, LARRY dnp

[] t128 MIZELL, WILMER
[] t172 REPULSKI, RIP
[] b53 RICE, DEL
[] t68 RICE, DEL
[] t93 RICE, HAL
[] t274 RIDDLE, JOHN
[] t168 SCHMIDT, WILLARD
[] bw1 SISLER, DICK
[] b17 STALEY, GERRY
[] t56 STALEY, GERRY
[] t180 STALLCUP, VIRGIL
[] t70 YUHAS, ED
[] t11 YVARS, SAL

1954

[] b206 BILKO, STEVE
[] t116 BILKO, STEVE
[] b142 BRAZLE, AL
[] b174 CASTIGLIONE, PETE
[] b126 CHAMBERS, CLIFF dnp
[] t192 DEAL, ELLIS
[] t151 GRAMMAS, ALEX
[] b94 HEMUS, SOLLY
[] t117 HEMUS, SOLLY
[] t26 JABLONSKI, RAY
[] t158 LOWREY, PEANUTS
[] b222 LUNA, MEMO

[] t142 POHOLSKY, TOM
[] b190 PRESKO, JOE
[] t135 PRESKO, JOE
[] b46 REPULSKI, RIP
[] t115 REPULSKI, RIP
[] b30 RICE, DEL
[] t147 RIDDLE, JOHN
[] t237 RYBA, MIKE
[] t194 SARNI, BILL
[] b67 SCHEIB, CARL
[] b14 STALEY, GERRY
[] b78 YVARS, SAL

1955

[] b257 ALSTON, TOM
[] b206 BEARD, RALPH dnp
[] b230 BRAZLE, AL dnp
[] t137 ELLIOTT, HARRY
[] b245 FLOWERS, BENNET
[] b186 GRAMMAS, ALEX
[] t21 GRAMMAS, ALEX
[] b107 HEMUS, SOLLY
[] t183 JACOBS, ANTHONY
[] t78 JONES, GORDON

[] b61 LaPALME, PAUL
[] b75 LAWRENCE, BROOKS
[] b62 LINT, ROYCE dnp
[] b76 POHOLSKY, TOM
[] b205 REPULSKI, RIP
[] t55 REPULSKI, RIP
[] b106 RICE, DEL
[] t98 RIDDLE, JOHN
[] b30 SARNI, BILL
[] t204 SMITH, FRANK

1956
(all topps)

[] 27 BURBRINK, NELSON dnp
[] 273 COOPER, WALKER
[] 211 DICKSON, MURRY
[] 141 FRAZIER, JOE
[] 37 GRAMMAS, ALEX
[] 308 HARMON, CHUCK
[] 26 HATTON, GRADY
[] 336 KINDER, ELLIS

[] 325 LIDDLE, DON
[] 337 MORGAN, BOBBY
[] 196 POHOLSKY, TOM
[] 201 REPULSKI, RIP
[] 247 SARNI, BILL
[] 323 SCHMIDT, WILLARD
[] 209 SURKONT, MAX
[] 78 WEHMEIER, HERM

1957
(all topps)

[] 47 BLASINGAME, DON
[] 359 CHENEY, TOM
[] 380 COOPER, WALKER
[] 273 DAVIS, JIM
[] 71 DICKSON, MURRY
[] 299 HARMON, CHUCK
[] 287 JONES, SAM
[] 363 KASKO, EDDIE

[] 182 LANDRITH, HOBIE
[] 350 MIKSIS, EDDIE
[] 298 NOREN, IRV
[] 206 SCHMIDT, WILLARD
[] 384 SMITH, BOBBY GENE
[] 111 SMITH, HAL R
[] 81 WEHMEIER, HERM

1958
(all topps)

[] 199 BLASINGAME, DON
[] 423 CLARK, PHIL
[] 168 CUNNINGHAM, JOE
[] 293 FREESE, GENE
[] 366 GREEN, GENE
[] 97 JACKSON, LARRY
[] 8 KASKO, EDDIE
[] 284 KATT, RAY
[] 24 LANDRITH, HOBIE
[] 53 MARTIN, MORRIE

[] 65 McDANIEL, VON
[] 231 MERRITT, LLOYD dnp
[] 143 MUFFETT, BILLY
[] 442 PAINE, PHIL
[] 402 SMITH, BOBBY GENE
[] 273 SMITH, HAL R
[] 239 STOBBS, CHUCK
[] 451 TAYLOR, JOE
[] 248 WEHMEIER, HERM
[] 237 WIGHT, BILL

1959
(all topps)

[] 491 BLASINGAME, DON
[] 211 BLAYLOCK, BOB
[] 539 BLAYLOCK, GARY
[] 296 BROGLIO, ERNIE
[] 231 BURTON, ELLIS dnp
[] 418 CIMOLI, GINO
[] 454 CLARK, PHIL

[] 337 CROWE, GEORGE
[] 285 CUNNINGHAM, JOE
[] 278 ESSEGIAN, CHUCK
[] 6 GRAMMAS, ALEX
[] 37 GREEN, GENE
[] 243 GRISSOM, MARV
[] 433 HARRELL, BILLY dnp

[] 527 HEMUS, SOLLY
[] 342 JABLONSKI, RAY
[] 399 JACKSON, LARRY
[] 81 JEFFCOAT, HAL
[] 101 KELLNER, ALEX
[] 538 KING, CHARLES
[] 379 MILLER, BOB
[] 549 NUNN, HOWIE

[] 135 OLIVER, GENE
[] 246 PORTER, J W
[] 137 RICKETTS, DICK
[] 162 SMITH, BOBBY GENE
[] 497 SMITH, HAL R
[] 286 STONE, DEAN
[] 544 TATE, LEE
[] 18 URBAN, JACK

Washington Senators / Nationals

1949
(all bowman)

[] 121 CHRISTMAN, MARK
[] 90 COAN, GIL
[] 106 EARLY, JAKE
[] 132 EVANS, AL
[] 144 HAEFNER, MICKEY
[] 151 HARRIS, MICKEY
[] 191 HAYNES, JOE

[] 16 KOZAR, AL
[] 74 McBRIDE, TOM dnp
[] 118 MELE, SAM
[] 140 SCARBOROUGH, RAY
[] 173 STEWART, ED
[] 189 WOOTEN, EARL dnp

1950
(all bowman)

[] 54 COAN, GIL
[] 107 DENTE, SAM
[] 144 EVANS, AL
[] 160 HARRIS, MICKEY
[] 17 HUDSON, SID
[] 15 KOZAR, AL

[] 5 KUZAVA, BOB
[] 52 MELE, SAM
[] 91 MICHAELS, CASS
[] 161 ROBERTSON, SHERRY
[] 143 STEWART, ED

1951
(all bowman)

[] 18 COAN, GIL
[] 96 CONSUEGRA, SANDY
[] 133 DENTE, SAM
[] 205 GRASSO, MICKEY
[] 202 GUERRA, MIKE
[] 311 HARRIS, MICKEY
[] 240 HAYNES, JOE
[] 169 HUDSON, SID

[] 97 KUZAVA, BOB
[] 206 MARRERO, CONRADO
[] 168 MELE, SAM
[] 132 MICHAELS, CASS
[] 95 ROBERTSON, SHERRY
[] 137 STARR, DICK
[] 192 WYSE, HANK

1952

[] t292 BAKER, FLOYD
[] b68 BUSBY, JIM
[] t307 CAMPOS, FRANK
[] b51 COAN, GIL
[] t291 COAN, GIL
[] b143 CONSUEGRA, SANDY
[] b234 FITZSIMMONS, FRED
[] b174 GRASSO, MICKEY
[] t90 GRASSO, MICKEY
[] b106 GUMPERT, RANDY
[] t247 GUMPERT, RANDY
[] b135 HARRIS, MICKEY
[] t207 HARRIS, MICKEY
[] b103 HAYNES, JOE
[] t145 HAYNES, JOE
[] b123 HUDSON, SID
[] t60 HUDSON, SID
[] t190 JOHNSON, DON
[] t132 KLUTTZ, CLYDE
[] t8 MARSH, FRED
[] b205 MASTERSON, WALT

[] t186 MASTERSON, WALT
[] b15 MELE, SAM
[] t94 MELE, SAM
[] b36 MICHAELS, CASS
[] t178 MICHAELS, CASS
[] b63 NOREN, IRV
[] b194 PORTERFIELD, BOB
[] t301 PORTERFIELD, BOB
[] t245 ROBERTSON, SHERRY
[] t298 ROSS, BOB dnp
[] b230 SHEA, FRANK
[] t248 SHEA, FRANK
[] t93 SIMA, AL dnp
[] t306 SLEATER, LOU
[] b246 SNYDER, JERRY
[] b227 SUKEFORTH, CLYDE
[] t71 UPTON, TOM
[] b210 WILSON, AL
[] t327 WILSON, AL
[] t139 WOOD, KEN

1953

[] b15 BUSBY, JIM
[] t123 BYRNE, TOMMY
[] t51 CAMPOS, FRANK
[] b34 COAN, GIL
[] t133 COAN, GIL
[] b77 GRASSO, MICKEY
[] t148 GRASSO, MICKEY
[] bw55 JOHNSON, DON dnp
[] t13 MARRERO, CONRADO
[] bw9 MASTERSON, WALT
[] t262 OLDIS, BOB
[] t256 PEDEN, LES
[] b22 PORTERFIELD, BOB

[] t108 PORTERFIELD, BOB
[] b141 SHEA, FRANK
[] t164 SHEA, FRANK
[] t241 SIMA, AL
[] t224 SLEATER, LOU dnp
[] t89 STOBBS, CHUCK
[] t159 TERWILLIGER, WAYNE
[] bw62 THOMAS, KEITH
[] t129 THOMAS, KEITH
[] b152 VOLLMER, CLYDE
[] t32 VOLLMER, CLYDE
[] b109 WOOD, KEN

1954

[] b8 BUSBY, JIM
[] b168 FITZGERALD, ED
[] t223 HAYNES, JOE
[] b120 HODERLEIN, MEL
[] t103 LEMON, JIM
[] b200 MARRERO, CONRADO
[] b52 McDERMONT, MICKEY
[] t91 OLDIS, BOB

[] b24 PORTERFIELD, BOB
[] t189 ROSS, BOB dnp
[] t33 SCHMITZ, JOHNNY
[] t204 SCULL, ANGEL dnp
[] b104 SHEA, FRANK
[] b216 SNYDER, JERRY
[] t185 STOBBS, CHUCK
[] t114 STONE, DEAN

[] t73 TERWILLIGER, WAYNE
[] b88 TIPTON, JOE
[] b88 UMPHLETT, TOM

[] b136 VOLLMER, CLYDE
[] t140 WRIGHT, TOMMY

1955

[] b166 BUSBY, JIM
[] b148 CHAKALES, BOB
[] b34 COURTNEY, CLINT
[] b208 FITZGERALD, ED
[] b117 GROTH, JOHNNY
[] b268 HAWES, ROY LEE dnp
[] t173 KLINE, BOB
[] b262 LEMON, JIM
[] b165 McDERMONT, MICKEY
[] t97 PAULA, CARLOS
[] b104 PORTERFIELD, BOB

[] b105 SCHMITZ, JOHNNY
[] t159 SCHMITZ, JOHNNY
[] b207 SHEA, FRANK
[] b74 SNYDER, JERRY
[] t136 STEWART, BUNKY
[] t41 STOBBS, CHUCK
[] t60 STONE, DEAN
[] b45 UMPHLETT, TOM
[] b13 VOLLMER, CLYDE dnp
[] t141 WRIGHT, TOMMY

1956
(all topps)

[] 329 BERBERET, LOU
[] 157 BRODOWSKI, DICK
[] 159 COURTNEY, CLINT
[] 198 FITZGERALD, ED
[] 322 OLSON, KARL
[] 51 ORAVETZ, ERNIE
[] 49 RAMOS, PEDRO

[] 234 RUNNELS, PETE
[] 216 SCHOONMAKER, JERRY dnp
[] 68 STOBBS, CHUCK
[] 87 STONE, DEAN
[] 237 VALDIVIELSO, JOSE
[] 327 WIESLER, BOB

1957
(all topps)

[] 293 ABERNATHY, TED
[] 315 BERBERET, LOU
[] 131 BOLLING, MILT
[] 294 BRIDGES, ROCKY
[] 261 CHAKALES, BOB
[] 320 CHRISLEY, NEIL
[] 51 COURTNEY, CLINT
[] 367 FITZGERALD, ED
[] 403 HYDE, DICK
[] 386 LUTTRELL, LYLE
[] 153 OLSON, KARL

[] 179 ORAVETZ, ERNIE dnp
[] 169 PLEWS, HERB
[] 326 RAMOS, PEDRO
[] 334 SCHOONMAKER, JERRY
[] 22 SNYDER, JERRY
[] 101 STOBBS, CHUCK
[] 381 STONE, DEAN
[] 356 THRONEBERRY, FAYE
[] 246 VALDIVIELSO, JOSE dnp
[] 126 WIESLER, BOB

1958

(all topps)

[] 405 ASPROMONTE, KEN
[] 458 BECQUER, JULIO
[] 383 BERBERET, LOU
[] 274 BRIDGES, ROCKY
[] 72 BYERLY, BUD
[] 303 CHRISLEY, NEIL
[] 382 CICOTTE, AL
[] 31 CLEVENGER, TEX
[] 92 COURTNEY, CLINT
[] 56 FISCHER, BILL
[] 236 FITZGERALD, ED
[] 455 GRIGGS, HAL
[] 156 HYDE, DICK

[] 137 KEMMERER, RUSS
[] 403 KORCHECK, STEVE
[] 369 LUMENTI, RALPH
[] 356 MALKMUS, BOB
[] 109 PLEWS, HERB
[] 331 RAMOS, PEDRO
[] 58 SCHULT, ART dnp
[] 239 STOBBS, CHUCK
[] 124 USHER, BOB dnp
[] 11 VALENTINETTI, VITO
[] 173 YOST, EDDIE
[] 422 ZAUCHIN, NORM

1959

(all topps)

[] 169 ABERNATHY, TED dnp
[] 424 ASPROMONTE, KEN
[] 93 BECQUER, JULIO
[] 84 BERTOIA, RENO
[] 298 CLEVENGER, TEX
[] 112 CONSOLO, BILLY
[] 451 CONSTABLE, JIMMY dnp
[] 483 COURTNEY, CLINT
[] 386 DELSING, JIM dnp
[] 124 DOBBEK, DAN
[] 230 FISCHER, BILL
[] 33 FITZGERALD, ED
[] 209 GREEN, LENNY
[] 434 GRIGGS, HAL
[] 498 HYDE, DICK
[] 191 KEMMERER, RUSS

[] 284 KORCHECK, STEVE
[] 316 LUMENTI, RALPH
[] 151 MALKMUS, BOB
[] 376 NARAGON, HAL
[] 291 PASCUAL / RAMOS
[] 373 PLEWS, HERB
[] 246 PORTER, J W
[] 78 RAMOS, PEDRO
[] 267 ROMONOSKY, JOHN
[] 242 SAMFORD, RON
[] 26 STOBBS, CHUCK
[] 534 THRONEBERRY, FAYE
[] 44 VALENTINETTI, VITO
[] 106 WOODESHICK, HAL
[] 311 ZAUCHIN, NORM

INDEX

i

INDEX

ii

INDEX

iii

INDEX

INDEX

INDEX

INDEX

INDEX